LITHUANIA
UNDER
THE SOVIETS

LITHUANIA
UNDER
THE SOVIETS

Portrait of a Nation, 1940-65

Edited by
V. STANLEY VARDYS

FREDERICK A. PRAEGER, *Publishers*
New York · Washington · London

FREDERICK A. PRAEGER, *Publishers*
111 Fourth Avenue, New York 3, N.Y., U.S.A.
77–79 Charlotte Street, London W.1, England

Published in the United States of America in 1965
by Frederick A. Praeger, Inc., Publishers

© 1965 by V. Stanley Vardys

Library of Congress Catalog Card Number: 65-14060

This book is No. 162 in the series *Praeger Publications
in Russian History and World Communism*

Printed in the United States of America

Contents

Introduction

Among the East European countries seized and dominated by the Soviet Union, Lithuania and the other Baltic states—Latvia and Estonia—have not yet received adequate attention from scholars. There are, of course, several good reasons for this relative neglect of Baltic studies, though only one of these need be suggested here. Lithuania, although generally identified with Eastern Europe, has since 1940 been occupied and frankly incorporated into the Soviet Union. This loss of statehood negatively affected Lithuanian research and publication in the West. On the one hand, Lithuania was frequently ignored by students of Eastern Europe on grounds that its postwar development was different from that of the other Communist-ruled East European nations. On the other, Soviet-affairs specialists tended toward the belief that the Baltic states were not typically Soviet. Yet it would seem that the opposite holds true. In arguing for a revival of scholarly interest in the Baltic countries, I would especially stress that they, as no others, offer a half century of perspective and basis for comparison so necessary for a meaningful study of the process and results of sovietization.

The purpose of this book is to examine the full cycle of this sovietization, from the destruction of Lithuania's independence and the "bourgeois" order to its complete integration into the Soviet state and society. To achieve this objective, the volume is organized in three parts. The major part deals with the twenty-five years of Soviet rule: the Lithuanian Communist Party; the administration of the republic—its economics, education, the arts, religion—and Soviet social engineering. This comprehensive scrutiny is preceded by material designed to give the reader the necessary historical background and perspective—i.e., a survey of modern Lithuania's rise to freedom after World War I, its independent life (1918–40), and the ensuing efforts of regaining that independence during World War II and its aftermath. This is the first such symposium to be published in the West and, hopefully, will be found useful; it fills a conspicuous gap in the field of Soviet and East European studies.

All the articles in this volume were specially prepared for this collection, with the exception of the essay on the partisan movement, which was originally published in the *Slavic Review*. I am grateful to the Editor of this journal for permission to include it here. Generally, this volume covers developments up to early 1964, that is, the time the manuscripts were submitted for publication. Revisions were made, of course, whenever events warranted them. It should be pointed out, however, that such instances were not numerous. Not even the change in Soviet leadership in October, 1964, produced specific new policies that would substantially affect the arguments in this book. The regime's objectives and the patterns of behavior and control that were established by Stalin and revised by Khrushchev have to date not been altered by the new leaders.

Although each author and he alone is accountable for his study and conclusions, I, as editor, am responsible for several features of the book, including its format and topical organization. It also was my task to secure translations where needed (some essays were originally written in Lithuanian), to eliminate overlapping, standardize the usage of names and terms, and many of the other things that had to be coordinated because of the distances that separated the contributors in two continents and three countries.

One of the most ticklish editorial problems arose as the result of the diversity of usage of Lithuanian and other regional names. Since the Baltic countries for years have been under convergent Russian, German, or Polish domination, there still exists among scholars a tendency to write local names in these rather than in the local languages. This practice has been further complicated by the frequent boundary shifts in modern times and the wholesale name changes that the Soviets introduced in some parts of the Baltic area after World War II. I attempted to untangle the situation by using presently accepted spellings and designations, except where there exists an established American usage, in which case the Americanized form has been used. For the sake of clarity, however, the old Russian, German, Polish, or Lithuanian versions are also given. The other problems, the transliteration of Russian words, was solved by following the system of the Library of Congress. No attempt, however, has been made to transliterate Lithuanian phrases. They appear in the original.

Finally, I am grateful to the many friends and colleagues for the aid and encouragement given me while working on this project, which, unforeseeably, took almost four years' time. I am thankful to the contributors for their willingness to undertake this long journey. I owe a special debt of gratitude to the American Foundation for Lithuanian Research, Inc., whose generosity helped make possible the publication of this book. I should also like to express my appreciation to the editors at Frederick A. Praeger for their invaluable assistance.

V. STANLEY VARDYS

January, 1965
University of Wisconsin-Milwaukee
Milwaukee, Wisconsin

PART I

Independence Won and Lost: 1918-40

1. Lithuania from Medieval to Modern Times: A Historical Outline

SIMAS SUŽIEDĖLIS

Lithuania is a small country situated on the eastern shore of the Baltic Sea. Its area is equivalent to the combined territory of New Jersey, New Hampshire, Connecticut, and Delaware; its landscape resembles that of Wisconsin, since both are of morain origin. The land is not rich in minerals; it is, however, suited for agriculture because of a reasonably long period of vegetation, the precipitation, and mild temperatures.

Lithuania's neighbors to the north are Latvians, to the east and south Belorussians and Poles, and to the southwest—since the end of World War II—Russians who have colonized the formerly German East Prussia.

Contrary to popular opinion, the Lithuanian people are not Slavs but Balts; their language is not related to Russian and the other Slavic languages. The only other kindred people to the Lithuanians are the Latvians, whose language is closely related to Lithuanian. Other related groups, like the old Prussians, who did not survive the colonization of their land (East Prussia) by the Teutonic Knights, were absorbed by the Lithuanians and Latvians. Linguistically, the Lithuanians belong to the eastern branch of the Indo-European language family. Lithuanian is one of the oldest surviving Indo-European languages; it is related to Sanskrit.

THE DEVELOPMENT OF THE MEDIEVAL LITHUANIAN STATE

The origins of Lithuanian statehood are to be sought in the closing years of the twelfth century. At that time, separate Lithu-

3

anian tribes inhabiting the Baltic coast between the Vistula and
Daugava (Russ. Zapadnaia Dvina, Germ. Düna) rivers began to
unite under one ruler. The early thirteenth century contest for
supremacy was won by Mindaugas (ca. 1236–63), who is considered the founder of the Lithuanian state. In 1251, Mindaugas
became a Christian, and two years later, by the authority of Pope
Innocent IV, was crowned King of Lithuania. Thus, under
Mindaugas, Lithuania became a Christian monarchy, the form of
government then dominant in Western Europe.

Mindaugas, although an able statesman, failed to unify the
kindred tribes. He was checked by German knights who, in their
northward advance along the Baltic coast, had already conquered
the Latvians and Prussians. The Latvians remained under German rule for about 400 years, and the Prussians were completely
annihilated. Only their name survived in the Germanized Prussian province (Preussen), which also included Lithuania Minor,
a part of Lithuania.

In 1263, King Mindaugas and two of his sons were assassinated
by two conspiring princes, but the state itself endured. A new
ruling family took over. It abandoned Christianity, which Mindaugas had introduced, but expanded Lithuania's power eastward
to the Black Sea, making the country's name known throughout
Europe. Rulers of this family, who made major contributions to
the growth of Lithuania's national power, were Gediminas (1316–
41), who gave his name to the dynasty; his sons Algirdas (1345–77),
and Kęstutis (1345–82), who for a long time ruled jointly (the so-
called diarchy), and Vytautas (1392–1430), a son of Kęstutis, known
as Vytautas the Great. A member of this family, Jogaila, son of
Algirdas (1377–92), became King Wladyslaw II, Jagiello, of Poland. He founded the Jagellonian dynasty that ruled united
Lithuania-Poland for two hundred years. Under Jogaila and
Vytautas, Lithuania returned to Catholicism (1387 and 1413).

Lithuania reached its greatest power and broadest expansion
under Vytautas. In the east, the Lithuanian state enveloped
Moscow from two sides. The Duchy of Moscow was ruled by
Vytautas' daughter Sophia, as regent; and, until his own death in
1430, Vytautas acted as protector of Sophia's son, Basil II (1425–
62). In the north, the large Russian trading republics of Pskov
and Novgorod belonged to the Lithuanian sphere of influence.
In the south, the Lithuanian state reached the Black Sea. Here, in
1399, Vytautas withstood the Tatar Golden Horde and checked
the Tatar invasion of the Christian West for all time. Such were

the political consequences of the battle at Vorksla, which, ironically, Vytautas had lost.

In the west, Vytautas stopped the German eastward expansion (*Drang nach Osten*). At the battle of Tannenberg (1410), famous in European history, the united Lithuanian and Polish armies, in the field commanded by Vytautas, defeated the Germans. The defeat was the death blow to the German knights and ended 200 years of ceaseless attacks on Lithuania and Poland. Although Polish and Russian historians, generally, tend to minimize Vytautas' role at Tannenberg, historical facts testify undeniably to his leadership in the battle.

The Polish interpretation arises from an old quarrel with the Lithuanians over the nature and advantages of the Polish-Lithuanian union established by Jogaila and the position of Lithuanian dukes, especially Vytautas, in it. In 1385, the Poles elected Jogaila their King on condition that he unite the two states. The next year, Jogaila was crowned King Jagiello of Poland and, of course, continued to rule Lithuania. In 1392, Vytautas succeeded in regaining power from Jogaila in Lithuania, but had to accept and renew Jogaila's act of union with Poland (1385). He ruled Lithuania, however, quite independently from the King, and the Poles did not like it; they were apprehensive that Lithuania, ruled by Vytautas, might escape the yet very fragile bond of union with Poland. In this union, the two states remained separate entities, but were ruled by a common sovereign (except for a brief interval) until the end of the Jagellonian (Gediminas) dynasty in 1572.

As the Jagellonian dynasty drew to a close, a new, more institutionalized tie between Lithuania and Poland was created. This was a federal union under an elective monarchy agreed upon at the Lublin meeting in 1569. Within the federation, Lithuania maintained its sovereignty; it had its own government (ministers), parliament, laws, courts, and currency. A single king ruled over both states; joint meetings of the parliaments of both countries were held alternately in Lithuania and Poland. This union survived until the end of the eighteenth century.

The main reason for this close alliance of Lithuania and Poland was the growing power of Russia. From the middle of the fifteenth century, the Duchy of Moscow began to gather various principalities around itself, detaching some from Lithuania. Because Russian lands were a part of the ancient Lithuanian state, certain Russian historians try to prove that it was a dual Lithuanian-Russian one. But this claim does not agree with historical fact.

Lithuania was a unitary state, ruled by one sovereign from its capital, Vilnius, but it was a multinational rather than a national state. Within it, the ancient order (*starina*) of the Slavic tribes, and their religion, language, and customs survived. Lithuania remained multinational even after the medieval multinational states of Europe became nation states.

Nationalism appeared in Russia with the rise of imperialistic tendencies. The dukes of Moscow proclaimed themselves Czars of all the Russias, and in the middle of the sixteenth century began to push toward the Baltic Sea, primarily through Estonian and Latvian lands, which were then a part of the German colony of Livonia. Moscow's first invasion of Livonia (1558) was countered by Lithuania-Poland in a twenty-four-year war with Czar Ivan IV (the Terrible, 1530–84). During this period, many Latvian and Estonian lands passed to the protection of Lithuania-Poland by the Treaty of Vilnius (1561), while others went to Sweden.

Swedish invasions of the eastern coast of the Baltic brought on long wars, from which Russia finally emerged victorious and firmly entrenched on the Baltic coast. The Russian invasion of Lithuania (1655–61) was frightful. Vilnius, the capital, was conquered for the first time, burned (fire raged for seventeen days), and looted. Thousands were massacred, and many other towns were destroyed. After the second Russian invasion, during the Northern Wars (1701–21), the garrisons of Peter the Great did not withdraw from Lithuania and Poland. The united Lithuanian-Polish Republic was destroyed from within and divided among its three neighbors—Russia, Prussia, and Austria—by three partitions (1772, 1793, 1795). Lithuanian lands, except for Lithuania Minor, were acquired by Russia.

During the Czarist occupation, which lasted for 120 years (1795–1915), an intensive policy of Russification and colonization was in effect: For forty years (1864–1904), publication in the Latin alphabet was banned, all societies and Lithuanian schools were abolished, and many tracts of land were taken over by Russian colonists. An attempt was made to obliterate the very name "Lithuania" by substituting the term "Northwestern Territory" (Severo Zapadnii Krai).

From the beginning of the eighteenth century, the name "Poland" was frequently used in western Europe to refer to the entire Polish-Lithuanian republic. As Lithuania gradually merged with Poland or Russia, its fame abated. In the nineteenth century, non-Lithuanian students of history, fearing that all trace might be lost of one of the oldest nations in Europe, hurriedly began to collect materials for the study of Lithuania's language, customs, and folklore. However, the fear was unfounded. In spite of the oppressive Russian occupation, the Lithuanian nation survived and strove for independence.

During the first Russian Revolution (1905), the Lithuanians declared for self-rule. The *seimas* (parliament or assembly) of Vilnius, composed of about 2,000 delegates, demanded autonomy for Lithuania, a demand that was repeated by the delegates to the Duma in St. Petersburg. World War I brought changes that led to demands for complete independence.

WORLD WAR I AND INDEPENDENCE

In the summer of 1915, the Russians were forced to leave Lithuania, and for three years thereafter the country was occupied by the German Army. The Germans planned to colonize the country after the war, just as they had previously colonized the area at the mouth of the Nemunas River on the Baltic coast in Lithuania Minor. However, Germany's defeat put an end to this plan.

The nationalist movement in Lithuania, like similar movements in eastern and central Europe, was greatly encouraged by Woodrow Wilson's speech of January 22, 1917, espousing the right of national self-determination. Although Wilson's Fourteen Points did not specifically demand Lithuanian freedom, his call for self-determination became the foundation of Lithuanian demands for independence.

Germany tried to shape this movement to its own uses. At the end of June, 1916, when a congress of captive nations convened in Lausanne, Switzerland (most of the delegates were from nations ruled by Great Britain, France, and Russia), Germany allowed a Lithuanian delegation from Vilnius to attend. The military authorities hoped that the Lithuanian delegation would help to stir up unrest in countries ruled by the Allies. But, contrary to German expectations, the Lithuanian delegation demanded independence for its own land, most of which was in German hands. This, the first public demand for Lithuanian independence during World War I, irritated the German Government, which at that time felt confident of victory and looked forward to colonizing Lithuania. The German Government's anger proved to be unwise, however, since the demands for freedom by the East

European nations could no longer be ignored. Four months later, on November 15, 1916, Germany and Austria-Hungary were forced to announce the re-establishment of the Polish state, effective as of the end of the war. The movement for Lithuanian independence, however, suffered a setback; the Polish Temporary Council, in its turn, sought to re-establish a Polish-Lithuanian state. A group of forty-four Poles, meeting in Vilnius on May 25, 1917, presented a memorandum to Bethmann-Hollweg, the German Chancellor, asking for the merger of Lithuania with Poland. Thus, Lithuania's historic ties with Poland worked against its claim to independence.

A further obstacle to Lithuanian independence grew out of the Russian Revolution. Socialist demonstrations against the monarchy, begun on March 8, 1917, in St. Petersburg, led to the abdication of Czar Nicholas II on March 15. The Provisional Government formed by the Fourth Duma, headed by Prince Lvov, declared for the self-determination of the nations of Russia. At that time, there were 200,000 Lithuanians in Russian territory not occupied by Germany. In their name, a Lithuanian delegation requested, on March 18, 1917, that the Provisional Government allow the Lithuanian Council to administer those parts of the Vilnius and Kaunas regions (*gubernie*) which were not under German occupation, to take over institutions evacuated from Lithuania, and to prepare for the founding of a democratic Lithuania. The request was neither refused nor granted. After a month, the Lithuanians decided to strengthen it by convoking a *seimas* of the Lithuanians in Russia.

The *seimas*, composed of 336 delegates, met in St. Petersburg (May 27–June 3, 1917). A majority resolution adopted on June 3 stated:

> Since Lithuania until the end of the eighteenth century had its own separate political life . . . and since it is now granted that nations have the right to choose what they want . . . it is therefore clearly declared to the whole world: the whole of ethnic Lithuania must become an independent state . . . its government and structure to be determined by a founding *seimas*, elected by a universal, equal, and secret ballot.[1]

This resolution was renewed at a congress of the national minorities of Russia, held in Kiev (September 6–16, 1917). The delegates concurred with the Lithuanian demands, drawing up the following resolution:

To obtain the Provisional Government's attention to the vital matter of enacting an appropriate law, which would recognize the right of Lithuanians to form a sovereign Lithuanian state from the Russian, Lithuanian-Prussian, and Suwalki regions, on the basis of the principle of self-determination.[2]

The Russian Provisional Government did not look favorably on national self-determination, which would have led to the dissolution of multinational Russia. Aleksandr Kerenski, head of the Provisional Government, after proclaiming a Russian Democratic Republic on September 5, 1917, expressed his opposition to the secession of Finland and threatened to use armed force to prevent it, adding that his forces had sufficient artillery to prevent any nation from seceding. But two months later, Kerenski was no longer in power: On November 7, the Bolshevik Revolution overthrew the Provisional Government and established the Soviet dictatorship.

The Soviet Government, headed by Lenin, Chairman of the Council of People's Commissars, declared on November 15, 1917, that all the nations of Russia had the right of self-determination, "including independence and the formation of sovereign government."[3] A separate Commissariat was formed for national affairs, headed by the Georgian Stalin. However, neither the declaration nor the Commissariat was a sign of good will. The real intent behind this propaganda mask was to keep Russia undivided, in a union of soviet republics. Nor did the Bolsheviks reject Russian imperialism.

On December 1, 1917, the Lithuanians in Russia formed a Supreme Council in Voronezh, to continue the work for Lithuanian independence. The Council hoped to use as a basis Lenin's recognition of the right of self-determination, which included the "formation of the sovereign governments." But that recognition was a mere fiction. The Bolshevik Government appointed its own Commissar for Lithuanian affairs, the Bolshevik Vincas Mickevičius-Kapsukas. The opposition of the Bolsheviks to Lithuanian independence was stated by Kapsukas in the following words:

We recognize the right of self-determination for all nations, but this does not mean independence. . . . We have in mind the needs of nations and of the Lithuanian proletariat. Since in an independent Lithuania these needs might suffer, we reject independence and fight against it.[4]

On April 18, 1918, a decree was published banning the Lithuanian Council in Voronezh and its branches in St. Petersburg, Moscow, and elsewhere. Later that year the Bolsheviks threw the Red Army into their fight against Lithuanian independence, an action made possible by the collapse of the German Eastern front. Until July 15, 1918, Germany held the military initiative, although it wavered between despair and hope. The despair was caused partly by the entry of the United States into the war early in 1917, but the hope was nourished by the two Russian revolutions of March 8 and November 7. Germany was able to transfer some of its forces to the Western Front, while seeking peace on the Eastern Front. These plans had a bearing on Lithuania's future.

Hoping to keep control of the eastern lands after the war, Germany tried to portray her own selfish aim as the will of the conquered nations. The military leadership gathered well-known people into an advisory council (*Vertrauensrat*), which ostensibly expressed the will of the conquered people. This maneuver succeeded in Courland, in Latvian lands, and in the Ukraine, but the Lithuanians rejected such collaboration and, on May 17, 1917, demanded elections and a conference. Elections were not allowed, but permission was granted for a conference of invited delegates.

The conference at Vilnius (September 18–22, 1917) was attended by 214 delegates from 33 districts. Lithuanians of all political tendencies were represented, including three delegates from Switzerland representing the Lithuanian Information Bureau, which had been active in Switzerland since 1916, rallying support for Lithuanian independence throughout Europe. The Bureau also maintained contact with the Lithuanians in Russia and America. In January, 1917, a group of Lithuanian immigrants in America (of whom there were about 700,000) had already presented a memorandum to President Woodrow Wilson and the European ambassadors in Washington, requesting that all of ethnic Lithuania be unified and granted independence after the war. The delegates to the Vilnius conference were aware of this action and of the June resolution of Lithuanians in Russia.

The Vilnius conference began only after the German observers had left the hall. On September 22, the conference unanimously resolved that:

> An independent Lithuania must be established within its ethnic boundaries, ordered according to democratic principles. . . . A constitutional *seimas*, meeting in Vilnius, will have to determine the foundations of the state and its relations with other states.[5]

This resolution was made while Lithuania was under German occupation, still uncertain of who would win the war. Political realism demanded that Germany, a powerful neighbor, be considered a power that might still conclude the war with favorable peace terms. The Vilnius conference therefore adopted a conciliatory supplement to the effect that if prior to the peace conference Germany were to agree to proclaim an independent Lithuanian state and support Lithuania's cause in the conference, then it would be possible for the future Lithuanian state to enter into certain relations, to be determined later, with Germany, without prejudice to autonomous Lithuanian growth. This was a promise of closer future ties with Germany than with other countries.

The conference elected a twenty-man council (*taryba*), but the German military authorities wanted to use it merely as an instrument for annexing Lithuania to Germany. The council insisted that it be allowed to establish relations with the Lithuanians abroad, and its representatives were given permission to visit neutral Sweden and Switzerland. Meetings with delegates of the Lithuanians in Russia were held in Stockholm (October 18–20), and talks went on in Berne (November 2–10) with delegates from the United States and Switzerland. In both cases it was agreed to consider the council the supreme representative of the nation.

On their way home from Switzerland, the representatives of the council conferred with the Ministry for Foreign Affairs in Berlin. There they agreed to a preliminary treaty, the so-called "protocol of December 1, 1917," granting permission to proclaim Lithuania's independence, though close ties to Germany were to be maintained. These ties would be based on four agreements, covering military matters, communications, customs, and currency. The protocol was to be ratified by a meeting of the whole Council. Although there were some differences of opinion, the council on December 7 decided as follows: The Lithuanian state was to be reconstituted with Vilnius as its capital, and the council itself would immediately take over the administration of internal affairs and relations with other countries. The proposed agreements with Germany were to be negotiated and finally ratified by a founding *seimas*.

However, the German military authorities in Kaunas did not accept this decision. They also rejected the Berlin protocol. Broadly speaking, there were two views on the subject in Berlin. In the Reichstag, Lithuanian independence was supported by the Catholic Center, Social Democratic, and Independent Socialist parties. On the other hand, the nationalist commander-in-chief,

General Erich von Ludendorff, advocated the incorporation of Lithuania into Germany. He still hoped that the war would end favorably for Germany, especially after the Bolsheviks, on November 28, 1917, offered an armistice on the Eastern Front.

Statements of the voluntary secession from Russia by the German-occupied countries were useful to Germany while preparations for negotiations with Russia went on. (Lithuania's wishes were, of course, well-known, having been frequently voiced in Lithuania and abroad.) But the German military staff in the eastern territories aimed at something more: incorporating Lithuania into Germany. Under German pressure, the council on December 11 adopted a resolution that, on the one hand, declared the reconstitution of the Lithuanian state and repudiated all past political ties to other countries, and, on the other hand, affirmed strong ties to Germany.

Some regard this resolution as the first declaration of independence.[6] But this is not the case, since it was never made public and was only a draft for further negotiations with Germany. The Council expected that Germany would recognize Lithuanian independence on the basis of the resolution, allow Lithuanians to take over the civil administration, and admit a Lithuanian delegation to the talks at Brest Litovsk, which had begun on December 2, 1917. Representations to that effect made to Georg von Hertling, Chancellor of Germany, failed to bear fruit.

As a result, the Lithuanian Council lost faith in Germany. It was clear that Germany was still aiming at complete annexation. When, on February 9, Berlin proclaimed an independent Ukraine, the Council decided to wait no longer. Rejecting any union with Germany, the Lithuanian Council, meeting in Vilnius, issued the following declaration of independence on February 16, 1918:

> The Lithuanian Council, as the only representative of the Lithuanian nation, basing itself on the right of national self-determination and the decision of the Vilnius conference of September 18–23, 1917, proclaims that it is re-establishing an independent, democratically ordered Lithuanian state with Vilnius as its capital and that it is separating that state from any state ties that have existed with other nations.
>
> The Lithuanian Council further declares that the foundations of the Lithuanian state and its relations with other states must be determined by a founding *seimas,* to be convened as soon as possible and elected democratically by all the people.[7]

This declaration was published in *Lietuvos Aidas,* a Vilnius newspaper. The German military censors immediately confiscated the issue. As a result, reprints had to be circulated secretly throughout the country and abroad. The declaration was reprinted by three major Berlin newspapers—*Tägliche Rundschau, Vossische Zeitung,* and *Kreuzzeitung*—and on February 20 was read in the Reichstag. In the debate that followed, it became clear that the German Government was still influenced by the military leadership, which was then, because of recent victories on the Eastern Front, even more eager than before to annex Lithuania outright.

The Lithuanian declaration of independence was made at a time when German-Russian negotiations had been suspended. The Soviet delegation, led by Trotsky, had left Brest Litovsk on February 10 with the statement that there was "neither war nor peace." The Russian Army was ordered to demobilize. Trotsky hoped that, in this way, nationalist movements favorable to the Soviet system would be encouraged behind the German lines. But on February 18, Germany began a new offensive and in a few days occupied the Ukraine up to the Black Sea, White Russia, Latvia, and Estonia, and was on its way to Moscow and St. Petersburg. The Bolsheviks sent a new delegation to Brest Litovsk, led by Sokolnikov, and a peace treaty was signed on March 3, 1918. Soviet Russia ratified it on March 15; Germany, on March 22. By the terms of the treaty, Russia renounced its claims to Finland, the Baltic states, Poland, the Ukraine, and part of the Caucasus.

While the Reichstag was debating ratification of the Russian peace treaty (March 17–22), the members of the Lithuanian Council were called to Berlin. A majority of Reichstag members (Catholic Center, Social Democrats, Independent Socialists) charged that the government was exerting undue pressure on Lithuania, but this protest was ignored. However, on March 23, 1918, Wilhelm II recognized the independent Lithuanian state, subject to two conditions: (1) that it pay part of the war costs, and (2) sign permanent agreements with Germany. That meant that Lithuania's independence was recognized not on the basis of the declaration of February 16, 1918, but on that of December 11, 1917. Somewhat later it became known that the Kaiser intended to delegate the Duke of Prussia or the Duke of Saxony to rule Lithuania as a vassal state.

At the same time, a conference of 1,500 American Lithuanians, meeting in Madison Square Garden in New York City on March 13–14, passed a resolution demanding complete independence for

Lithuania. This resolution was presented to President Wilson, who promised to support Lithuania's claim at the peace conference and to free Lithuania from all ties to Germany.

The majority leader in the German Reichstag, Matthias Erzberger, a member of the Catholic Center who was favorably inclined to Lithuania, suggested that the situation be resolved by electing an independent monarch. Wilhelm von Urach, Duke of Württemberg, a Catholic, was proposed as a candidate. On June 4, 1918, the Lithuanian Council set forth the conditions under which von Urach could assume the Lithuanian crown under the name of Mindaugas II. Wilhelm von Urach accepted the conditions on July 1 in Freiburg im Breisgau, and on July 13 he was elected King of Lithuania by a majority vote of the Lithuanian Council.

German nationalist newspapers strongly attacked the Lithuanian Council for acting without the consent of the German Government. On July 29, 1918, the *Deutsche Zeitung* wrote that Lithuania could not have its own separate dynasty and that part of its territory had to be incorporated into Prussia to ensure an overland link with Courland, Latvia, and Estonia. Germany still wanted to keep control of the coast from the Nemunas (Russ. Nemen, Germ. Memel) to the Narva rivers, so as to colonize the area later. But, because of German reversals on the Western Front, this plan could not be realized. Max von Baden, Chancellor of Germany, declared in the Reichstag on October 5, 1918, that the occupied countries had the right of self-determination.

On October 20, a Lithuanian delegation in Berlin obtained Germany's permission to take over control of Lithuania. On November 2, a temporary constitution was adopted. The question of the invitation to Wilhelm von Urach was to be settled by the founding *seimas*. The Presidium of the Council took over the functions of government (Antanas Smetona, chairman; Justinas Staugaitis; and Stasys Šilingas). Augustinas Voldemaras formed the first cabinet on November 11, the day that World War I ended.

THE WARS FOR INDEPENDENCE

But the fight for independence was not yet over; it lasted until the end of 1920. Three large neighbors—Germany, Russia, and Poland—had designs on Lithuanian territory, and, in the beginning, the Western Allies upheld the claims of "indivisible Russia" and Poland.

On November 13, 1918, immediately after the armistice, Soviet Russia repudiated the Treaty of Brest Litovsk and began a new war for the introduction of the Soviet system throughout Europe. The initial aim was to occupy Finland, the Baltic states, and Poland.

To mask the occupation of the Baltic states, Soviet Russia formed Bolshevik "governments" in Estonia, Latvia, and Lithuania. The Lithuanian "government of workers and peasants" was formed on December 8, 1918, with Vincas Mickevičius-Kapsukas at its head. Russian recognition of the Baltic Soviet "republics" was announced (December 22–24, 1918). All these gestures simply meant that Soviet Russia was planning to deprive the Baltic states of their freedom, using the opportunity created by Germany's defeat.

Article 12 of the armistice agreement, signed at Compiègne on November 11, 1918, obliged Germany to remain in the eastern territories until local administrations could take over.[8] But owing to the disorganization of their armies, the Germans could not fulfill this obligation. They retreated, and the Red Army marched in after them. Bolshevik forces occupied Vilnius (January 5–6, 1919) and looted it extensively. The Lithuanian Government withdrew to Kaunas. Between Kaunas and Vilnius, the Soviet advance was halted by hastily organized Lithuanian volunteers with the help of German military units.

Although the Lithuanian forces, commanded by General Silvestras Žukauskas, lacked sufficient weapons and clothing, they were patriotic and brave. Behind the Bolshevik lines, the people rose against the new enemy, and partisans became active. The war with the Bolsheviks ended on August 30, 1919, with the Lithuanians having advanced to the Daugava River in Latvia. Forced out of Latvia and Estonia as well, the Bolsheviks requested armistice talks with the three states. Estonia signed a peace treaty on February 2, 1920; Lithuania, on July 12; Latvia, on August 11. Soviet Russia renounced all claims on the Baltic countries, the eastern boundaries of which were drawn up by the treaties. The Lithuanian-Russian border ran 100 miles east to Vilnius and Grodna (Lith. Gardinas).

The Bolsheviks later admitted that they found no support in the Baltic states for a Communist revolution. The Soviet system, in other words, could not be established without the Red Army.[9]

If the Soviet Union now claims that it intended to liberate the Lithuanian people from the oppression of the bourgeoisie and German imperialists, it is simply distorting historical facts.

In 1919–20, Germany no longer had any power in Lithuania; the government and military forces of the country were in the hands of the Provisional Government in Kaunas, and on April 16, 1920, Antanas Smetona became President. A military mission of the Western Allies visited Kaunas, saw the reconstruction of the Lithuanian state, supported the war against the Bolsheviks, and supervised the evacuation of German units, some of which tried to stay on in the Baltic area.

One of the retreating German commanders, General Rüdiger von der Goltz, after fighting the Bolsheviks in Finland, transferred his forces to Courland under the pretext of helping the Baltic states against the Bolsheviks. But behind this move lay the German design to keep the Baltic coast for Germany. In the summer of 1919, an adventurer-officer under von der Goltz's command, Bermondt-Avalov, a Siberian German, led German units in an invasion of northern Lithuania. These units were defeated by Lithuanian forces commanded by General Kazys Ladyga, in a battle at Radviliškis (November 21–22, 1919). General Frank P. Crozier, a British officer, acted as military adviser. The Lithuanians wanted to chase the enemy to the mouth of the Nemunas and occupy the Lithuanian Klaipėda (Ger. Memel) region, but they were held back by General Henri A. Niessel, the head of the Allied mission.

The Klaipėda region, which lies north of the Nemunas, is part of Lithuania Minor. It had been ruled by Germany for 700 years, but many of the inhabitants on both sides of the river had kept their Lithuanian identity. During the Czarist occupation, nationalist ideas spread from Lithuania Minor to Lithuania Major. The city of Tilsit (Lith. Tilžė, present-day Sovetsk), on the south bank of the Nemunas, was the center of underground resistance to foreign rule. Soon after World War I, on November 16, 1918, a conference of Lithuanians from Tilsit called for union with Lithuania Major. A petition was presented to the Paris peace talks with detailed evidence of the region's Lithuanian character. On March 20, 1920, four delegates from Lithuania Minor entered the Lithuanian State Council (provisional parliament) in Kaunas.

The Treaty of Versailles (Article 99) stipulated that only the territory north of the mouth of the Nemunas River be separated from Germany. This included Klaipėda Harbor. But because of

French-Polish maneuvering, the area did not come into Lithuanian possession until 1923.

In the east and south, Poland had already occupied a third of ethnic Lithuania, including the capital, Vilnius, and Grodna (Lith. Gardinas) and Suwalki (Lith. Suvalkai). After liberating themselves from Germany, the Poles sought to re-establish Poland's boundaries before the first partition (1772). The Lithuanian-Polish state then controlled a large part of the Ukraine, all of White Russia, and part of Latvia up to the Daugava. Lithuania's refusal to renew the old union with Poland was the main obstacle to the realization of this aim.

At the Paris Peace Conference, to which Lithuania had been refused admittance, Poland argued that few Lithuanians remained in the area it had occupied, and that most of them already spoke Polish. On January 29, 1919, Roman Dmowski suggested in the name of Poland that Lithuania be formed out of Courland and the regions of Kaunas, Vilnius, and Suwalki, but that it be joined politically to Poland.[10] This project was rejected only because the Allies had not yet decided to separate the Baltic countries from Russia. The Bolshevik Revolution seemed only a passing incident.

In order to realize its territorial aims, Poland resorted to armed force. On April 19, 1919, while the Lithuanians were forcing out the Bolsheviks, Polish forces led by Józef Piłsudski, a landowner of Lithuanian extraction, occupied Vilnius and advanced as far as the upper Daugava. In the east, Polish armies were pushing the Bolsheviks out of White Russia and the Ukraine, but in the north, the Poles were attacking Lithuania. Twice the Allies laid down demarcation lines, both of which were violated by Poland. By the summer of 1920, Polish divisions were 25 miles from Kaunas, the seat of the Lithuanian Government, and only an unexpectedly severe blow by the counterattacking Bolsheviks prevented the capture of the city.

The Bolsheviks had crossed into Lithuania for a second time, occupying Vilnius on July 15, 1920, only three days after the signing of the Lithuanian-Soviet peace treaty. The Red Army, however, withdrew to the boundaries stipulated by the treaty, and on August 26, the Lithuanian Government began to move from Kaunas to Vilnius. The government's action was not based on the belief that the Soviets would abide by the terms of the treaty and thus permanently leave Vilnius in Lithuanian hands. Rather, the government was convinced that the Bolsheviks withdrew because of their resounding defeat at Warsaw by the Poles, whose strategy had been directed by the French General Maxime Weygand and whose forces had been strengthened by equipment from the Allies.

As agreed at the peace conference with the Soviets in Riga, Lithuania remained neutral in this final stage of the Soviet-Polish war. But Poland charged that the Lithuanians supported the Bolsheviks and attacked Lithuania again, though the Poles themselves were negotiating a peace treaty with the Bolsheviks. This time the Allies stopped the new Polish invasion, and on October 7, Poland and Lithuania signed an armistice, which left the city of Vilnius and a small part of Vilnius region in Lithuanian territory. Two days later, however, Poland started a new attack.

The invasion was led by General Lucjan Zeligowski, who claimed to be leading rebellious "Lithuanians and White Russians." Marshal Piłsudski later admitted having given the orders. On October 9, Polish forces occupied Vilnius and advanced on Kaunas. But on November 19, at Širvintos, and on November 21, at Giedraičiai, they were defeated by Lithuanian forces, leaving the way open for the Lithuanians to advance on Vilnius. The Lithuanian advance was halted, however, by order of a League of Nations commission, which promised to resolve the dispute peacefully.

The wars of independence were thus over, but the Vilnius region remained in Polish hands. The League of Nations did not force Poland to withdraw, and direct Lithuanian-Polish negotiations proved unavailing. In protest, Lithuania did not establish diplomatic relations with Poland.

RECOGNITION OF THE FREE STATE

Lithuania re-established its independence largely through its own efforts. These efforts were successful mainly because of the favorable situation in Eastern Europe following the war, a situation rarely duplicated in modern history. Both empire-minded giants, Germany and Russia, had collapsed and were unable to impose their will on the Baltic countries. Lithuanian forces, although weak, could assert themselves, especially after efforts by the Western Allies to restore imperial rule in Russia had failed. In the existing balance of forces, Lithuania could maintain itself against Poland, which at the time was one of the main foes of Lithuanian independence.

In an attempt to save what remained of its influence for the future, Germany, which up to the very end of the war had sought to incorporate Lithuania, was now the first to recognize its independence (March 23, 1918). After the Compiègne armistice, Germany's forces, although disorganized, helped to turn back the first Bolshevik invasion. Germany also granted a loan of 100 million marks. This fell far short of covering even the war damages, but in the circumstances it represented salvation.

In the beginning, England and France supported Estonia and Latvia more readily. They recognized both governments *de facto* in 1918 and *de jure* on January 26, 1921. Both England and France were afraid that either Germany or the Bolsheviks might establish themselves in the area. England was the first to grant *de facto* recognition to Lithuania, in September, 1919, and was also the first Allied power to grant a loan. Recognition was delayed as a consequence of Polish claims. France, for one, wanted an ally against Germany in Eastern Europe and hence supported Poland.

The United States recognized Lithuania *de jure* on July 27, 1922. England and France followed suit on December 22. (Lithuania had already become a member of the League of Nations on September 21, 1921.) American recognition, which was given partly as a consequence of petition to the President (with a million signatures) by American Lithuanians, came late and followed the collapse of all hopes to restore an "indivisible" Russia and the withdrawal of Japanese forces from Russia in the Far East. Thus, countries within the former Russian Empire were left to their own fate. Nevertheless, the United States became one of the most faithful supporters of Lithuanian independence. Recognition, once granted, was never withdrawn; nor has the present Soviet occupation regime ever been recognized. To this day, the Lithuanian diplomatic service functions freely in the United States as well as in Canada and a number of other Western countries.

2. Independent Lithuania:
A Profile

V. STANLEY VARDYS

The violence that the Kremlin inflicted on the Lithuanian state and society by sovietizing them can be fully understood only by taking into account the period of Lithuania's independence (1918–40). Independence after World War I differentiates Lithuania, as well as Latvia and Estonia, from the other non-Russian captives within the Soviet Union that did not escape Russian rule for any length of time. This chapter will offer a necessary albeit brief sketch of the Czarist background and the development of Lithuania's sovereign self-government.

Independent Lithuania was distinguished by three features, which in some ways were shared by all the new states established between the Baltic and Black seas after World War I, but which gave Lithuania a personality all its own. Socially and economically, Lithuania was a progressive country; the system destroyed by the Kremlin was almost completely a product of independence. Politically, in 1939, its government was an eclipsed democracy, slowly returning to democratic processes. In foreign policy, Lithuania was nationalistic; like many other old European nations whose independence was restored only in modern times, it emerged with blurred boundaries, a geopolitical fact that shaped its concept of national security, its relations with the neighboring states, and its domestic developments.

SOCIAL AND ECONOMIC DEVELOPMENT

The Land and the People. For sixteen years (1923–39), the free Lithuanian state[1]—one of the smallest in Europe, although larger than either Holland or Denmark—had an area of 21,489 sq. mi.

21

The peace treaty with Soviet Russia in 1920 recognized Lithuanian sovereignty over an area of 33,937 sq. mi. About one-third of this area, however, was occupied by Poland; and since Lithuania was unable to regain it, Lithuania in the early 1920's (1920–23) controlled only 20,389 sq. mi. In 1923, an additional 1,100 sq. mi. was gained by the capture of the province of Klaipėda. In October, 1939, part of the Vilnius region (2,569 sq. mi.) was returned by the Soviet Union, but in March of that year, Lithuania had lost the province of Klaipėda to Germany. Nevertheless, the gain more than offset the loss, and, at the time of the Soviet occupation, Lithuania controlled a territory of 22,958 sq. mi. The size of the population varied with the changing boundaries. In 1939, before the territorial changes, Lithuania's estimated population was 2,575,363. With the return of a part of the Vilnius region, the population increased to 2,879,070. In March, 1939, 80.6 per cent of the total population were Lithuanians. The largest non-Lithuanian group were the Jews (7.15 per cent), followed by the Germans (4.1 per cent), Poles (3.04 per cent), Russians (2.34 per cent), Latvians, and White Russians. More than 80 per cent of the population was Roman Catholic; about 10 per cent, Lutheran; 2.6 per cent, Orthodox; and 7 per cent, Jewish.

Since the land was poor in the mineral resources required for industrial development, the main occupation was farming. Although in the nineteen years between 1920 and 1939 slightly more than 10 per cent of the total population moved from villages to the growing cities, three-quarters of the people still lived in rural areas in 1939, and only 23.3 per cent in towns.

The Czarist regime, which had ruled Lithuania for 120 years, hindered the modernization of Lithuanian society. The country's agricultural economy and village society were dominated by large landowners who, to make matters worse, were not Lithuanian in outlook; they were either Polonized Lithuanians or noblemen of Polish origin. Some of them were absentee Russian nobles. Industry was undeveloped. Czarist economic policy put the province at a disadvantage compared with the other parts of the Russian Empire. In 1913, only seven industrial enterprises in the entire region employed more than a hundred workers each; only one employed more than a thousand.[2] The country's culture was kept at a low level by a variety of measures, among them the ban on print in the Latin alphabet imposed in 1864 and enforced until 1904. During this period, Lithuanian books in the Latin alphabet had to be smuggled in from Germany or the United States and were read at the risk of punishment. The rate of illiteracy was very high; the number of schools very small. Local self-government was denied until after the 1905 revolution. In addition, the country's economy was ravaged by the self-defeating and imprudent policies of Germany, which occupied Lithuania during World War I.

Thus, Lithuanian independence started in rather unfavorable conditions, which were aggravated by the needs of military and, later, diplomatic defense. The twenty-two years of political freedom, however, gave the country's young leaders the opportunity, unique in Lithuanian history, to carry out a program of fundamental social and economic reform.

Reform of Agriculture. The chief measure of the program was the land reform, unanimously approved by the Constituent Assembly in 1920, even before the passage of the reborn nation's permanent constitution. In 1922, a detailed reform act was adopted and put into effect under the Reverend Mykolas Krupavičius, Minister of Agriculture and the reform leader of the Christian Democrats. The reform produced far-reaching social, economic, and political results.[3] First, it stilled the land hunger in the villages and thus gained the strong loyalty of the peasants for the new state. Before the reform, many peasants did not own the land they tilled; 40 per cent of all the land was in the hands of a small group of landlords, with about 20 per cent being owned by 450 families, mostly Polish and Russian. Many of these were absentee owners who cared nothing for efficient production. The land reform created the attitudes and conditions making for a greatly increased yield of crops, butterfat, and other farm products. It also eliminated the centuries-old influence of Polish and the more recent importance of Russian landowners, thereby destroying the basis of feudalist conservatism. Most important of all, the reform established the middle-sized family farm at the center of Lithuanian agriculture. About 50 per cent of the land was put into the hands of farmers whose holdings ranged in size from 37.5 to 125 acres. In this way, 45,000 families (about 200,000 people, or about 10 per cent of the population) were "raised to a new status of respectability and self-reliance."[4] Only 0.6 per cent of the farmland was eventually organized into farms of more than 250 acres.[5] Later, a maximum limit of 325 acres (originally, 200 acres) on farm holdings prevented land accumulation and speculation. The land reform accelerated the movement from villages to farmsteads, with the result that Lithuanian society was founded anew on strongly independent, medium-sized, gradually prospering farms. This kind of society was considered the best guarantee of stability. The total area redistributed was about 1.8 million acres, for which the former owners, unlike those in Latvia, were compensated with long-term state bonds.[6] The new owners had to pay for the land in interest-free installments spaced out over thirty-six years.

Network of Education. A second fundamental reform was the establishment of a system of public education. The Czarist government did not operate a single university in Lithuania. About 40 high schools and 1,000 primary schools made up the bleak educational picture in 1919. Twenty years later, the Lithuanian Government ran 2 universities, 5 other academic colleges and institutes, and a military academy. In 1939, the government or private organizations supported 93 high schools and 76 professional schools.[7] The number of primary schools tripled. The 20 per cent of the annual national budget spent on education was supplemented by subsidies from counties, districts, and municipalities for the construction and maintenance of schools. The system of public education was aided by the private schools sponsored by the Catholic societies and by the Jewish, German, Polish, Russian, and Latvian minorities. Education was centered on the humanities, especially after the 1936 reform, which unsuccessfully attempted to lengthen pre-university education from twelve to thirteen years. The government was criticized for not giving sufficient attention to vocational schooling. The country's production machinery needed men trained in technical skills rather than high-school graduates with six years of Latin. The Lithuanian Army at least partially filled this need; it was not merely a defense force supported by 23 per cent of the nation's budget, but also a means of education in literacy, citizenship, and technical skills.

The great progress in education stimulated sufficient interest in culture for the state to organize and finance two theaters, an opera and ballet company, at least two symphony orchestras, radio stations, and other cultural media. A growing body of literature, sculpture, paintings, scientific journals, and newspapers also attests to a cultural revival unequaled in Lithuanian history.

Decision on the Economic Structure of the Country. In the late 1920's, the government decided to develop Lithuania into a dairy and livestock country similar to Denmark. This meant, of course, that industrial growth would lag behind. To this day, the Communists criticize Lithuania's leaders for this policy, charging that they intended to keep Lithuania "backward." The government's decision, however, suited the country and the times. The land did not yield the raw materials for heavy industry; and, since little industry had been developed in Lithuania before World War I, and because few skilled technical workers were available, the creation of highly specialized industries that did not need large quantities of iron and coal was also out of the question. Furthermore, the world-wide economic depression of the late 1920's precluded the entry of a new industrial producer into international competition. On the other hand, the prospect for dairy farming and meat production looked very promising.

Thus, the government wisely shifted from grain crops to dairy products and livestock.[8] Ironically, more than three decades later, on March 19, 1963, Nikita Khrushchev, the chief Communist critic of prewar Lithuania's leaders, ordered that Lithuanian agriculture develop in the same direction. The growth of dairy farming during the period of independence can be seen from the fact that, whereas in 1928 Lithuania produced only 1.6 million tons of butter, in 1939 it produced 19.6 million tons and exported more than 18 million. The number of milk cows doubled, although the number of cattle increased only about 20 per cent between 1913 and 1938. However, there was a 100 per cent increase of milk yield per cow.

Progress in other agricultural sectors was somewhat less impressive, with the exception of hog raising. The number of hogs tripled, despite the agricultural depression of 1932–36, which hit hog breeders hardest by reducing their markets abroad, especially in England. The quality of Lithuanian bacon, moreover, steadily improved until it became competitive with the highest-grade products of older bacon-exporting countries. Lithuania's exports of bacon increased 200 per cent between 1924 and 1939. Such success was achieved because the government encouraged improvement of quality and also developed a canned-meat industry, which had been practically nonexistent. Another factor in the rise of exports was the development of a new system of marketing. The government concentrated on creating industries that used domestic products and resources. For example, the government introduced the growing of sugar beets and constructed Lithuania's first sugar refineries. A similar policy was pursued in the field of manufacturing.

These new industries and the marketing network were created by the state and cooperatives in partnership, thus introducing a social sector in the otherwise free economy of Lithuania. One of the strongest marketing companies (Lietūkis, established in 1923) was a cooperative handling 85 per cent of the total grain and 27 per cent of the flax export, while importing all fertilizer, 80 per cent of agricultural machinery, 40 per cent of the petroleum products, 42 per cent of the cement, etc. It also owned 45 per cent of the stock in the largest and most modern meat-processing company (Maistas, established in 1923), which operated five large plants. All remaining stock in this company was owned by the state. Similarly, the government held a majority of the stock of the sugar company (Lietuvos Cukrus, established in 1932). Processing and marketing of dairy products and eggs was the function of still another cooperative (Pienocentras, established in 1926), which held a virtual monopoly (96 per cent) of exports of dairy products and eggs. Cooperatives were also numerous in the fields of credit, insurance, and manufacturing.

It must be also pointed out that the Lithuanian food industries and agricultural enterprises were not emphasized to the exclusion of manufacturing, though the government did not promote manufacturing the way it did the meat, dairy, and sugar industries, which by 1939 constituted 41 per cent of Lithuania's entire industrial production. The government's fiscal, credit, and monetary policies were geared primarily to the support of the farmer and farm production, though at the same time Lithuania's conservative monetary policies made credit needed by the farm and business people scarce and prohibitively expensive. The litas (unit of Lithuanian currency) was not devalued, even during the depression. On the other hand, the national budget was always balanced, and inflation was hardly felt; Lithuania's foreign debt remained far smaller than that of the other more developed but also more acutely depression-stricken European countries. It also should be added that the power resources for a more radical industrial development were much too scarce and costly; the governments of the 1920's and the 1930's, oriented toward agriculture and conservative in finances, never accumulated enough investment capital to expand those resources, although plans were made. Also, government economists hesitated to involve much greater foreign capital than the small West European and American investments then working in the country. Thus, manufacturing was built and expanded primarily by private entrepreneurs—some foreign, but mostly Lithuanian. Foodstuffs, textiles, clothing, metallurgy, woodwork, paper, and chemicals, in that order of importance, were the chief products of domestic industry; and the state was directly engaged in paper- and glass-making, in addition to food-processing.

Recently, even the Soviets have conceded that between the two world wars Lithuania's industrial capacity more than doubled (2.2).[9] This estimate, however, seems very low, because the number of workers in Lithuanian industries between 1913 and 1939 increased about sixfold. Between 1928 and 1939, the number of textile workers, for example, increased fourfold as a result of new factory construction; in the metallurgical and chemical industries, the number doubled; in food processing, it tripled. In 1913, paper and textile industries employed 300 workers each; in 1939, textile workers numbered 7,019, paper workers, 2,404. Industrialization continued even during the depression, whereas it stood still in most other countries. During the years of the depression (1928–39), industrial production increased three and one-half times;[10] this is a much greater increase than the 2.2 given by the Soviets for the years from 1918 to 1940; furthermore, in 1936, the growth of industrialization began to accelerate rapidly. Nevertheless, in absolute terms, industrialization did not advance very far, because the starting point had been very low. In early 1939, there were only about 40,000 industrial workers.

It is easily understandable, then, why Lithuania imported industrial and manufactured goods and exported farm products. Exports varied, of course, with the change in agricultural production. Just after World War I, grain and timber were the most important exports. Twenty years later, dairy products had supplanted grain. In addition to timber, which still was high on the export list, bacon, eggs, flax, and, of course, grain were the leading exports. By then, however, most of the exported timber was partially or completely processed. The main export was foodstuffs, which constituted 60 per cent of the total; the remainder included timber and its products, flax, and unprocessed wool. Imports included machinery and machine parts, motor cars, coal, cement, scientific instruments, woolen yarn, cotton and woolen fabrics, and other manufactured goods. Only twice during the decade 1929–39 did the country buy more than it sold. Generally, it had a comfortable trade surplus. Only a small fraction of its trade (5–8 per cent) was conducted with the Soviet Union. Lithuania's main trading partners were Great Britain and Germany.

Needless to say, improved agriculture and industrialization increased the real income of wage earners.[11] In 1938, the weekly wages of an industrial worker bought 1.7 pairs of shoes in Lithuania, compared with only 0.35 in the Soviet Union; a Polish worker, in contrast, could buy 1.2 pairs, a Latvian, 1.9 pairs. Weekly wages bought 60 lbs. of meat in Lithuania, but only 4.3 lbs. in the Soviet Union; in Poland, weekly wages bought 38 lbs., in Latvia, 56 lbs. Weekly wages, furthermore, paid for 0.33 per cent of a woolen suit in Lithuania, but only 0.09 per cent in the Soviet Union. The Latvian figure was 0.55; the Polish, 0.42.

Social Organization. While the land reform prevented the rise of a large village proletariat, industrialization was not widespread enough to encourage the growth of an important class of industrial wage earners. As a result, the number of rural and industrial workers was relatively small, quite insufficient for any class-oriented division of the country and inadequate to give meaningful support to political radicalism. The "middle-class" farmer dominated the countryside, thus giving it a stable outlook of political moderation. In the cities, a new middle class arose: the intelligentsia, the businessmen, the bureaucrats, the military officers. Numerous workers also came together in the larger cities, which contributed to the changed character of the cities. However, they were not yet overcrowded or congested, because the population movement from village to town was moderate; between 1920 and 1929, slightly more than 10 per cent of the population moved to the towns. Competition between city life and village life, however, was already felt. The most important, though not the largest group in both cities and villages was the intelligentsia, including the clergy, professionals, and teachers. Most of these were politically moderate, nationalistic, and strongly oriented toward Western Europe, to which Lithuania was bound not only by economic interests but also by cultural ties. It should be added that the Lithuanian-educated intelligentsia shared with its largely Russian-educated predecessors the spirit of social reform.

This brief survey of Lithuanian society would be incomplete without a discussion of the influence of the Roman Catholic Church. Its importance in Lithuania was comparable to that in

Ireland, Italy, or Poland. Before World War I, the priest commanded the highest respect; during the period of independence his influence was still dominant, but the other professions were beginning to gain importance too. The Church's traditions and customs were part of the folkways; its moral code dominated public opinion. At the end of the nineteenth century, the Church largely freed itself from Polish domination, and its clergy provided much of the leadership of the movement for independence and, afterward, for radical social reforms. Naturally enough, a Catholic group became the dominant political force. As a consequence, Lithuania's first permanent constitution was very favorable to religion and protected certain traditional prerogatives of the Church. For example, the constitution provided for compulsory teaching of religion, except in private schools sponsored by nonsectarian organizations. Thus the state financed the teaching of the Catholic as well as the Protestant and Jewish religions in public primary and secondary schools. Furthermore, churches were granted exclusive jurisdiction over marriage laws, each denomination being allowed to apply the law in its own way. As in present-day Italy, civil marriage was unknown in Lithuania between 1918 and 1940; for Catholics, this meant that divorce was impossible. In addition, denominational schools were eligible for state aid, and in the early 1920's, the Christian Democrats passed a law guaranteeing salaries for the clergy. Similarly, the state supported a Catholic theological-philosophical school (its curriculum was not confined to theology) and a Department of Protestant Theology at the University of Kaunas.

Although all religious denominations enjoyed equal protection before the law and no religious tests were required for holding any public office, the constitutional provisions and laws favorable to religion strengthened the position of the Catholic Church, which was already economically independent by virtue of its ownership of land. The Church remained the most important social force in Lithuania and could not be combated successfully by mere political means. Thus, the plans for reducing the Church's financial strength that were advocated in 1926 by the ruling Social Democratic–Populist coalition failed to materialize. Equally fruitless were the later efforts of the authoritarian Nationalist League of Antanas Smetona to curb the Church's influence by banning and restraining some Catholic organizations, and by restricting the work of the Catholic theological-philosophical school.

It is important to add that during the period of independence, the Church became indissolubly wedded to Lithuanian nationalism, and a majority of the clergy, including the hierarchy, had already supported democracy before World War I. In the 1920's, for example, the clergy-dominated Christian Democratic bloc briefly broke off diplomatic relations with the Holy See, because of the decision of Pope Pius XI to incorporate the Vilnius diocese into Poland's ecclesiastical organization. Furthermore, after a period of flirtation with the Nationalist League (1926–28), the Church opposed the authoritarian regime of Antanas Smetona.

The Whirl of Domestic Politics

The Early Democratic Radicalism. Although Lithuania, because of Czarist opposition, did not have a tradition of self-government, all the groups that participated in the Lithuanian national revival at the end of the nineteenth century favored the establishment of a democratic Lithuanian state. Organized authoritarianism in Lithuania developed only after independence was won. During the two years, 1919–20, however, "everyone saw salvation only in democracy. It was the alpha and omega of . . . political wisdom. Like a sort of holy spirit, democracy was expected to enlighten the masses with political wisdom and confer upon them the gift of political infallibility."[12] In part, this sweeping democratic faith was rooted in the peasant origins of the new leaders; it also reflected the theoretical views of the largely Russian-educated Lithuanian intelligentsia, most of whom had matured during the movement for popular government in Russia before World War I. To a certain extent, this democratic conviction was merely a symbol of the nationalist passion for Lithuanian self-government; largely, it was sustained and kindled by the radicalism of the Russian Revolutions of 1917. Lithuanian refugees returning after wartime evacuation to Russia injected an especially large dose of this democratic radicalism.

The Lithuanian Council which proclaimed Lithuania's independence on February 16, 1918, was formed as democratically as wartime circumstances permitted. Its mandate was renewed in 1919 at a conference of provincial delegates held in Kaunas. A year later, even before the end of the wars for independence, a Constituent Assembly was formed, elected by universal suffrage, with an estimated 85 to 90 per cent of registered voters casting their ballots.

The Constituent Assembly was a remarkable legislature. On the one hand, its membership faithfully reflected Lithuania's ideological, political, and ethnic diversity; on the other hand, the system of proportional representation that was used did not deny the Assembly a firm working majority. Of the 112 members, 28 belonged to the Populist party, 12 were Social Democrats, 11 represented ethnic minorities (7 Jews, 3 Poles, and 1 German), 2 were independents. The absolute majority of 59 were Christian Democrats. The legislature's stability was assured by a coalition between the dominant Christian Democrats and the Populists. This coalition proved to be the backbone of the Lithuanian democracy. After the demise of this Christian Democratic–Populist partnership in 1924, democracy itself perished.

Although the independence wars prevented the Constituent Assembly from continuous work, within three years it was able to hold 257 plenum sessions and pass about 300 laws.[13] Two of these, authorization of the land reform and the Constitution, were of historical significance.

The Constitution was adopted on August 1, 1922, and went into force five days later.[14] Like the constitutions of many other Central East European countries at the time, it provided for the assembly type (the traditional French type) of democracy, with the legislature controlling the executive branch of government. The president and the members of the *seimas* were to be elected for three years. The president appointed the chairman of the council of ministers, but the council collectively and the ministers individually were responsible to the legislature. The judicial system was independent of both the council and the legislature. In Lithuania, as in other European countries with a similar form of government, legislative supremacy left the government at the mercy of the political parties, because assembly-type government actually meant party rule. The new nation had selected the most difficult form of democracy, a choice which later endangered the democratic system itself.

The Politics of Democracy. Although the Christian Democrats had an absolute majority in the Constituent Assembly, Lithuania generally had a multiparty system. The basis of partisan division was neither economic nor social but ideological (*weltanschaulich*). The spectrum of ideology ranged from Catholicism through anticlerical Liberalism to Marxism. To compound the political diversity, ideological competition was very severe and frequently

fanatical. It did not, however, come from class antagonism. With
the exception of the Social Democrats, who claimed to represent
the working class, the appeal and membership of the others was
mixed. The dominant Christian Democratic bloc (composed of
three parties: the Christian Democrats, the Farmers Union, and
the Labor Federation) enjoyed the support of both farm and labor
groups; it appealed equally to the city dweller and the farmer.
Although divided into the "liberal" and "conservative" wings,
the bloc supported reform leading to a welfare state within the
limitations of the country's agricultural economy. Its chief com-
petitor—because most akin to it—was the Populist Party. The chief
difference between them was ideological. While the Christian
Democrats protected the prerogatives of the religious denominations and the interests of the Catholic Church, especially in
education, the Populists opposed them. It was primarily this
ideological attitude, not economic or other issues, which brought
the Populists close to the Social Democrats. In Lithuania, the Social Democrats were more radical than the other parties, but
similarly committed to parliamentarianism and nationalism; in
other words, they were Marxist, but not revolutionary. The Communists had split off from the Social Democrats in 1917 and been
outlawed, though sometimes they ran candidates under labels of
other (front) organizations.

Thus the extreme Left in Lithuanian politics was occupied by
the Marxist Social Democrats. The Populists and the Christian
Democratic bloc occupied the Center (the Left Center and Right
Center, respectively), while the Right was made up of the Farmers
Party and, especially, the Nationalists, first elected to the third
seimas in 1926. Moderately conservative in economic and social
policy, the Nationalists were at first ambivalent toward democracy, but then turned against it, introducing authoritarian rule.
The political spectrum was completed by representatives of the
minorities, who jealously guarded the liberal rights granted the
minorities in the early 1920's. (Those rights were curtailed somewhat a decade later.) Generally, they voted with the Populists and
the Social Democrats to offset the Christian Democratic domination.

Understandably, it was not easy to organize majorities in such
a divided legislature. Once formed, they were, moreover, unstable
and kept the executive weak, while interparty divisions continued
to intensify. Disagreements were caused primarily by ideological
differences. The constitution of 1922, for example, was adopted

solely by Christian Democratic votes, because the Populists and the Social Democrats disagreed with provisions concerning religion and education. Elections[15] to the first regular *seimas* in 1922 brought in a membership divided (thirty-nine to thirty-nine) between the Christian Democratic bloc and the others. These others—that is, the opposition to the Christian Democrats—even refused to recognize the election of a new President, Aleksandras Stulginskis, a leader of the "conservative" wing of the Christian Democratic bloc. This necessitated a new election two years before the legislature's term expired. This time the Catholic bloc won a marginal majority of only two in a house of seventy-eight members. As this majority was too small for effective government, the Christian Democrats managed to woo the Populists back into a working coalition, and in this way guaranteed the country a spell of political stability. However, the new friendship soon ended in ideological disagreement on matters of education; in 1924, the two partners separated, to the great detriment of democracy, which they both cherished. In the regular election of 1926, the ruling Catholic bloc suffered a resounding defeat. The issues of economic recession, clericalism, partisan spoils, and corruption in government were successfully used by the opposition parties to reduce the representation of the bloc to thirty-five out of eighty members of the new *seimas*.

However, in this last free election, in May, 1926, the gains of the Center-Left opposition were small, and somewhat complicated by the appearance of two new splinter groups—the Nationalists, who won three seats in alliance with the Populists, and the Farmers Party, which elected two representatives. Under these precarious conditions, originally poisoned by the extremely bitter campaign of the spring of 1926, the Populists, twenty-two of whom had been elected, would not consider renewing the coalition with the Christian Democratic bloc, but allied themselves with the more radical Social Democrats instead. However, since their combined strength was still short of the necessary majority (the Social Democrats, though they had gained in the elections, had merely fifteen deputies), the coalition needed additional support. Repaying the Populists' favor, the Nationalists gave a vote of confidence to a Populist-Social Democratic cabinet. However, the support ultimately needed by the new ministry was given primarily by the deputies of the minority groups. Seeking the support of these deputies to form a Populist–Social Democratic coalition appears to have been a fatal mistake. In a country as nationalistic as

Lithuania, it was inviting trouble to form a government and stake its stability on the votes of the Polish and German minorities (and the Jewish minority too, though this did not arouse any suspicions), groups whose mother countries were involved in conflicts with Lithuania. Just seven years earlier, Poland had attempted to overthrow the Lithuanian state from within with the help of the Polish minority; a local German plot against Lithuania had also been uncovered in Klaipėda only a short time before.

The new cabinet, headed by the Populist leader Mykolas Šleževičius, an energetic and idealistic stalwart of Lithuanian politics, who had headed a differently constituted coalition Cabinet during the dangerous years of the wars of independence (1919–21), immediately proceeded to reward coalition partners and supporters and initiated or planned a number of policies designed to cut expenditures; unfortunately, these seemed (and some were) devised to redress the domestic balance of power, which until then had favored the Christian Democrats. Some of the measures were intended to normalize certain democratic procedures. However, these policies estranged influential segments of society and irritated the citizenry, thus producing effects quite contrary to those intended. For example, the elimination of restraints on the right of assembly and on the press, which dated back to the war period of 1920, and an amnesty for prisoners convicted for violation of these restraints benefited the Communist Party almost exclusively. Its activities now aroused fears of Communist domination, especially since the Social Democratic Minister of the Interior, in the name of freedom, even allowed attacks on, and blackmail of, law-enforcement agencies. These fears were intensified by plans, advocated primarily by the Social Democratic coalition partner, to reconsider the place of religion in the schools (the Minister of Education was also a Social Democrat), to discontinue the clergy's salaries, and even to cut the size of the Church's landholdings. The dissatisfaction of the clergy and other groups with these developments, and with radically Leftist tendencies generally, was shared by many Army officers, who feared not only the regime's Leftism, but also plans for a reduction in the armed forces, which they considered a threat to national security. Finally, the coalition incurred universal disfavor by allowing an increase of Polish schools (though they cost the government nothing) as a reward for Polish support. This favoritism was shown at a time when the Polish Government was closing down Lithuanian schools in the occupied Vilnius region; the country was very angry. These anxieties and emotions easily engulfed the youth, who began demonstrations against the government, and by the fall of 1926, the country was a powder keg.[16]

Finally, several police actions against demonstrating students ignited this powder keg, and on December 17, a revolt, earlier planned by a group of army officers, was set into motion.[17] President Kazys Grinius, in office just six months, was compelled to appoint the Nationalist Professor Augustinas Voldemaras as Prime Minister and then was requested to resign. The *seimas,* with the coalition parties boycotting the session, elected Antanas Smetona, the former Provisional President of the Republic, again to head the state. The Christian Democratic bloc voted for both men; several of the group's politicians themselves had participated in the coup, and now they joined the Voldemaras cabinet. However, this incidental partnership did not last. Christian Democrats did not regard the new cabinet as permanent and sought an immediate return to parliamentarian rule. However, the Nationalists, catapulted to supreme power, did not intend to quit; instead, they outsmarted their Christian Democratic and Farmers Union collaborators, who had no choice but to leave the Cabinet within a year after the *coup d'état.* The third member of the Christian Democratic bloc, the intractable Labor Federation, was forced out in 1929. Meanwhile, to quiet the country, the Smetona-Voldemaras regime promulgated a new provisional constitution (1928) that provided for a legislature and also strengthened the executive. However, Smetona delayed elections indefinitely, and after about three years of behind-the-scenes maneuvering, indecision, and confusion, settled for an authoritarian government.

The late 1920's and early 1930's were inauspicious for Central East European democracies; they declined everywhere save in Czechoslovakia, giving way to autocrats—some strong, some weak. However, democracy in Lithuania did not lose, as it later did in Latvia, Estonia, and even Germany, as a direct result of strains imposed by the economic depression of the 1930's. Although some of the Populist–Social Democratic policies were unnecessarily provocative and thus inspired fear and undermined confidence in the government, the eclipse of democracy reflected, as historian Juozas Jakštas correctly explains,[18] the crisis of the assembly-type system, the lack of political maturity, the failure of the largely apolitical farmers to understand and appreciate the workings of democracy. Generally conservative, they quickly tired of partisan competition and the spoils system. To this should be added that party leaders were short-tempered and frequently intolerant of decisions they did not like; majorities did not understand the limits they must not exceed if they wished to retain the confidence of the minority. Finally, the frequent deadlocks in the *seimas* hurt the executive's stability, thus breeding dissatisfaction with the system itself. In fairness, however, it should be said that the executive's initiative was stifled less than it seemed at the moment; on the contrary, the early and mid-1920's witnessed an outburst of creative energy. The *seimas* and the numerous cabinets not only designed and began the execution of land reform, but also established a sound currency, organized financial institutions, reformed local government, established the foundations of a cooperative economic system, created a university, founded an opera house and drama and ballet companies, and in six years almost tripled the number of primary and secondary schools. Their many accomplishments also included the successful termination of the wars of independence, the weathering of stormy conflicts over Vilnius and the seizure of Klaipėda, and the bolstering of Lithuania's security by a nonaggression pact with the Soviet Union.

Authoritarian Rule. The regime of President Smetona derived its support[19] primarily from the Army and the Nationalist Party, which called itself the Nationalist "League" to emphasize its claim that it was not just another partisan association. In the late 1920's, there was a danger that Prime Minister Voldemaras, a very colorful as well as aggressive politician, widely known in Europe for his eloquent and brusque defense in the forum of the League of Nations of Lithuania's claim to Vilnius, would establish a Fascist dictatorship. But the moderating influence of Smetona prevailed, although Voldemaras had to be removed from the government, then arrested, and eventually pensioned off to live in exile. Smetona saw some good in Fascism, but he considered it alien to Lithuania and therefore did not copy it too closely. He opposed National Socialism outright and condemned it publicly. It is, however, quite clear that Smetona was not a democrat. In 1935, a series of previously passed restraining laws on the press and the right of assembly culminated in the formal outlawing of all non-Nationalist political parties. In 1938, Smetona promulgated a new constitution that strengthened the presidency, but refused checks to the president's power. Provision for a legislature, moreover, was offset by extensive limitations on suffrage. Though a legislature was chosen the same year, it acted as a mere rubber stamp for presidential decisions. The regime that the Nationalists created defies easy definition. It certainly was not totalitarian; opposition, though outlawed, functioned unofficially, and many opposition leaders were strongly entrenched in the universities and schools and in a number of large state-supported cooperatives. Although controlled and hampered, several thousand associations continued their work and only a small part of the press was in Nationalist hands. Press censorship existed, but it was not absolute. Arrests of opposition leaders, although numerous in the early 1930's, almost ceased by 1938. Economic activity was completely free. Minorities were protected. Attempts to overthrow the regime were put down, yet capital punishment against conspirators was extremely rare and only Communists were held in prisons for extended periods of time. The regime was certainly more moderate than Mussolini's and gentler than Piłsudski's personal dictatorship in Poland. It has been dubbed a "semidemocracy, semidictatorship," with only some attributes that today we identify as totalitarian.[20] Indeed, the Nationalist regime could not introduce totalitarianism, because the forces of democratic opposition were too strong and had to be handled by less extreme methods. A mild-mannered man, Smetona could not be compared to Mussolini, Hitler, or even Piłsudski. He kept the regime in power largely by using political patronage and cleverly playing off the competing governmental institutions and political forces, including his own supporters, against one another.

The regime was constantly subject to pressures at home. Finally, in 1938, it was shaken by Poland's ultimatum demanding resumption of diplomatic relations, and in 1939, it was much weakened by Germany's unconditional demand for the return of the Klaipėda region. Following the Polish ultimatum of March, 1938, Smetona needed broader support and appointed a nonpolitical General, Jonas Černius, to head a government composed not only of Nationalists and neutral technicians but also of the previously persecuted Populists and Christian Democrats. Although in 1939 the prime ministership was returned to the Nationalist party by the appointment of the moderate Nationalist Antanas Merkys, cooperation with the Populist and Christian Democratic opposition survived. Some elements within the Nationalist Party, it is true, disliked this course and urged resumption of complete control once the national crises were over; however, the floodgate was already open. The start of World War II endangered the country's very independence; the opposition by now was so strong in economic institutions, schools, and even in the army that the liberalizing trend could not be reversed. After a twenty-year cycle, the country was groping for a new form of self-government that would steer clear of the radical democratic and the authoritarian extremes.

In Europe Between the Wars

Foreign Policy Objectives and Techniques. Generally, Lithuania pursued three objectives of foreign policy: It sought to protect its independence, defend and secure its territorial integrity, and to support the European *status quo* created at Versailles as a condition for its own security. In the early 1920's, military means as well as diplomacy were employed to fight off enemies of independence and then to achieve a favorable solution of the Klaipėda (Memel) question. After 1923, however, military power was not used; policy-makers and the public were divided even on its employment against the Soviet aggression of June 15, 1941, which admittedly occurred under quite unorthodox circumstances. Broadly speaking, for self-protection Lithuania first and foremost relied on the collective-security arrangements of the League of Nations, later supplemented by unilateral, bilateral, and regional action. After the start of World War II, along with Latvia and Estonia, Lithuania placed its hope for security in the policy of neutrality.

Admitted to the League of Nations in 1921, Lithuania, then recognized by only six states, became a faithful member and an enthusiastic signatory of League-sponsored international agreements. Lithuanian affairs frequently were the subject of speeches delivered in the League. The Lithuanian Government also submitted important cases to the International Tribunal at The Hague.

Problems discussed in these international forums concerned the questions if Vilnius and Klaipėda. The old capital city of Vilnius and an area of 13,000 sq. mi., was lost to Poland. The city of Klaipėda, with a strip of Baltic shoreland, was regained from Germany. Both conflicts created tensions and crises in Lithuanian-Polish and Lithuanian-German relations that endangered Lithuania's international situation and threatened domestic tranquility. Lithuania's refusal to abandon its claim to Vilnius induced Poland, then an important ally of France, to obstruct the acceptance of Lithuania by the West European states. Polish maneuverings were largely responsible for Lithuania's late recognition *de jure* by France and Great Britain. Conflict over Klaipėda with Germany resulted in German accusations against Lithuania in the League of Nations and elsewhere, in economic boycotts that hurt Lithuania's foreign trade, in hostile propaganda, and in diplomatic pressures. These conflicts also contributed to the failure of a Finnish-Estonian-Latvian-Lithuanian-Polish confederation against the Soviet Union and considerably delayed Lithuania's alliance with the two other Baltic states of Latvia and Estonia. Germany could and did foment unrest and difficulties through the German population in the Klaipėda area and elsewhere, while in the early 1920's, Poland, with the help of the Polish minority, attempted to overthrow the Lithuanian state itself (the Polska Organzacja Wojskowa affair of 1919).

However, Lithuania was willing to suffer the propagandistic, diplomatic, and economic disadvantages caused by these conflicts. It is important to note that on this issue all political groups were united. Explanation of these strong commitments to regaining Vilnius and keeping Klaipėda, commitments sometimes labeled unrealistic or "supernationalistic," is not found merely in the nationalist feelings of a newly reborn nation, though these naturally aroused the masses, thus making a flexible policy of any government very difficult. There were other, more substantial reasons for continuing on this course. First, the Polish occupation of Vilnius meant a substantial loss of ethnic Lithuanian population. In the past centuries, the Lithuanian language was being replaced by Polish in the south and the east, and a nation of 2 million people could hardly afford a further massive cut of its ethnic trunk. Further substantial losses had occurred to the Germans in East Prussia and the Klaipėda region. Although, according to the German census of 1910, the population of the Klaipėda region was still almost evenly divided between the German- and Lithuanian-speaking groups, many of these Lithuanians were culturally tied to Germany and were loyal to the Kaiser rather than to Lithuania. Moreover, without Klaipėda, Lithuania would no longer have commercial access to the Baltic Sea and thus would suffer enormous economic loss.

Collective Security and the Conflict over Vilnius. The Lithuanians felt the loss of the Vilnius region especially acutely because it did not occur on the battlefield but was effected by breaking a valid agreement. On October 7, 1920, an armistice agreement was signed with Poland, leaving Vilnius and its environment to Lithuania. Two days later, however, the "independent" Polish General Lucjan Zeligowski, on orders from Piłsudski,[21] who had recognized the legitimacy of Lithuania's claim to Vilnius, broke the armistice and marched on Vilnius, expelling the unsuspecting Lithuanians. Piłsudski planned to have Zeligowski penetrate as far as possible into Lithuanian territory. However, some days later, Lithuanian regulars stopped the Polish advance. Zeligowski's troops were in full retreat when the pursuing Lithuanians halted at the order of a commission of the League of Nations, which wanted to stop the hostilities at any price. The League promised a peaceful solution of the conflict, and the Lithuanians took the case to Geneva. There the Assembly decreed, as was the custom in those days, that the local population decide their fate by plebiscite. Lithuania agreed, but demanded the withdrawal of the Polish troops. Warsaw also consented to the plebiscite, but refused to leave the occupied area. Actually, neither side was interested in the proposed plebiscite: The Lithuanians did not consider elections a proper method for determining the fate of their capital city, which they claimed as theirs anyway, and the Poles insisted on the right of current possession.[22] Piłsudski, a native of the area (he requested in his will that his body be buried in Cracow but his heart in Vilnius, where it still rests), would not take any risks.

The League of Nations then suggested direct Polish-Lithuanian negotiations under the chairmanship of the League's representative, the Belgian delegate Paul Hymans. The Belgian diplomat worked out a proposal that provided for the cession of Vilnius to Lithuania if the latter agreed to permanent political, military, and economic ties to Poland. Hymans thus sought to re-establish a form of the long-defunct Polish-Lithuanian union. This was in fact the main goal of Polish and French foreign policy. Two versions of the proposal were considered. After the first version failed of acceptance, Hymans revised the plan, but at the end of 1921, the revision was also rejected. Actually, neither Poland nor Lithuania cared for the plan. Poland objected to the region's coming under Lithuanian sovereignty, while Lithuania opposed a union with Poland that provided, among other matters, for the equality of the Polish language on Lithuanian territory. After the collapse of negotiations, the League abandoned the case. Shortly afterwards, Poland held an election in the occupied area, under the supervision of its troops, and of course won. Lithuania's proposal to have the dispute settled by the World Court at The Hague was rejected, and Lithuania then decided (early in 1922) not to establish diplomatic relations with Poland. The new border was closed to traffic and remained shut even after the Conference of Ambassadors formally recognized the Polish gains in 1923.[23]

Warsaw, however, continued its attempts to open the Lithuanian-Polish border, and finally persuaded the League of Nations to charge Lithuania with violating international obligations by refusing Poland transit. Lithuania appealed to the World Court at The Hague, and in 1931, the Court declared Lithuania to be within its sovereign rights. After this decision, Lithuania was left in peace, but not for very long.

Poland renewed its pressure on Lithuania early in 1938. Then allied with Germany, the Polish Government, shocked by Hitler's *Anschluss* of Austria, sought to compensate Poland and, presumably, to contain Germany by gaining access to the Baltic Sea through Lithuania. On March 17, 1938, Poland handed Lithuania an ultimatum[24] demanding resumption of diplomatic relations and the opening of the frontier. Poland warned that it would use force if Lithuania refused to comply. The Lithuanian Government had hardly any choice but to submit, and on March 31, the forced intercourse was renewed. The Lithuanians, however, did not accept their submission as a renunciation of their claim to Vilnius.

The new situation, however, did not continue for very long. In September, 1939, Poland lay in the deadly grip of the German-Soviet pincer, with thousands of its defeated troops seeking refuge in Lithuania, where, only a year earlier, they threatened to enter as conquerors. After having been interned, most of the Polish troops and civilians were permitted by Lithuania to flee to the west, though some fell victim to the Soviets, together with their Lithuanian hosts who lost their independence just a short while later. Thus ended the unfortunate quarrel between the two historic partners.

The Question of Klaipėda and Unilateral Action. Lithuania's relations with Germany were hardly less turbulent and unhappy. Difficulties with Germany arose over the question of Klaipėda. After 700 years of German domination, this old Lithuanian province was detached from Germany by the Versailles Treaty and administered under the authority of the victorious Allied powers. Since the region was separated from the Reich on the ground that a majority of its population was Lithuanian,[25] it was presumed that the Conference of Ambassadors, which ultimately had to decide Klaipėda's fate, would transfer it to Lithuanian sovereignty. The Conference, however, hesitated, because not only Lithuania but also Poland, backed by France, sought domination over the area. Poland and France offered Klaipėda to Lithuania in return for the latter's recognition of Polish claims to Vilnius and for permanent Lithuanian ties with Warsaw, as one version of the Hymans proposal provided. The Lithuanians, however, did not consider such a trade advantageous. Consequently, after the Hymans plan was rejected, the Big Powers did not know what to do with the region. The Poles, previously willing to see it go to Lithuania because Lithuania itself would belong to them, now tried to keep it out of Lithuanian hands. With French help, they hoped to convert Klaipėda into a free state like Danzig. Such a solution was the best guarantee of Polish and French influence in the region and its harbor, Klaipėda.

But Lithuania knew of this plan and did not wait. It had lost faith in the solution of such conflicts by negotiation and immediately following the French march into the Ruhr, on January 15, 1923, struck out to seize the Klaipėda region by force. On that day, the Lithuanians of the region staged a revolt[26] against the French administration. The revolt was engineered in Kaunas. The rebels, with disguised help and leadership from the Lithuanian Government, immediately and almost without bloodshed took over the area. It is important to note that at that time Berlin's interests in Klaipėda coincided with those of Lithuania. Germany rightly foresaw that it would have more influence in the region under Lithuanian rule than in a free state under Polish-French domination, and therefore encouraged the Lithuanians to seize control of the area. German intelligence began dropping hints to this effect as early as 1922, and during the actual revolt, the Germans facilitated, wherever they could, border crossings by Lithuanian insurgents.[27] After the seizure of Klaipėda, Weimar Germany continued friendly relations with Lithuania, though, of course, at a price. This, it should be added, was never understood by the Germans of the Klaipėda region; during the first years of Lithuanian rule in Klaipėda, they therefore created disturbances, much to the chagrin of Berlin.

Reactions to the Lithuanian seizure of Klaipėda were almost exactly as expected in Kaunas, by now quite familiar with Allied behavior. There were protests, threats, ultimatums, but Lithuanian firmness induced negotiations. However, since pressures mounted from the French-Polish side, from their allies, and from Germany, the Conference of Ambassadors did not flatly transfer the region to Lithuanian sovereignty, but recognized it only under very broad local autonomy, which considerably limited the authority of the Lithuanian Government. Lithuania, moreover, was "punished" by the Conference of Ambassadors; it formally recognized Polish rule over the Vilnius region.

Although the Klaipėda region, economically and otherwise, prospered as never before, Lithuania experienced political difficulties in Klaipėda.[28] The Lithuanian Government soon found that numerical strength in the area did not bring equivalent political power, because the native Lithuanians were more Germanized than had been expected; nationalistic Lithuanian parties could not muster majorities in the region's legislature. Local Germans, moreover, never became reconciled to being Lithuanian citizens. To complicate matters, Germany interfered in local politics through its diplomatic representatives. Secession plots were uncovered by the Lithuanians. Germany, on the other hand, charged Lithuania with the violation of the Klaipėda statute. Debates in the League of Nations led nowhere. Finally, in 1931, Lithuania brought the matter of statute violation to the World Court at The Hague. As in its dispute with Poland, this time too Lithuania won, but as Europe was not governed by court decisions, trouble in Klaipėda continued.

After the rise of Nazism in Germany, political difficulties in Klaipėda quickly became serious. Nazi and Nazi-front organizations took over the leadership of German nationalism and promoted *Anschluss*. In 1934, the Lithuanian Government accused them of conspiracy against the state, and thus the first European trial of the Nazis took place in Kaunas. Many defendants were found guilty. Hitler was furious and retaliated by scrapping a trade agreement with Lithuania. Since Germany was at that time the largest buyer of Lithuanian farm products, the Führer's vengeance brought economic loss and hardship to the Lithuanian farmer.

Lithuanian resistance to German pressures, however, could not continue indefinitely. Immediately following the occupation of Czechoslovakia, in March, 1939, the German Foreign Minister, von Ribbentrop, presented the Lithuanian Foreign Minister, Juozas Urbšys, with an ultimatum demanding that Lithuania cede the Klaipėda region to Germany. Upon consultation, it appeared that the Western powers counseled acceptance, and Lithuania again submitted to superior force. A pale and seasick Hitler arrived on March 22, 1939, to receive Klaipėda into the Reich. It appeared that he had boarded the destroyer "Deutschland" even before the Lithuanians agreed to the ultimatum and became sick while waiting at sea for the final signing of the protocol.[29] In accordance with the "voluntary" transfer of Klaipėda to the Reich, Germany granted Lithuania a free harbor zone and the rights of transit. This concession, however, was withdrawn after Lithuania was occupied by the Soviet Union.

Search for Bilateral and Regional Security. Although the little country remained a faithful member of the League of Nations, the treatment it had received from the League and its French and Polish supporters in the cases of Vilnius and Klaipėda caused it to doubt that the *cordon sanitaire* then organized by the Poles with French aid was a suitable arrangement for Lithuania. In 1919, Lithuania was an enthusiastic supporter of the idea of a Baltic confederation composed of Finland, Estonia, Latvia, Lithuania, and Poland, which was to serve as a safety valve against the Soviets and, to a lesser degree, as the final link of a chain checking German expansionism. However, Lithuania left the negotiations on the confederation after Poland occupied the Vilnius territory. Persistent Polish efforts to normalize relations with Lithuania for the purpose of drawing it back into the negotiations were fruitless. Meanwhile, the Soviet Union anxiously watched Poland's actions. The Soviet Union accused Poland of forming an aggressive bloc against it and sought to shatter the projected defense chain by offering security to individual prospective members of the Baltic-Polish group. After first easing the atmosphere with the conclusion of a nonaggression pact with Germany (August 24, 1926), the Soviet Union successfully negotiated a nonaggression treaty with Lithuania.[30] The treaty, signed on September 28, guaranteed Lithuania's frontiers (as laid down by the peace treaty with Moscow in 1920) and pledged neutrality in case of attack by a third party. Thus, the treaty reaffirmed Lithuania's claim to the Vilnius region, although this had been denied by the Conference of Ambassadors. For this reason, Lithuania considered the treaty a diplomatic victory; it checkmated Poland, which now would find it more difficult to carry out its diplomatic design in the Baltic area. The treaty was even more useful for the Soviets. It meant the disruption of Warsaw's plan to deal collectively with the Soviet Union by the Polish-led bloc of Baltic nations. Lithuania was therefore criticized for signing the pact; foreign observers, aided by Polish diplomacy, accused Lithuania of upsetting the *status quo* and thus endangering European security against the Soviet Union.[31] Looked at from the perspective of time, it is easy to see that such a judgment was incorrect; the collapse of the *cordon sanitaire,* which was to be headed by Poland, could not be blamed on Lithuania. In the first place, it could not exist without a strong commitment from England and France, which was never given; in the second, the chosen leader of the bloc, Poland, did not succeed in organizing it, although Poland could have without Lithuanian participation. The Lithuanian-Soviet agreement, supplemented by a definition of aggression, was renewed after Hitler's rise to power in 1933, and then extended to 1944, only to be broken by the Soviets long before its expiration.

Changes in the European situation in 1934 offered Lithuania further opportunity to strengthen its position on the Baltic coast. Hitler had risen to power in Germany, and Nazi propagandists called for a German return to the Baltic area. Fears of this new *Drang nach Osten* were augmented by Hitler's refusal to sign an Eastern Locarno pact, which would have provided, among other matters, a joint German-Soviet guarantee of the Baltic states. Instead, the Führer signed a nonaggression pact with Piłsudski, thus affecting a very unlikely German-Polish alliance. Latvia and Estonia, which had relied on Warsaw and so were reluctant to cement relations with Lithuania because of the latter's conflicts with Poland as well as with Germany, now themselves felt threatened by Germany and miffed by Poland's attitudes; thus they accepted Lithuania's proposal to establish a Baltic entente by admitting Lithuania into the already-existing alliance between Latvia and Estonia. A treaty of "entente and collaboration," signed in Geneva on September 12, 1934, provided for coordinated political and economic policies, though not for military assistance. The Lithuanians hoped, however, that the entente would become one of "the important factors stabilizing peace in that corner of Europe between the large states of Russia, Poland, and Germany."[32]

Experience soon proved, however, that these arrangements were insufficient for the stabilization of peace. The independence and territorial integrity of Lithuania, like that of the other states, needed stronger protection. This could come only from England and France. These two allies supported the independence of the three states, and in the fateful summer of 1939, refused to deliver them to the Soviet Union in exchange for an Anglo-French-Soviet treaty of alliance. At the same time, however, they committed their military power to defend only Poland's independence. The Baltic states were left to their fate.

3. Aggression, Soviet Style, 1939-40

V. STANLEY VARDYS

In the summer of 1939, the Nazis and the Soviets decided jointly to complete the destruction of the Versailles organization of Europe, at which until then each had been nibbling away individually. This destruction was set in motion by means of the nonaggression pact of August 23, 1939, which unleashed Germany against the Western powers and sealed the fate of Eastern Europe, including Lithuania.[1] The pact's secret protocol provided for a division of Poland and for Soviet domination over Latvia and Estonia. Initially, Lithuania was allocated to the German sphere of influence, but by a supplementary provision of September 28, it was transferred to the Soviets. The Germans, pressed by their Russian ally, traded Lithuania for the Lublin province of Poland (which was seized by the Soviets) and for an additional compensation of 7.5 million dollars in gold. Berlin had lost interest in Lithuania after the Kaunas government, anxious to remain independent from both Berlin and Moscow, rejected von Ribbentrop's invitation, at the price of an alliance with Germany, to attack Poland and capture Lithuania's old capital city and region of Vilnius.[2] General Jonas Černius, the Lithuanian Prime Minister, publicly declared that Lithuania would seek to regain Vilnius only by peaceful means.

History has many ironic moments and this was one of them: Lithuania had suffered diplomatically and economically for refusing to abandon Vilnius, but now it declined to take it, although invited to do so. Instead, together with the other Baltic states, Lithuania declared its neutrality, thus hoping to weather the storm of the war. This, however, appeared to be impossible.

By declining to join the war against Poland, Lithuania avoided the status of German protectorate that Hitler usually imposed on smaller nations allied with Berlin; however, by rejecting German "protection," Lithuania delivered itself into the hands of the Soviet Union.

THE FIRST STAGE OF THE DRAMA: THE SOVIETS MOVE IN

The Kremlin's "Limited" Objective. Moscow proceeded carefully. Although Soviet military maps[3] began showing Lithuania as a Soviet Socialist Republic in the fall of 1939, at first the Soviets demanded of Lithuania (as well as of Latvia and Estonia) only a mutual-assistance pact that would allow the Kremlin to maintain land and air bases and 20,000 Red troops. To make this demand more palatable, Stalin sugar-coated it with a promise for the return of the city of Vilnius and a portion of the surrounding territory, which had been recognized as Lithuanian by the peace treaty of 1920—territory that just weeks before had been wrested from the terrified Poles. Thus it happened that, unwilling to seize it directly, Lithuania now had to accept the city from the Soviet Union.

Although the mutual-assistance pact, signed on October 10,[4] guaranteed that the Soviets would not interfere in Lithuania's domestic affairs, rumors about an impending seizure of the Baltic states began to spread immediately, and Foreign Commissar Molotov felt it necessary, in a speech to an extraordinary session of the Supreme Soviet, to "declare that the foolish talk of sovietization of the Baltic states is useful only to our common enemies and to all kinds of anti-Soviet provocateurs."[5]

At first, Soviet behavior seemed to confirm this solemn assurance. The troops that entered Lithuania in accordance with the "mutual-assistance" treaty conducted themselves reasonably well. The underground Communist Party was apparently ordered to tread softly; in the negotiations on the bases, Stalin had given the Lithuanians freedom to deal with the Lithuanian Communists however they liked. But, this attitude of sweet reason lasted only as long as the Soviets were fighting the winter war against Finland, which had refused to accept a mutual-assistance pact of the sort foisted on the other Baltic states. Once the Finns were subdued, the Communists in Lithuania started fomenting strikes on Soviet military base sites; military commanders began complaining to Lithuanians about alleged failures to provide promised food supplies; Soviet soldiers were allowed to mingle with Lithuanian civilians, with whom they would become involved in tavern brawls. At the same time, the Soviets, in a show of strength, transferred substantial military equipment to their bases near Kaunas. Their true intent became clear when, on May 16, 1940, *Izvestiia* excitedly came out against the cornerstone of the current Lithuanian (and Baltic) policy of neutrality, then very much the talk of Baltic diplomats. "The recent war events [the occupation of Belgium, the Netherlands, and Luxembourg by the Germans] once more proved," the Soviet newspaper wrote, "that the neutrality of small states, which do not have power to support it, is a mere fantasy. Therefore, there are very few chances for small countries to survive and to maintain their independence. All considerations of small countries on the question of justice and injustice in relations with the Big Powers, which are at war 'to determine if they are to be or not to be,' are at the least, naïve." The Lithuanian minister in Moscow, Ladas Natkevičius, reported that "a black cat crossed the path of Lithuanian-Soviet relations."[6]

The Squeeze and the Occupation. These premonitions were well-founded, for on May 28, the day the Belgian King surrendered to the Germans, Moscow accused Lithuania of kidnaping two Soviet soldiers and causing them to desert the Red Army. The accusation was repeated the next day by General Loktenev, the Deputy Commissar for Defense. Lithuanian authorities reacted immediately, and on the General's information found one of the soldiers happily spending nights with a local lady. With him was another Red soldier, not named in the note. Kaunas proposed a joint Soviet-Lithuanian commission to investigate the affair. However, since this proposal did not agree with Soviet plans, it was ignored; instead, three days later, on May 30, the Soviet Government publicly accused Lithuania of kidnaping Soviet soldiers and of adopting a "provocative" attitude that might have "grave consequences."[7] Immediately after the publication of this warning, the Lithuanian Government decided to send its Foreign Minister to Moscow to clarify the situation and propose methods to avoid such incidents in the future. The Soviets, however, seized on their own provocative acts as a *casus belli* and demanded the visit of the Prime Minister. Russia needed to act at once if its designs on Lithuania and the other Baltic states were to come off smoothly; time was short, but Russia's timing was perfect. The Germans, busy with their invasion of France, were far too occupied to restrain Moscow in the Baltic area. Amid the noise and excitement over the war in the West—as it happened, the collapse of Paris and France itself—Russia found it easy to swallow the Baltic states without opposition from Germany or the rest of the world.

On his June 6 trip to Moscow, Prime Minister Antanas Merkys and his aides were refused elementary diplomatic courtesy[8]—a bad omen for the travelers—although they regained some of their optimism after being met in Moscow with official honors. The initial meeting at the Kremlin was set for 9:00 P.M. on June 7.[9] In this first confrontation, Foreign Commissar Molotov did not yet completely spell out Soviet demands, but he bitterly accused the Lithuanian press, some of the ministers, and several organizations of hostile attitudes. He did not seem to care about the results of the investigation of the alleged kidnapings, but required "a 100 per cent pro-Soviet policy" and the dismissal of the Lithuanian Minister of the Interior and the Director of Security, the alleged culprits in the incidents involving Soviet soldiers. At the second meeting, on June 9, Molotov brought forth more startling charges and demands. He accused Prime Minister Merkys of organizing a military alliance with Latvia and Estonia and intimated that Merkys, too, should be dismissed, and a new, more pro-Soviet government established. When all of this was communicated to Kaunas, the Cabinet, together with the President, decided to assure the Soviets of Lithuania's "unquestioned and firm" loyalty. The President also promised to reorganize the Cabinet. Furthermore, he was persuaded to write a letter of similar assurances to Mikhail I. Kalinin, the Chairman of the Presidium of the Supreme Soviet. In addition, Foreign Minister Juozas Urbšys was sent to Moscow to answer allegations about the Baltic military alliance (which did not exist). Upon his arrival, a third meeting was held in Moscow, but this could not relieve the mounting tension, because the Soviets did not want it to. Urbšys' frantic visits to Kalinin and later to V. G. Dekanazov, the Deputy Foreign Commissar, did not diminish the gravity of the threat either.

Finally, the artificial tension was resolved by its creator. On June 14, Molotov handed the Lithuanian envoy an ultimatum[10] demanding in effect Lithuania's self-liquidation. In less than twenty-four hours, Lithuania was to allow "a free entry" into Lithuania for any Soviet divisions the Kremlin considered necessary to "assure the enforcement" of the mutual-assistance treaty. Furthermore, a new government was to be formed, "able" and "determined" to "fulfill" the treaty and to "suppress firmly" the treaty's alleged enemies. To justify these unwarranted demands, the Soviets attributed them to so-called Lithuanian "provocations" against Soviet soldiers; they also called for the arrest and trial of the Lithuanian Interior Minister, Kazys Skučas, and Director of the Department of Security, Augustinas Povilaitis. Thus, the Soviets finally showed their true intentions. After more than two decades of pretended friendship, they now sought to destroy Lithuania, despite their earlier solemn promise, in the treaty of 1920, to abandon their claims on Lithuania "forever," a promise elaborated in the nonaggression pact of 1926, and finally reaffirmed in the mutual-assistance pact of 1939 itself.

The choice faced by the government in Kaunas was difficult. In an emergency cabinet meeting, President Smetona proposed to reject the ultimatum and to resist.[11] However, he did not get the majority's support. It was clear that resistance to the Soviet forces rushing into the country from their bases close to the largest Lithuanian towns and from across the Eastern border would be merely symbolic; practical-minded men dreaded the price. It seems also that the chief of the army, General Vincas Vitkauskas, who had just been appointed by the President to replace General Raštikis, whose political influence the President thus sought to reduce, was a turncoat. Some well-intentioned ministers, furthermore, did not think that the Soviet protectorate would be severe; they felt that during the war the small country would not be able to maintain its complete independence anyway. It also seems likely that President Smetona could not get unity now because his motives were suspect as a result of his authoritarian rule during the previous decade. (Yet the division in the coalition Cabinet of Merkys was not based on political "position" or on "opposition" to the Nationalist rule of Smetona.) The President, of course, could have ordered resistance; however, this might have added to the difficulties rather than resolved anything. Therefore, he agreed to accept the Soviet demands, specifying that he, not the Soviets, would appoint the new Prime Minister. The Soviets, however, rejected both the suggestion and the person (General Raštikis) Smetona named to the post. Instead, they sent V. G. Dekanazov, the Deputy Foreign Commissar, to take charge of matters in Lithuania.

From this the President understood that his own and his country's freedom were at an end. Unwilling to become a Soviet tool, he left the country in protest, and came to the United States via

Germany and Switzerland, where he was received by President Roosevelt. (He died here in a hotel fire in 1942.) Meanwhile, some 300,000 Soviet troops rushed into the country in their steam-driven trucks. From June 15 on, all power in the country belonged to the Red Army and to Dekanazov, the Kremlin's emissary, operating from the Soviet Legation in Kaunas. The government that Dekanazov installed, and even the Lithuanian Communist Party (which was soon legalized), were mere tools in Soviet hands, although some individual politicians at first viewed them as relatively free Lithuanian agents.

THE SECOND STAGE: LEGALIZATION OF AGGRESSION

Operation Confusion. The Soviet design for Lithuania did not include an immediate revelation of Soviet plans for the future of the occupied country. Although the issue apparently had been decided by the Kremlin, all public talk of Lithuania's incorporation into the Soviet Union was silenced and denounced. At the moment, the Soviets were concerned with "legalizing" their aggression. The local population had to be confused so that there would be no violent opposition to the planned incorporation, and foreign countries had to be reassured so that "incorporation" would be recognized. In this respect, Smetona's departure created the first problem. A way had to be invented "legally" to appoint Soviet collaborators without the Presidential approval. This was found by declaring that Smetona had resigned from his office (which was not true) and by manipulating the constitution to ease a Soviet puppet into the position of acting President and Prime Minister.[12] On June 17, Dekanazov chose Justas Paleckis, known as a moderately Leftist journalist, to take over both Smetona's and Merkys' posts. Vincas Krėvė-Mickevičius, a famous Lithuanian writer, very popular throughout the land, became Deputy Prime Minister and Minister of Foreign Affairs. His consent to join the new administration gave to the new rulers the prestige they needed and at first confused some of the intelligentsia. Five other members completed the Cabinet, which was almost immediately enlarged to Communist advantage. On June 19, the group consisted of four Communists, two fellow travelers, and two democrats. Within two weeks, three additional Communists were appointed, giving them an absolute majority. This cabinet, labeled a "people's government," was to smooth sovietization. However, at the beginning not all the members of the Cabinet were aware of their real function.

The Communists encouraged this ignorance. Mečys Gedvilas, the Communist Minister of the Interior, who may have been kept in ignorance himself, promoted this confusion by declaring that the government would create a "people's republic."[13] This view was spread by rumor and circulated, interestingly enough, even among the Red Army soldiers. (These rumors were traced to Soviet *politruks*—political commissars in the Red Army.) All of this exposed the deception used by the Kremlin on the native Lithuanian population and on their own collaborators. The latter raised false hopes among the people that Lithuania would not be sovietized or deprived of its free national status. All the Soviets wanted, they said, was to destroy the Smetona regime, which did not suitably enforce the Lithuanian-Soviet treaty. Some political opponents of the President wishfully thought that the Soviets merely provided the opportunity for getting rid of the unpopular Smetona and hoped that the end of the Nationalist League's rule did not mean the end of Lithuania's independence. For a few weeks, until the Communists entrenched themselves in the governmental apparatus, such views suited the Soviets very well.

The mistake, however, and thus Moscow's trickery, was discovered sooner than Moscow liked, albeit too late to warn the nation. The most illustrious example of the deceived intellectual was the Deputy Prime Minister, Vincas Krėvė-Mickevičius. He regarded the Paleckis government as a legitimate successor to Prime Minister Merkys, who had been arrested, and to President Smetona, who had fled abroad. A deeply patriotic man, however, Krėvė soon found out that the country was ruled by Dekanazov, not by Paleckis or himself. But the old man thought that Moscow did not know what was going on[14] and decided to inform the Kremlin. He could not get himself to believe that Moscow really wanted to liquidate Lithuania's independence. On June 24, therefore, Krėvė asked for a conference with Molotov. At first, Molotov referred him to Dekanazov, but Krėvė persisted, and on July 2, he was received privately by the Foreign Commissar at the Kremlin. Molotov was in turn polite, evasive, and thoughtful with the stubborn little writer who had a reputation of being strongly Leftist and pro-Russian. However, Molotov's hints were too obscure for the adroit and undiplomatic Krėvė, so Molotov put his cards on the table. Krėvė himself has related the conversation:

> "You provoke my candor, Mr. Minister," he [Molotov] said at last, glancing up at me. "You force me to say something which I had no

wish to say at this time. Therefore we shall speak openly without sentimentality of which there is already enough. You must take a good look at reality and understand that in the future small nations will have to disappear. Your Lithuania along with the other Baltic nations, including Finland, will have to join the glorious family of the Soviet Union. Therefore you should begin now to initiate your people into the Soviet system, which in the future shall reign everywhere, throughout all Europe; put into practice earlier in some places, as in the Baltic nations, later in others."

Although I had been warned in advance by Mr. Natkevičius [the Lithuanian envoy in Moscow] that I might hear such things, I was completely abashed by Molotov's flat statement. My throat felt dry, my lips frozen, and for some time I was speechless.

It appeared that Mr. Molotov perceived my condition. He telephoned and ordered some tea.

"When these things become evident, there will be great confusion among our people, perhaps even armed resistance," I began, not realizing what I was saying. "The German Government, without doubt will make use of this, for it will not tolerate the instigation of the Soviet system on its border."

"Germany swallowed the occupation of the Baltic States without choking, and she will have to digest their incorporation," Molotov snapped back. "They are having too much trouble in the West now to want a war with the mighty Soviet Union. I also will not conceal from you that in regard to these matters we have already come to an agreement with them."[15]

The Commissar then continued, suggesting that the Soviets would soon take Europe and thus could not tolerate a small oasis in their backyard, "with a form of government that will have to disappear." When Krėvė countered that the United States would not allow Europe to become Soviet, the Commissar characterized the United States in an extremely uncomplimentary manner, explaining that "we shall find means to help the leaders of American politics make mistakes, when these mistakes will be to our advantage. . . . All those who put their faith in them [the Americans] will be greatly disillusioned."

Upon hearing all this, Krėvė declared that he would resign from the "people's government." Molotov warned the Lithuanian to think twice before doing so. Indeed, Krėvė found it difficult to quit. After returning to Kaunas, he sought to delay the planned elections for a new diet, but the Communists already had a majority in the Cabinet, and he failed. Then he resigned together with Galvanauskas—the only other democratic member of the

Cabinet—but Krėvė's resignation was not accepted. Instead, he was given two weeks' leave to look after his health. The Communist Gedvilas took over Krėvė's position. The disillusioned writer fled Lithuania at the end of the war and eventually came to the United States, where he taught at the University of Pennsylvania. (He died in 1954.)

The Softening-Up for Incorporation. Dekanazov and the "people's government," meanwhile, worked around the clock, because the Soviets had a strict timetable. All actions in the three Baltic states were synchronized to prepare for their collective "admission" to the Soviet "family of nations" within a period of six weeks. The reason for this Soviet haste has never been offered. Presumably, the Kremlin wanted to take the people by surprise and thus prevent organized opposition; also, Moscow had to push ahead while the Germans were busy in the West.

Preparation for extracting consent to the country's sovietization now proceeded in two ways. First, the Soviets brought their fifth column out into the open and used it as an auxiliary force; second, they intimidated and isolated the non-Communist forces in preparation for the election of the "people's diet." Thus, on June 25, the Communist Party became a legal organization. Four days later, the new rulers set up a Komsomol and Communist trade unions. The Party immediately announced its platform,[16] which called for confiscation of large landholdings and their distribution to the landless and the poor; furthermore, the Communists demanded the destruction of independent Lithuania's constitutional system, insisted on the arrest of "enemies of the people," and urged purges of the administration, the police, and the army. The platform did not mention incorporation into the Soviet Union, but otherwise spelled out immediate Soviet policies, which were adopted by Dekanazov and enforced by the "people's government."

While the Communist Party and its fronts now were pushed into the open, the activities of all the other political organizations were suspended; most of them were formally outlawed before the elections to the diet. Within days, some newspapers were closed down; others were taken over and used in the electoral campaign and then shut down or replaced by Communist publications. In addition, the Lithuanian Army was purged and completely reorganized before the elections. It became the "people's army," under the supervision of *politruks.* The Department of State Security had been taken over the very first day of the occupation and was now controlled by the NKVD, with Antanas Sniečkus, the Communist Party's first secretary, acting as its director. Purges of the police force, the civil administration, the officer corps, and the schools followed, and the heads of the main political parties and organizations. Immediately before the election, during the night of July 11–12, the Soviets began a roundup of some 2,000 political opponents, a "softening-up" before the election of a "people's diet."

This election represented the culminating objective of the immediate occupation policy. It was necessary for the production of a diet that would express "the will of the people," that is, would rubberstamp the Moscow-made decision on Lithuania's "joining" the Soviet Union. The announcement of the election on July 5 provided another interesting proof that Lithuania's political life was being controlled by Moscow. Tass announced the election on July 3, while in Kaunas the formal acceptance of the decree was held up by the stubborn Krėvė-Mickevičius, still acting as Deputy Prime Minister.[17] Thus, the passage of Lithuania's electoral decree came two days after its adoption was announced in Moscow.

To achieve the desired results, the new rulers had to pass a new electoral law. This was done on July 6, with elections scheduled for July 14. The nominations and the campaigning thus had to be squeezed into a week's time. Such speed obviously pointed to a guiding hand reaching directly from the Kremlin into the Soviet Legation in Kaunas.

The electoral law[18] of July 6 provided for a Soviet system of elections. Candidates had to be nominated at mass meetings held at the county level and approved by the Republic's electoral commission, which was controlled by people loyal to the Communists. The deadline for nominations was July 10. Since the Communist Party was then the only legal political group, nominating meetings for candidates were held under its auspices. The list of candidates included as many names as there were seats to be filled. It was not, however, under the Communist label, but designated as a coalition group—the Union of the Working People of Lithuania—formally sponsored by five groups, one of which was the Communist Party. The others were the Komsomol, the trade-union bureau, the tenants association, and the freethinkers. It has since been ascertained that some of the "nominated" candidates had not even consented to be nominated, although they did not dare publicly to protest their involuntary participation. Even at this late time, the platform of this Communist front did not call for Lithuania's incorporation into the Soviet Union. Indeed, a few eager Communist speakers who demanded an *Anschluss* were silenced, and posters hailing Lithuania as the sixteenth Soviet Republic were torn from utility poles and stands. However, this glaring "omission" of the real purpose of the elections did not stop the Soviets from insisting later that the issue of joining the Soviet Union had been decided by a plebiscite.

The balloting was conducted under equally questionable circumstances. The electoral law made voting mandatory; thus, passports of voters were stamped at the polling places. Aliens as well as citizens were allowed to cast ballots. Furthermore, local electoral commissions did not maintain definite registration lists, thus making their manipulation very easy; teenagers, for example, were encouraged to vote, although the minimum voting age was twenty-one; finally, election commissions counted all spoiled ballots, or simply stuffed ballot boxes. Yet on July 14, the designated election day, only an estimated 20 per cent of the voters came to the polls. Paleckis then extended the voting time to 10:00 P.M. of the next day, and the supreme electoral commission warned against "provocations," which meant throwing ballots on the floor, and making "other harmful demonstrations." On July 17, the commission claimed that 95.1 per cent of all voters actually cast their ballots and that the candidates were elected by 99.19 per cent of the votes cast.[19] These figures were unquestionably false.

Aggression Formalized. The developments following the election were anticlimactic. On July 21, the elected diet of seventy-nine members held its first and only session; there, in the Kaunas Opera House, the "elected" members, seated together with the plainclothesmen and visitors, raised their hands to petition the Supreme Soviet for admission into the Union of Soviet Socialist Republics. The petition did not conceal the causes of the diet's decision. It stated, in part, that "now the people, with the help of the powerful Red Army, have broken the yoke of Smetona's masters and established Soviet rule."[20] A paragraph later, the diet confessed that all of this was possible "thanks to the Soviet Union."

The Supreme Soviet approved the petition on August 3, together with similar petitions from Latvia and Estonia. Abroad, however, Lithuania's forcible incorporation into the Soviet Union

was not universally recognized. On July 23, even before the incorporation formalities were completed, the U.S. Department of
State issued the now-famous statement, signed by Sumner Welles,
condemning the "devious processes whereunder the political independence and territorial integrity of three small Baltic republics—
Estonia, Latvia, and Lithuania—were to be deliberately annihilated by one of their more powerful neighbors."[21] The United
States still continues its policy of nonrecognition of the incorporation of the Baltic states into the Soviet Union. This example
is followed by a number of other nations. Passports issued by
Lithuanian legations and consulates in the United States, Canada, Uruguay, and the Holy See are recognized as travel documents by many American, European, and Asian states.

PART II

World War II and Its
Aftermath: Resistance

4. Lithuania During the War: Resistance Against the Soviet and the Nazi Occupants

ZENONAS IVINSKIS

The failure of the Lithuanian Government to oppose the invasion of the Red Army by armed force did not signify Lithuania's acquiescence in the fact of foreign occupation. It took the Soviet occupant another decade to subdue the Lithuanians to the Communist regime. Indeed, the period of 1940–52, one of the bloodiest in Lithuania's history, was one of resistance, first, against the Soviets (1940–41), then against the Nazis who held the country occupied for three years (1941–44), and then again against the re-established Soviet rule (1944–52).

The purpose of this study is to describe Lithuanian reactions to the loss of independence and then to depict the development and activities of articulated Lithuanian resistance against the Soviets during the first occupation, and then against the Nazis.

RESISTANCE AGAINST THE SOVIETS, 1940–41

Crystallization of Opposition. It should be stressed from the outset that the resistance against the Soviets (and later against the Nazis) was of an intensely nationalistic character. A century of national revival, culminating in the establishment of an independent state, produced among the Lithuanians strong commitments to national ideas and to the national state. The younger generation especially, sensitive to the medieval traditions of Lithuanian statehood, took modern Lithuania's independence as an axiomatic fact and therefore refused to reconcile itself to its loss. This dedication to the national Lithuanian ideals, combined

61

with traditional dislike of the Russian rule and fears of persecution by Communist Russians soon crystallized into active opposition to the Kremlin's occupation.

Resistance groups quickly won approval and support from virtually all strata of the Lithuanian population. This support grew in direct proportion to the increasing political suppression, economic expropriation, and decline of the standards of living that swiftly followed the introduction of the Soviet regime. Furthermore, the increasing highhandedness and unrelenting terrorism of Moscow's rule, ultimately resulting in mass deportations of civilians, caused the Lithuanians to look for salvation abroad, first of all in Germany, its nearest and most powerful neighbor. Generally, the anti-Soviet opposition fed on hope that the Communist occupation would not last. Such hope was kindled not only by expectations of war between Germany and the Soviet Union but also by the news that a number of Western countries had refused to recognize Lithuania's forcible incorporation into the Soviet Union. Encouragement was found in the declaration of the American Under Secretary of State, Sumner Welles, on July 23, 1940, which condemned the destruction of Baltic independence by the Soviet Union and assured that "the people of the United States are opposed to predatory activities no matter whether they are carried on by the use of force or by the threat of force."[1] Further comfort was derived from President Roosevelt's sanguine prediction to the Lithuanian-American Council, made three months later, on October 15, that Lithuanian independence was not lost. "Lithuania's independence," he said, "has only temporarily been put aside. Time will come and Lithuania will be free again. This will happen much sooner than you expect."[2]

The resistance took diverse forms. The bulk of the population resorted to passive opposition, which consisted primarily of boycotting the numerous political activities the regime introduced and of verbal ridicule of the Communist system and the Russians. Within a year, a large body of anti-Soviet folklore developed.* At the same time, active resistance to the Soviets began

* This included anecdotes deriding the fashions of Soviet women, the table manners of Soviet officers, and Soviet reactions to the food and amenities of life they found in the capitalist country they immediately labeled "Little America." Words of ridicule were substituted for the texts of patriotic and romantic Soviet songs. Stalin and the Party were derided in sovietized versions of the Lord's Prayer, the Credo, etc.

among the country's youth. Patriotic loyalties of young Lithuanian army officers and soldiers were the first to be challenged, because after the Lithuanian Army's incorporation into the Red Army, the military was required to pledge loyalty to the Soviet Union. Many refused openly.³ Furthermore, elections to the "people's diet" brought out large numbers of anti-Soviet leaflets designed to counter the false Communist propaganda and to unmask Soviet objectives. These leaflets, sponsored by locally organized secret patriotic organizations such as the Force for Lithuania's Defense (Lietuvos Gynimo Rinktinė), the Front for the Restoration of Lithuania (Lietuvos Atstatymo Frontas), the Battle Band (Kovos Būrys),⁴ were extremely emotional. For example, a sheet signed in the name of the Force for Lithuania's Defense, dated July 8, 1940, said: "A true Lithuanian would die rather than vote for Lithuania's traitors. Do not go to the polling places, because there you'll be forced to betray your brethren, your freedom, and your religion." Underground publications spread more widely after students returned to schools in September, 1940. Senior high-school and university students formed secret societies. Mimeographed leaflets and even periodicals appeared in both Vilnius and Kaunas. Lithuanian educators also voiced their opposition to the regime. On August 14–15, 1940, a congress of 8,000 teachers in the Kaunas sports palace staged an unexpected patriotic demonstration. The regime had called this congress to begin a "reorientation" program for teachers, but the delegates concluded the congress by singing Lithuania's banned national anthem.

The most energetic centers of active resistance were organized by the students of Kaunas and Vilnius universities, in close cooperation with junior staff members. However, resistance activities were not yet coordinated. Furthermore, the underground groups lacked experience in protecting themselves from *agents provocateurs* and informers.* Therefore, on October 9 in Kaunas, at a secret meeting of the Kaunas and Vilnius resistance groups, the delegates not only discussed their aims, but also sought ways

* A number of resistance members fell into the hands of security agents and the NKVD. Retreating in June, 1941, the Bolsheviks carried out extensive executions among those who survived in prisons at Petrašiūnai (near Kaunas), at Rainiai forest, near Telšiai (where the prisoners, among them several high-school students, were killed by unspeakable torture), Panevėžys, Pravieniškės (Kaišiadorys), and other localities.

of introducing a greater degree of planning and more conspiratorial measures into the movement.

Unification of Resistance Groups. However, the activities of most underground groups were centralized not through the initiative within the country but through the efforts of Colonel Kazys Škirpa, the former Lithuanian Minister and Military Attaché in Germany, who had many contacts in German military and diplomatic circles. Aided and advised by Lithuanian politicians, officers, and intellectuals who had fled to Germany to escape Soviet arrest in Lithuania, Colonel Škirpa won approval from the Germans, and on November 17 established a nucleus for a united organization named the Lithuanian Activist Front (Lietuvių Aktyvistų Frontas, LAF).[5] The Communists, fabricating the history of the resistance, claim that the LAF was merely a German "fifth column" in Lithuania.[6] The fact is, however, that the organization was formed and operated for the sole purpose of restoring Lithuania's independence; its connection with the Germans was merely incidental, conditioned by the circumstances of the day.

From Berlin, Colonel Škirpa commanded the LAF with the assistance of an advisory council. The organizers worked out the basic rules for this underground resistance organization as well as a political program for the re-establishment of a free Lithuanian state. The group produced a series of articles and proclamations on this program, but these had little influence in Lithuania, because only a small part of this material could be smuggled into the country.[7] Also, Colonel Škirpa was forced by the Germans to remain in Berlin after Lithuania was taken by the Germans. Thus, he was isolated from the events of the summer of 1940 and could have little influence on the course of politics in his homeland. Of much greater importance to the anti-Soviet underground than political advice and planning were the military suggestions and directions by the leadership of the LAF on how to prepare and execute a revolt against the Soviets. On March 24, 1941, all instructions of this type were summarized in a paper entitled "Directives for the Liberation of Lithuania."[8] These instructions were so secret that their memorized contents were entrusted only to the most reliable couriers.[9]

Preparation for the Insurrection Against the Soviets. The leadership of the LAF in Berlin based its instructions to the Lithuanian underground on the assumption that there would be a German-Soviet war and on the evaluation of German trustworthiness as an ally. Once the Germans cross the Lithuanian frontiers, the directives ordered, the Lithuanian underground was to stage an insurrection against the Soviets, and in any event, even if the Germans demurred, establish a provisional Lithuanian government. In this way, even if the Germans should refuse to grant Lithuania independence, they would be confronted with a *fait accompli*.[10] Such caution (and optimism that such forcing of the German hand might succeed) was based on Škirpa's experiences with the German military, the Nazi Party, and the Foreign Ministry, who made nebulous and indefinite promises that aroused his suspicion, and prompted him, fortunately, to provide for an unexpected eventuality that nevertheless occurred.

In preparation for the insurrection, the LAF organized in Lithuanian cities and towns a conspiratorial system of "threes" and "fives" (units of three and five persons) linked to one another and thus to a central leadership through overlapping membership of unit leaders. Thus, a far-reaching, hierarchically organized chain of units was established that guaranteed maximum secrecy, the main characteristic of the LAF. A regular member of an underground unit knew only his own group. The rule that governed the dangerous underground activity was to know just what was necessary, and no more, to carry out the assigned task.[11] Local units were given instructions how, in case of insurrection, to take over police stations, telephone communications, hospitals, and other important institutions. The network of these units was somewhat impaired by the mass deportations of June 14, 1941, but the organization was not substantially crippled. It was estimated that in 1941 this network numbered about 36,000 members.

Two major centers of command—one in Vilnius, the other in Kaunas—were formed to carry out the revolt and establish a provisional government, even against the German will. "These functioned on a parallel basis so that if one was liquidated, the other could continue alone. Liaison between the leadership in Berlin and the two centers in the country was maintained through trusted couriers, thus assuring that all the activities would be adequately coordinated."[12]

The LAF did not immediately unify all existing resistance units. Before LAF instructions reached Lithuania, various groups and regional organizations had arisen in the late summer of 1940 and later, e.g., Lithuania's Defense League in the Tauragė district, the Iron Wolf in Šakiai, the Lithuanian Freedom Army in the Šiauliai district.

The last-named, organized in a military manner and led by army officers, was very active during the Nazi occupation and even more so early in the second Soviet occupation, especially with its famed partisan units Vanagai (Falcons). On December 26, 1940, representatives of liberal-nationalist youth, especially of students, founded the Union of Lithuanian Freedom Fighters, which joined the LAF in April, 1941, and played an active part in the revolt of June 23.

During this time, Lithuania was completely sealed off from the outside world and found itself in a tightly shut propaganda "pot." It was therefore imperative that the resistance movement maintain contacts abroad, especially to learn when to expect a Soviet-German war, which seemed to promise the only opportunity for getting rid of Communist oppression. The first courier from Berlin did not reach Kaunas and Vilnius before the middle of December, 1940. He brought with him the pamphlet *From Bolshevik Slavery to a New Lithuania,* published in Berlin on December 5. He also brought news of the coming war, instructions, and other information.*

If the revolt were to succeed it was necessary that the date of the war be known at least approximately, but the long-awaited day was continually being postponed. News arrived from Berlin that German military operations would begin during the first ten days of May. However, intensive preparations for the revolt had to be stopped[13] since the Reich spent several important weeks settling accounts with Yugoslavia, which had just then broken away from the Axis. Such delays not only affected the morale of the resistance but were also costly in casualties. Arrests took place even among the Vilnius staff. Yet, when the day came at last, the revolt took its successful course.

THE REVOLT OF JUNE 23

A New Declaration of Independence. Germany attacked the Soviet Union on the morning of June 22, 1941. As expected, the news of the war, even in the zones of military action, was greeted

---

* Several weeks later, while returning, he was betrayed at the border. After suffering torture in the Kaunas prison, he was moved to Minsk prison and there executed soon after the start of the war. See Antanas Pocius, "Kap. Pranas Gužaitis ir pogrindis," *Į Laisvę* (Chicago), No. 8 (1955), pp. 34–36; also Adolfas Damušis, "Pasiruošta ir Įvykdyta," *Į Laisvę* (Chicago), No. 3 (1954), pp. 4–5.

by the Lithuanians with unconcealed joy. The nation, furthermore, was electrified by the Kaunas radio broadcast a day later
—June 23—proclaiming the revolt against the Soviets, the restoration of Lithuanian independence, and the formation of a
Provisional Government. All this took place while uniformed Russian soldiers were still walking the streets of Kaunas and Red
Army units were still close to the radio towers. The station was
captured by a special detail of insurrectionists. On the same day,
the insurrectionist forces took over police stations and several
arsenals in Kaunas (very many automatic rifles were found in the
exhibition pavilion), saved the city's automatic telephone exchange from demolition by the Soviets, and freed political prisoners. In two days, the rebels won complete control of the city, so
that on June 25, the army of General (later Field Marshal) Friedrich Wilhelm von Küchel entered Kaunas in parade order. For
this "capture" of the city, the Führer awarded General von Küchel the order of Knight of the Iron Cross. The award citation
scrupulously refrained from mentioning Lithuanian help. The
German high command (Oberkommando der Wehrmacht) similarly claimed that the Kaunas radio station was captured by a
German lieutenant named Flohret. But in fact the station had
already been in the hands of Lithuanian rebels for a day and a
half when Flohret, accompanied by two privates, came to the
station and announced its seizure.

From Kaunas the revolt swiftly spread into the country. Many
cities and villages were cleaned of Bolshevik troops days before
the Germans occupied them. It is estimated that about 100,000
partisans took part in the insurrection, a number about three
times the size of the membership of underground organizations
under the leadership of the LAF. This massive participation indicated, of course, that the revolt had national, spontaneous support. Local leaders could and did display initiative and acted
independently of the central leadership of Kaunas, which could
not enforce uniform discipline or control the actions of local
units.

What caused this dramatic rejection of Soviet rule by the Lithuanians? As previously mentioned, resistance against the Soviets
was nurtured by nationalist ideals, by hopes of outside help and,
finally, by the oppressive policies of the Soviet regime. These de-
serve a more detailed description. In the brief span of a few
months, the Communists had nationalized all business enterprises, thus expropriating, displacing, and impoverishing a siz-

able and important social group. Most peasants lost at least some of their farm acreage, because the regime allowed an individual family only 75 acres of land; furthermore, the farmers were burdened by discriminatory requisitions of agricultural products that led to their financial ruin (for a more elaborate discussion see pp. 143–44). Factory workers suffered from the steeply increased cost of living and disappearance of goods from the stores. The clergy and the traditionally religious population were subjected to religious persecution. Furthermore, thousands of suspected oponents of the regime were crowded into Lithuanian and Russian prisons. Finally, in a mass operation, the Soviets deported over 35,000 civilians, including women and children. As was found out later, this deportation was the first in the planned deportion of an estimated 700,000* of the country's population to slave-labor camps. This first deportation occurred just a week before the outbreak of the German-Soviet war, on June 14–15, a fact that convinced many Lithuanians that a *modus vivendi* with the Soviet regime was impossible—and irrevocably excited anti-Soviet feelings. Against this background, it is easy to understand the population's support of the insurrection and the enthusiasm with which it greeted the war, the German troops, and the creation of the Provisional Lithuanian Government. Whatever happened now could not be worse than what had occurred under the Soviets. Furthermore, fresh memory of Soviet cruelties disposed the people and its leaders to attempt to find a way for a peaceful coexistence with the Germans.

The new declaration of independence, proclaimed by the insurrectionists on June 23, 1941, of course cost casualties. Two thousand partisans fell in battle; in other words, the casualties during the revolt were greater than those suffered during the 1919–20 wars of Lithuanian independence. About two hundred insurrectionists fell in Kaunas alone. The Provisional Government, however, was flooded with emotional messages of congratulations and support from the provinces. Many of these messages were signed by shop and factory workers who were no less appalled and frightened by the Soviet regime than was the rest of the nation.

The Six Weeks of Provisional Government. However, Lithuania's joy over the successful insurrection was premature. During the

---

* This estimate is based on the size of social groups the Soviets marked for deportation. For more details about deportations, see pp. 87, 91 .

first days of German control, it became clear that neither the restoration of Lithuanian sovereignty nor the establishment of a Provisional Government was welcome to the Nazis; Lithuanian independence was to them undesirable, the Provisional Government a bone in the throat that they would not swallow. Shortly before the German attack, Colonel Škirpa had been warned not to establish any government without German consent, and he was strongly reprimanded after such a government was created. On June 25, General Pohl, the Wehrmacht field commander in Kaunas, frankly told the representatives of the Provisional Government that he was not authorized to enter any discussions with any Lithuanian government. However, General Pohl, an Austrian, tolerated Lithuanian authorities where these did not interfere with German institutions and policies. He also kept out of the machinations that the SD (Sicherheitsdienst) and the Gestapo continuously planned for the removal of the "stuck bone."

To accomplish this purpose, the Germans at first refrained from using any force. News of the insurrection and the Provisional Government had created a sensation in Scandinavia and had reached the United States, and its liquidation by force would have been embarrassing and inconvenient. The Government, furthermore, was immensely popular in Lithuania; also, it included several national figures whose suppression would have a bad psychological effect on the Lithuanian population. The Nazis therefore decided to remove the unwelcome Government quietly, by boycotting and obstructing its activities and by pressuring it either to liquidate itself or to enlist into the service of the civil administration (Zivilverwaltung) that was soon to take over the administration of Lithuania.

The Germans therefore deprived the Government of its means of transportation and communication and denied it the use of radio facilities and the press for the publication of its decrees. Furthermore, they ordered the disbanding of insurgent formations that the Provisional Government hoped to use as a nucleus for a restored Lithuanian Army; Lithuanian leaders optimistically calculated to gain recognition of Lithuania's independence from the obviously reluctant Germans in exchange for Lithuanian military contribution to the war effort against the Soviets. The Germans, however, rejected such a trade. At the same time, the Gestapo isolated the leader of the insurrection and the formally pronounced Prime Minister of the Provisional Government, Colonel Škirpa. While Kaunas impatiently awaited the

Colonel's return, the Germans would not permit him to leave Berlin. Škirpa was interned in his apartment. He complained to Field Marshal von Brauchitsch, commander of the German Army, thereby greatly intensifying the Gestapo's enmity toward himself.[14] Until then, he had optimistically trusted his German acquaintances in the various Berlin offices, as they had trusted him. Yet his optimism appeared unwarranted. General Stasys Raštikis, the former commander of the Lithuanian Army, who in the spring of 1941 was in a position to observe Škirpa's relations with the Germans, has noted with insight that Škirpa, who had "so completely assumed the role of Lithuania's liberator and leader of the Lithuanian nation and state, thought out every detail, conscientiously and carefully prepared for his future activity, when the time came, was abandoned, kept away from his mission and even isolated by the very same German friends [who ostensibly had trusted him]."[15]

However, neither the denial of the necessary facilities nor the isolation of Colonel Škirpa destroyed the Provisional Government. The cabinet functioned without its formal head. Professor Juozas Ambrazevičius, a prominent literary historian, provisionally assumed the Prime Ministership, in the hope that Škirpa eventually would be allowed to return to Kaunas. Ambrazevičius bore his difficult burden patiently, and considering the conditions of the period, successfully, to the end. The cabinet met daily. Deprived of public means for communication with the provinces, it used the same couriers that had been employed by the underground during the Soviet occupation and published its decrees and programs in some provincial newspapers not immediately subject to German military censorship.

Noting that boycott and obstruction failed to produce results, the Germans now resorted to pressure. Dr. Greffe, a representative from the SP and SD headquarters (Hauptamt der Sicherheitspolizei und des Sicherheitsdienstes), took pains to convince the government that it should suspend its operation. Greffe's successor from the Foreign Bureau of the National Socialist Party, Dr. Peter Kleist, used threats. According to the underground newspaper *Į Laisvę*, he pressured Lithuanian negotiators by "banging the table with his fist and variously threatening [their safety]."[16] Kleist also demanded that the government disband or transform itself into an advisory group for the Zivilverwaltung. But such negotiations with acting Prime Minister Ambrazevičius and Defense Minister Raštikis, whom the Germans brought to

Kaunas in the hope that he would let himself to be used for their purposes, yielded no results.

The Germans, however, would not give in. Still hesitant to apply direct force, the Gestapo now attempted to liquidate the government with Lithuanian help. A small group of extremist supporters of the former Lithuanian politician Augustinas Voldemaras had collaborated with the Gestapo as early as 1938, and now they failed to resist the Gestapo's lure of seizing the reins of government from Ambrazevičius' cabinet. This group had long believed that it held a monopoly on the wisdom of advantageous collaboration with the Germans, and with their help a *Putsch* was attempted on the night of July 23–24 to overthrow the Provisional Government. Unfortunately for the Germans, the venture failed.

Thus, when Hitler established Ostland for the administration of the Baltic states and Belorussia, and when, on July 28, the newly appointed Reichskomissar für Ostland, Heinrich Lohse, announced the establishment of a civil German administration in Lithuania, the Provisional Government was still there. Still hesitant to liquidate it by arresting its members, the Germans once more attempted to persuade them to serve under German leadership. The General Commissar for Lithuania, Adrian von Renteln, in the only official meeting with the Provisional Government *in corpore,* proposed that the government turn itself into a council of trustees to the Zivilverwaltung. However, the government, with the exception of three members, refused this request. Nevertheless, it became clear to the stubborn Lithuanian leaders that there was no hope of achieving any *modus vivendi* with the Germans and that it would be useless to continue the Provisional Government's existence. Therefore, after lodging a written protest against the instituted German policies with von Renteln, the government on August 5 declared itself involuntarily suspended. Then the government members placed a wreath on the tomb of the unknown soldier and dispersed.

The Germans, thus, finally succeeded in choking off the Provisional Government. It is important to note, however, that the group survived for six weeks under the heel of the strongest war machine in Europe.

A complete evaluation of the revolt and the work of the Provisional Government will be possible only much later, from a greater perspective of time, after the series of occupations will have ended. At present, suffice it to say that the government was not able to influence the German occupation policies, though it tried, nor could it restrain the activities of the Gestapo, though it repeatedly protested to the German authorities against the mass executions of Lithuanian Jews.[17] However, having only limited freedom of action, the government, boycotted and obstructed, had to confine itself to areas that were of no immediate concern to the Germans. Its most fruitful achievements, therefore, are found in the field of education. The government's greatest accomplishment was its very tenacity in surviving for six weeks under heavy German pressure and in voicing Lithuanian determination to seek independent statehood, free not only from the domination of the Soviets but also from the dictates of the Nazis.

THE NATIONAL SOCIALIST POLICIES IN LITHUANIA

Within months it became clear why the Germans denied the Lithuanians the political fruits of their insurrection against the Soviets. Berlin had plans for colonizing Lithuania with Germans and then partly Germanizing and partly deporting or destroying its native population.[18] The Nazis, therefore, did not intend to share power with anyone, in order to be free to act when the time came.

Lithuania and the other parts of Ostland were run by a German civil administration under Nazi leadership. This administration kept a tight political control, took over the economy, refused to restore to its owners the land and industrial and commercial property previously expropriated by the Soviets, and established strict supervision of Lithuania's cultural and religious affairs.

Political and Economic Administration. Politically, the Germans, in the hope of minimizing Lithuanian disillusionment, established a council of "trustees," composed of Lithuanians, thus giving the Lithuanians, Latvians, and Estonians respectively an institution and a measure of administrative autonomy that was denied to the other East European areas occupied by the Germans. After the Provisional Government chose to disperse rather than permit itself to become such a council, von Renteln established a council on his own. He appointed General P. Kubiliūnas, a Voldemaras sympathizer who had served a prison term for a previous *Putsch* attempt against President Antanas

Smetona, to head this council (Generalrat) and invited individual members of the Provisional Government to join the Kubiliūnas group. To the surprise of the population, three out of fifteen members accepted,[19] though it should be added that the Germans later sent one of these three (Mečys Mackevičius) to the Stutthof concentration camp. Eight other councilors of varied political background were appointed in the fields of economy, finance, agriculture, education, justice, communications, labor and social security, and administrative control. This type of "self-government" was aimed primarily at the better integration of Lithuania into the war economy of the Reich.

Thus the plans for political autonomy of the Baltic nations, drawn up before the Barbarossa expedition (German code name for attack on the Soviet Union) against the Soviet Union began, were buried in the offices of Eastern specialists and officials in Berlin. Hitler rejected any such ideas.[20] Lithuanian inquiries about their country's future, however, continued to be answered in nebulous terms, as they had been during the first weeks of occupation by Dr. Greffe and Dr. Kleist: First it was necessary to defeat Communism, and then the Führer would reward those nations which helped in it.

However, soon the overconfident Nazi propagandists betrayed the secret: Independence for Lithuania did not figure in their plans. Even in Lithuania itself, the Germans, especially the Gestapo functionaries, promoted the view that in Lithuania only the intelligentsia was interested in statehood. The Lithuanian farmer, the Germans claimed, did not care for independence; he merely wanted to tend his land and obtain good prices for his crops. Furthermore, the Gestapo considered this Lithuanian intelligentsia corrupted by its alliances and friendships with the Anglo-Saxon countries and consequently sought an opportunity to "teach the intellectuals a lesson." Warnings were given in the German-controlled press on several occasions in the summer and fall of 1942. Furthermore, Nazi functionaries in Lithuania attempted to convince the inhabitants that small nations could not be independent. This thesis was even expounded in a work of fiction, for the Gestapo found a "writer" who described life in independent Lithuania as a mire[21] (*Bala,* in Lithuanian; the title of the novel), seeking thus to blacken Lithuanian life during the period 1918–40. In promoting their own vague, half-formulated plans for the Baltic area, the Germans actually were unable or unwilling to see that the Lithuanian commitment to independence was rooted not only in the traditions of a national renaissance and in love of the nation's history, but also in the twenty-two years of Lithuanian independence, during which a new Lithuanian generation grew up, a peasantry and intelligentsia that could not be told that their independence was a mire.

In the economic field the Germans similarly did not show any sign that they intended to share the fruits of Lithuania's labor with the Lithuanian people. All industrial and business firms previously nationalized by the Bolsheviks now came under German control.[22] Thus, a company for agricultural cultivation (Landbewirtschaftungs-Gesellschaft) administered all farms that formerly belonged to the state, to persons deported by the Soviets, to native Germans repatriated to the Reich during the Soviet occupation, and to Jews. Another company, the Zentral-handels-Gesellschaft Ost, took over slaughter houses, sugar and flour mills, breweries, etc., among them the largest Lithuanian enterprises, Lietuvos Cukrus (Lithuanian Sugar) and Maistas (Food). Shareholding companies like Grundstück-Gesellschaft, Tabakindustrie, Ostland-Faser ran seventy-four textile mills, paper mills, cigarette factories, and other concerns. These enterprises were managed by German trustees, usually members of the NSDAP.

The Lithuanians were further antagonized by the German refusal to return to private owners the land nationalized by the Soviet regime. Hitler himself opposed denationalization of Baltic farms. Consequently, some farms were directly managed by the Germans, others were managed by the former owners, who now did not have the title to their property. Only very few property titles were returned for bribes or for special "services." Soon it became clear why the Germans refused to eliminate this by-product of the Soviet occupation: They had made up their minds to colonize the area immediately. While the rightful owners were denied their property rights, former German repatriates and outright colonists were imported from the Reich to settle in selected farms. Colonization first began in the districts of Tauragė, Šiauliai, and Vilkaviškis, and continued steadily, so that by the fall of 1942, 16,300 German colonists had been established on choice Lithuanian farms.[23] This policy quickly created restlessness in all three Baltic states (the same policy was carried out in Latvia and Estonia), and some Germans became skeptical about its results. On September 16, 1942, Karl Litzmann, the German Generalkommissar for Estonia, reported to his superiors that "the dualism of our policy—economic measures as if we were operating in a Gau reintegrated into the Reich, while leaving the population in the dark about their future—is bound to lead to tensions and have the opposite effect of what we aim at."[24] In Lithuania, this tension was already manifest a year earlier, that is, in the autumn of 1941.

In addition to this economic expropriation, exploitation, and colonization, the Lithuanian economy was burdened by requisitions of products and manpower.

Recruitment of Manpower. Mobilizations of laborers started in the spring of 1942 after Marshal Göring, Fritz Saukel, and other high Nazi functionaries repeatedly reproached Heinrich Lohse, the Ostland Reichskomissar, for his alleged failure to provide the necessary manpower from the Baltic states.[25] In the spring of 1942, Dr. J. Paukštys, the Lithuanian Councilor for Labor and Social Security, was ordered by the Germans to mobilize 100,000 Lithuanian workers. On May 2, 1942, a decree was issued demanding the registration of all Lithuanian males and females between the ages of seventeen and forty-five. Those failing to register were subject to a 1,000 RM fine and three months imprisonment[26] in forced labor camps in Pravieniškės, Dimitravas, and Pabradė. In addition, in each district camps were established to imprison farmers failing to deliver various requisitions. The population, however, did not respond, and Dr. Paukštys was able to conscript only 5 per cent of his quota. In addition to this mass mobilization, there were others that produced equally meager results. The Zivilverwaltung, for example, issued a regulation requiring university freshmen to serve in the German youth labor force, the Reichsarbeitsdienst (RAD). The Kaunas and Vilnius universities, however, strongly resisted this requirement, obviously designed to choke off future university work, and on August 23, 1942, six members of the senates of both universities were arrested by the Gestapo and intimidated during a three-day confinement. However, with the help of the Lithuanian councilors, the universities were able to fend off this attack, and the German plan failed. Another tactic used by the Germans was to surround churches during Sunday services and seize people for work in Germany. On September 10, 1943, for example, at the small town of Žiežmariai, twenty German gendarmes, armed with machine guns and carrying grenades, forced their way into the local Catholic church to conscript laborers for the Reich.[27] At first, such incidents were scattered, but beginning in the late fall of 1943, they became weekly occurrences.

Thus personal existence became insecure, although frequently ways were found to "beat the Germans": Many German administrators and even Gestapo men could be bribed (this was impossible with Soviet functionaries in 1940–41); many lower Lithuanian administrators and the police intentionally performed their duties carelessly. However, the absence of basic security hurt education and the development of cultural activities, which already were much curtailed by censorship, limitation on publications, etc. It should be also added that prisons were again filled with political prisoners, as during the Soviet occupation; furthermore, the Nazis engaged in a full-scale annihilation of Lithuanian Jews. By the middle of 1943, German rule had deteriorated so much that an influential underground newspaper, *Nepriklausoma Lietuva*, was led to wonder whether the Bolsheviks or the Nazis "were the more inveterate murderers of innocent people."[28]

The Development of Anti-Nazi Resistance

The Rise of the Underground. How did the population react to these policies of the Zivilverwaltung? Generally, this type of German behavior upset the people. It produced growing dissatisfaction and opposition. Soon resistance to the Germans became universal. Resistance forces worked through a number of organizations and newspapers that had their origin in the Lithuanian Activist Front. The LAF's life had been short. The organization survived its own creation, the Provisional Government, but dissolved several weeks later. In the late summer of 1941, the LAF presented Hitler and the German military command with a memorandum on Lithuanian independence signed by a large number of persons, and the Germans responded on September 21 by arresting the LAF chief, Leonas Prapuolenis, and deporting him to the Dachau concentration camp. The next day they outlawed the organization itself. By liquidating the LAF, the Germans destroyed an institution that in the anti-Soviet underground, during the insurrection, and later, until the midsummer of 1941, had been the spokesman for all the resistance groups.

For at least two years, there would be no central leadership of the Lithuanian resistance against the occupier.

All but one anti-German resistance group sprouted from the LAF trunk after the organization was banned by the Germans. The one that had broken away from the LAF while it still was officially tolerated was the "Voldemaras group," named after the pro-German former Lithuanian politician. On June 29, this group officially registered as the Lithuanian Nationalist Party. It imitated the Nazi party; its members were used by the Germans to execute a Gestapo-planned *Putsch* against the Provisional Government. Four months later, however, the Germans banned the Voldemarists because they had dared to issue a memorandum criticizing the evils of the Zivilverwaltung system. But the group would not be silenced; it continued its activities, now in opposition to the Germans. This, of course, meant that it had to go underground.

In October, another group, the Freedom Fighters (Laisvės Kovotojai), issued an open letter to the German-controlled Lithuanian councilors formally condemning the Kubiliūnas course and began the publication of a widely read underground paper, *Laisvės Kovotojas* (*Freedom Fighter*). Later, it established liaison with friends and allies abroad, and early in 1944 organized a secret radio station, "Free Lithuania's Radio Vilnius." The remaining part of the LAF re-formed in October–November, taking the name "Lithuanian Front" (Lietuvių Frontas). Although its leadership was dominated by *ateitininkai,* an old (though outlawed under the Germans) Catholic Action group, the organization comprised groups beyond Catholic Action circles in all sections of the country. In January, 1943, this group began publishing *Į Laisvę* (*Toward Freedom*). For special political commentary the group disseminated the mimeographed *Lietuvių Biuletenis* (*Lithuanian Bulletin*). Individual units of the Lithuanian Front published another paper, *Vardan Tiesos* (*In the Name of Truth*), and a satirical publication, *Pogrindžio Kuntaplis* (*The Underground Pantofle*). The organization also printed *Lietuvos Judas* (*Judas of Lithuania*), giving the names of German collaborators who sought to please the German occupation authorities against Lithuanian interests. In the fall of 1942, students of the university in Kaunas organized the Lithuanian Union Movement and published a paper, *Atžalynas* (*The Sapling*), which attracted students and teachers of various ideological views from the universities of Kaunas and Vilnius. Several more influential anti-Nazi publications appeared in provincial towns, e.g., *Lietuva* (*Lithuania*), published in Šiauliai. Former members of the Riflemen's Association printed *Lietuvos Laisvės Trimitas* (*Lithuania's Freedom Trumpet*). The list of underground papers included *Laisvės Žodis* (*Word of Freedom*), *Lietuvos Kelias* (*Lithuania's Way*), *Baltija* (*The Baltic*), *Jaunime Budėk* (*Youth Be Prepared*), and others. One of the most influential and popular underground papers was *Nepriklausoma Lietuva* (*Independent Lithuania*), published by the Populist Party (Valstiečiai Liaudininkai) since the fall of 1941.

These underground newspapers, printed for the most part by clandestine printing presses, with circulations running into many thousands of copies, publicized the crimes of the occupation authorities, gave news about the war, and combated German propaganda. They further angered the Nazis because of their openly pro-Anglo-Saxon orientation, which then dominated the thinking of underground resistance leaders. In December, 1943, for example, *Į Laisvę* editorialized:

> The Anglo-Saxons, by proclaiming the Atlantic Charter, which was more kind to the interests of small nations than the Germans, knew how to stir up the expectations of small nations. Although attempts are made to convince our people that the Charter is useless, that the Anglo-Saxons have sold the small nations to the Bolsheviks, our people remember how the principles of free self-determination of nations after World War I were proclaimed in America and realized. Now also the hope will not betray us, especially when we remember that a million American Lithuanians are doing their utmost for the benefit of their home country.[29]

In addition to the profession of such optimistic trust in the Western Allies, these newspapers oriented the population on important issues of the day and warned about future German mobilizations and other dangers. As will be shown, the underground press was very influential in determining the population's response to the various German directives; its handling of German decrees was conspicuously demonstrated in 1943, when the Germans ordered mobilization of a Lithuanian Legion of the Waffen SS.

Boycott of the SS Legion. In the summer of 1941, the Germans felt certain that they would defeat the Soviet Union before the onset of winter and therefore they did not consider any outside help necessary; for such help they would have to make political concessions that might interfere with their plans of colonization.[30] Therefore, they very carelessly rejected the proposal made by the Lithuanian Provisional Government to join in the war against the Soviet Union, and felt satisfied with organizing several Lithuanian batallions for police and guard duties. But in the second half of 1942, when the Eastern Front required more and more cannon fodder and when a withdrawal from the Caucasus became necessary, the Germans changed their minds about the need for larger Baltic military forces. After successfully organizing Latvian and Estonian SS Legions at the end of 1942, and especially after the Stalingrad disaster in early 1943, the Germans directed their attention to Lithuania. According to German estimates, Lithuania could provide more armed men than Latvia, which had about 150,000 soldiers in its Legion.[31]

The mobilization was marked for March 6, 1943. All men of seventeen and over had to register for induction into the Legion. The entire German propaganda machinery, including the cinema and the theater, was used to facilitate smooth conscription. The Germans promised that the Legion would fight only in the northern sector of the Eastern Front and not be sent to more distant areas. The Legion, it was pledged, "will fight as a unit and will have all types of weapons: Its own armor, artillery, reconnaissance, and other auxiliary units."[32] Village elders were responsible for bringing prospective soldiers to the recruiting stations. But recruiting officers waited in vain. Sometimes, only an invalid or two would show up in the course of a day. University students gave an example of how to avoid the draft. The youths hid, changed residence, and took to the forests, completely frustrating the German campaign.

The German occupation authorities felt insulted by this behavior. The office of the Zivilverwaltung, and possibly von Renteln personally, had promised Hitler a Lithuanian SS Legion, but they could not deliver it. This explains why the Generalkommissar's office, not the Gestapo, drew up the list of intellectuals who were blamed for von Renteln's fiasco. These were singled out for deportation to concentration camps in Germany, and on the night of March 16–17, arrests began. Forty-six Lithuanian intellectuals were shipped off to Stutthoff. Thus they joined other Lithuanians in the Reich, among them important political leaders who had been interned in Germany or kept in its prisons since 1942, or even earlier.* The Gestapo considered these people, arrested to revenge the failure of military mobilization, parasites because of their alleged trust in the English and the Americans. The group included educators, priests, lawyers, university professors, and agronomists. Among them were three councilors to the Zivilverwaltung whom von Renteln himself had appointed.†

These arrests were a warning to the Lithuanian intelligentsia, a foretaste of possible massive punishment. On March 17, the arrests were followed by the closing of all schools of higher education. The Germans also seized school and office inventories. Various institutes at the universities of Kaunas and Vilnius were among the major victims.

Communist Lithuanian historians, who as a rule rewrite Lithuanian history to suit the interests of "big brother," have for once correctly stated that "Lithuanian youth massively resisted three mobilizations into the German armed forces . . . all mobilizations failed."[33] The Communists, however, refused to give the real reasons for this failure. They did not explain why the Germans publicly announced on March 17 that the recruitment for the SS Legion was being stopped and angrily charged that Lithuanians were unworthy to wear SS uniforms. The official German communiqué blamed the intelligentsia.[34] Indeed, the voice of this intelligentsia was clearly heard throughout the land in the underground press and its organizations. People responded to this voice, completely disregarding the Germans' advice not to participate in politics.

Eventually, the situation became very grave. Trying to ease it and to save the intelligentsia from further deportations—the Gestapo had drawn up a list of 200 persons, but spoke of an

---

* These included the former Lithuanian President, Dr. Kazys Grinius; the Christian Democratic leader and author of the Lithuanian land reform, Msgr. Mykolas Krupavičius; and former Minister of Agriculture, Jonas Aleksa. They presented to the Germans a memorandum protesting the colonization of Lithuania, the failure to restore the property nationalized by the Bolsheviks, and the persecution of the Jews and the Poles.

† Mečislovas Mackevičius, Justice; Pranas Germantas-Meškauskas, Education (died in concentration camp); Stasys Puodžius, Administrative Control (died in concentration camp). At the same time, the former Councilor for Economics, Professor Vladas Jurgutis, was sent to the Stutthof concentration camp. His memorandums, addressed to von Renteln, criticized not only the commissar's policies but the whole administrative apparatus. Copies of one such memorandum were widely circulated in the country. Its author inevitably came into conflict with the *Generalkommissar* and resigned his position. In 1943, together with other intellectuals, he was arrested.

eventual 30,000 deportees[35]—at least twenty-four prominent persons signed a declaration on March 27 calling for an "all-Lithuanian" conference. This declaration was drafted by the Germans; the signers, however, succeeded in greatly modifying it because the Germans themselves now were trying to find a way out of this complicated and tension-laden situation. The proposed conference convened on June 5; however, its 100 delegates were not elected but simply appointed by the Lithuanian district chiefs of the civil administration. This conference resulted in the creation of an advisory council attached to the First Councilor, General Kubiliūnas. To lend it an aura of respectability, the council was named after the historical National Council of 1917–18. However, this group had neither authority nor influence among the Lithuanians, although it included some prominent and honorable men. Thus, its pronouncements could not help any future German plans of mobilization.

Unification of Resistance Organizations. After a wave of repressive German measures, the people closed ranks more than at any other time since the insurrection against the Soviets and followed the directives of the underground press. The temper of the underground was defiant and contemptuous of the Germans. *Laisvės Kovotojas* lectured: "Germans, open your eyes and look around you, to see what is happening in the battlefronts and all around you. The midnight hour is approaching." In the same vein it consoled the people: "And you, young Lithuanian men and women, take strength from the hope and knowledge that only desperate rulers whose hours are counted and who don't know any longer what to do can employ such methods of suppression."[36] In such an atmosphere, another German conscription, ordered on June 7 by von Renteln and demanding registration "for military work" of all men born between 1919 and 1924, was destined to fail. The German reminder of the March 17 arrests did not help.[37]

The German tightening of the already oppressive occupation regime had a salutary effect on the numerous underground organizations: They consolidated their ranks. After all, the aim of these organizations was the same, namely, to keep the nation as intact as possible, ensuring its physical survival so that its manpower and resources would be available for an eventual restoration of independence. Two committees for Lithuania's liberation functioned during the second half of 1943. One of them, the Supreme Lithuanian Committee (Vyriausias Lietuvių Komitetas), united Leftist groups; the other, the Lithuanian Council (Lietuvos Taryba), represented the Catholic-oriented organizations. These two committees now merged to form the Supreme Committee for Lithuania's Liberation (Vyriausias Lietuvos Išlaisvinimo Komitetas). On October 14, 1943, the seven groups that made up the two committees issued a joint announcement that led eventually to the formation of a single institution of leadership. On February 16, 1944, this newly formed committee published a declaration explaining the status of Lithuanian sovereignty. It said, in part, that

> the sovereign Lithuanian state did not disappear either because of the Soviet or the present occupation by the Reich; only the functioning of the organs of the sovereign state has been temporarily impaired. This functioning, interrupted by the Soviet occupation of June 15, 1940, and by acts committed by force and fraud under the violent pressures of this occupation, was temporarily restored by the national insurrection of June 23, 1941, and by the work of the Provisional Government.[38]

In the same declaration, the Committee also explained the purpose of the German mobilization boycotts:

> The Committee asks those subject to the German drafts not to surrender to the fear of terrorism. This, like all other evil designs the occupier has devised against us, must be answered by all Lithuanians with a courageous and united NO! The draftees and those persecuted [by the occupation authorities] should not surrender but continue in hiding, thus saving their lives for the re-establishment of Lithuania's independence. The Committee urges all Lithuanians to help those in hiding.

Until the end of the German occupation, the Committee united all the political and paramilitary forces of the underground. It included representatives of political parties active in the past (Christian Democrats, Labor Federation, Farmers Union, the Populists, the Social Democrats, the Lithuanian Nationalist League, or Tautininkai), and delegates from the four most prominent paramilitary resistance organizations established under the German occupation (the Lithuanian Front, Freedom Fighters, the Nationalist Party, the Lithuanian Union League). Unfortunately, the Gestapo accidentally learned the composition of this new committee.* A majority of its members were arrested

---

* The Committee sent an arms specialist with previous contacts with Swedish munitions makers to purchase weapons in Sweden. On April 22, 1944, how-

and confined in Bayreuth prison (Bavaria), where they remained from April, 1944, until their liberation on April 14, 1945. The Committee, however, continued its activities with replacements.

The Tragedy of the Territorial Force. The deterioration of the military situation in the East forced the Germans to seek more and more manpower for work in Germany. The German Wehrmacht, possibly mindful of the recent experience of von Renteln, sought to provide for itself without the help of the Zivilverwaltung. Major General Emil Just, former German Military Attaché in Kaunas and now Wehrmacht Oberfeldkommandant for Lithuania, an officer whom the public did not equate with the SS, the Gestapo, and the Zivilverwaltung because of his attitude toward Lithuania, succeeded in organizing several engineering and construction batallions.

Furthermore, intensified activities by Soviet partisans in East Lithuania inspired the Germans to establish a permanent Lithuanian force for dealing with them. Such a force was created as a result of negotiations between the highly popular Lithuanian General Povilas Plechavičius and the German police General Friedrich Jeckeln, SS and police chief for Ostland, with his aides in Riga. Plechavičius agreed to form twenty batallions of the Territorial Defense Force (Litauische Sonderverbände). These batallions were to be composed of volunteers commanded by Lithuanian officers. They were supposed to be used against the widespread banditry and Soviet partisans in Lithuania, and also for rear-guard action in the northern sector of the Russian front (from Narva to Vilnius). The results of General Plechavičius' appeal on February 16, 1944, surprised the Germans: the promised number of batallions was formed immediately. Many applicants had to be turned away. This success was due partly to Plechavičius' personal magnetism, but primarily to the support given Plechavičius by the underground organizations and their press. They advised Lithuanian youth to join the batallions.

However, the Lithuanians' hope that from now on the Germans would allow them honorably to defend their native land against the Bolsheviks was in vain. The Germans immediately pressed for more manpower. Field Marshal Model demanded 15

---

ever, the courier was arrested during a police raid in Tallinn, Estonia. After torturing him, the Gestapo found out the names of those members of the Supreme Committee for Lithuanian's Liberation that the man knew.

new batallions (9,000 men), primarily for servicing military air-ports in the rear of the Eastern Front. On April 6, after General Plechavičius refused, von Renteln demanded 80,000 workers for the German war industry. In addition, the Germans pressed for a contingent of 30,000 men for air-force duty. Although this time General Plechavičius submitted to the demand, the underground organizations and the press resisted, and the Germans again failed. The occupation authorities now turned against the batal-lions of Plechavičius' own Territorial Force. A new German police chief for Lithuania, SS Brigadeführer General Major Hintze, who had replaced SS General Harm (dismissed for his failure to organize the SS Legion), ordered the incorporation of the Lithuanian Territorial Defense Force batallions into the auxiliary police service of the SS, and even introduced the SS manner of saluting. This, of course, meant that the Force would come under the direct command of the SS and would be used solely for SS purposes. General Plechavičius and his staff resisted, as they had previously resisted the German demand that these batallions be used on the Western Front. The Germans, however, were by now exasperated with the Nationalist general, and on May 15, SS General Jeckeln personally arrested him and his staff and sent him to the Salaspils concentration camp, near Riga. From May 17 to May 21, the Germans terrorized Plechavičius' troops by indiscriminately executing 100 soldiers as a warning that the now leaderless troops had to obey the German masters. However, most of the troops fled and went into hiding, taking their weapons with them, and the Germans succeeded in detain-ing only 3,500 troops, who were forced into Luftwaffe uniforms and sent for various duties to West German military airports.[39]

After thus breaking their word and abusing the Territorial De-fense Force, the Germans could not hope for any further coopera-tion, and they did not receive it. The Plechavičius troops who had gone into hiding disregarded the German order to return their weapons. Similarly disregarded was Kubiliūnas' demand on June 10, 1944, that all young men register for military duty. The Germans were equally unsuccessful in organizing new Lithuanian troops in the fall of 1944, when most of Lithuania had already been overrun by the returning Soviet Army; nor did their recruit-ing efforts succeed among the Lithuanian refugees who fled to Germany as the Soviet Army advanced.

Thus ended the resistance against the Nazis and the German occupation itself.

5. The Partisan Movement in Postwar Lithuania*

V. STANLEY VARDYS

Organized partisan resistance in Lithuania lasted for eight years (1944-52),[1] conveniently divisible into two periods: four years of strength (1944-48) and four of gradual decline (1949-52). During the first period, the partisans reached proportions of an underground army and fought open battles. Rising spontaneously in the summer of 1944, the movement spread very quickly, and by the spring of 1945, its ranks included an estimated 30,000 active fighters with other thousands ready to join in case of need.[2] Partisan groups were especially strong during 1945-47, when they dominated the countryside, withstanding the squeeze by combined Soviet security and regular army forces. The main formations of the movement, according to Soviet sources, could not be broken till the end of 1948.[3] During this period (1944-48), the movement underwent many organizational and tactical changes, necessitated by the losses suffered at the hands of the Soviet pursuer and the strategies he adopted against the partisans. At this time, too, main questions concerning the leadership and tactics of the movement were decided and attempts were made to unite all partisan groups on a national basis. However, success at unification eluded the partisans till the end of 1946. The achieved unity, furthermore, was more formal than actual, because intensified Soviet countermeasures prevented consolidation of organizational gains. Early in 1949, partisan groups reorganized into Lietuvos Laisvės Kovų Sąjūdis (LLKS), or Movement of Lithuania's Struggle for Freedom,[4] adopted tactics more suitable to small conspiratorial groups and continued resistance until destroyed sometime

* Reprinted, with permission, from an article originally published in the *Slavic Review*, XXII, No. 3 (September, 1963), 499-522. (Slight changes of an editorial nature have been made.)

around 1952. The last leader of the movement, A. Ramanaus-kas-Vanagas, an American-born former teacher, however, seems to have escaped capture till 1956, when he was arrested and executed.[5]

The scope of the hostilities can be judged from estimates of losses suffered in life and property. The director of the Lithuanian Communist Party's history institute at Vilnius told an American journalist in 1961 that during the partisan war "about 20,000 bandits [partisans] were killed and about an equal number of our own people."[6] Lithuanian nationalist sources put the figure at 30,000 for the partisans alone.[7] Neither of these figures includes liquidated or deported partisan families and supporters, which ran into tens of thousands. Property losses also were quite extensive. They included destroyed bridges, telephone lines, houses, livestock, crops. As a result of partisan activities in 1944–47, acreage of cultivated land was sharply reduced.[8] It has been claimed also that owing to conditions created by the guerrilla-style war, newly established kolkhozes in Lithuania started in greater poverty than those in the other Baltic states.[9]

CAUSES OF ARMED RESISTANCE TO THE SOVIETS

Armed resistance to the Soviets began during the summer and late autumn of 1944, immediately after the armies of the Third Belorussian Front, led by General Ivan Cherniakhovsky, reconquered Lithuania from the Germans. Partisan groups emerged spontaneously, without a preconceived central plan, though in the northwestern part of the country they organized shortly before Cherniakhovsky's armies overran the area.

The explanation of such an immediate and violent response to the renewed Soviet occupation is to be found in the peculiarly Lithuanian experiences and attitudes, shaped by the turbulent events of World War II. These experiences and attitudes may be summed up under five headings: (1) Lithuanian acquaintance with Soviet rule in 1940–41 and its overthrow in mid–1941;[10] (2) analysis and appraisal of the war and the international situation; (3) persistence of nationalist idealism and pro-Western orientation among the leaders of the intelligentsia, including former army officers; (4) experience, tradition, and momentum developed by previous organized nationalist undergrounds, first against the Communists in 1940–41, and then against the Nazis from the summer of 1941 to the end of the German occupation; (5) the

Kremlin's quick pace of sovietization, purges, and reprisals suffered by large segments of the population under the renewed Soviet rule.

Since 1940–41, Lithuanian relations with the Soviets had been poisoned by Soviet designs on Lithuania, and experiences with the Soviet regime had created an abyss between an overwhelming majority of the population and the Communists. In 1940, the Kremlin had forcibly incorporated the small country into the Soviet Union, communized much of the nation's life, and introduced a regime of terror that on June 13–14, 1941, culminated in the deportation of some 35,000 people to remote labor camps in Soviet Russia. Such measures had shocked the people, and in 1944, memories of these events were still very fresh. The returning Red Army was therefore greeted not with joy but with considerable apprehension and fear. Reconciliation with the victorious Soviets in 1944 did not seem possible or even feasible, particularly because all ties with the Bolsheviks had been visibly cut by an armed insurrection against the regime on June 23, 1941.[11] During their first occupation, the Bolsheviks had so alienated diverse strata of the population that a broadly based anti-Soviet underground sprang up and finally rose in an armed revolt. A force estimated at 100,000 men rebelled against the Soviets on the evening of the day Germany attacked the Soviet Union, and the arriving German armies found most localities, including the central cities, under Lithuanian insurrectionist control. The objectives of this rebellion were strictly nationalistic. Fearful that Germany would not recognize Lithuania's new independence, the rebels attempted to force the Germans to accept a *fait accompli*. Thus two days before the German columns reached the administrative capital, Kaunas, the rebels, using the seized broadcasting system, announced the restoration of the Lithuanian state and the establishment of a provisional government. But for the Germans this was a nuisance. Extremely confident of their own power, the Nazis denied all nationalist claims, disarmed the rebels, and dispersed their government, substituting for it a *Zivilverwaltung* under a Nazi commissar. Thus, although the insurrection had considerably quickened the pace of their blitz in the Baltic area, the Germans completely frustrated the political aims of the rebellion and by so doing forfeited Lithuanian cooperation.

The anti-Soviet rebellion nevertheless exerted a lasting and intoxicating effect on the Lithuanians. On the one hand, it demonstrated the existence of virulent nationalism and showed that

nationalist convictions could be translated into a reasonably powerful force. On the other, it proved to the satisfaction of the
masses that the Red regime was not invincible. If it cracked in
1941 under the whip of an invading European power, supported
by the native population, it could lose again under similar circumstances. Thus, though by January 28, 1945, Soviet armies had
completely overrun the Lithuanian territory, large segments of
the country, especially the intelligentsia and the farmers, still
clung to a conviction that the new Soviet occupation was only
temporary.[12]

In 1944, a majority of Lithuanians believed that the Soviets
would be thrown back by a coalition of Western Allies and Germany; the Germans were expected to overthrow Hitler and
make a separate peace treaty with the United States and Great
Britain.[13] When this hope vanished with Germany's capitulation,
invasions sponsored by the United States, alone or with England,
were expected.[14] This widely held Lithuanian view that the
Soviet regime was of a transient nature was enhanced by a fatally
unrealistic appraisal of the emerging international situation.

The leaders of anti-Soviet resistance inherited the political interpretation of World War II from the former anti-Nazi underground. According to this view, the war was not fought by two,
but by three parties: Germany, the United States with Great
Britain, and the Soviet Union. The Atlantic powers and the
Soviets were not really allies, it was maintained, but merely co-
belligerents, accidently thrown together in an incompatible coalition which would soon break up in disagreement over the postwar
organization of the world. The emerging conflict between the
wartime partners was expected to explode into a new world war
which the Soviets would lose, thus leaving Lithuania independent.[15] This analysis, generally speaking, influenced the choice of
action suggested for the intelligentsia during the fateful summer
of 1944, when a decision had to be made by many whether to
stay under the returning Soviets. Important national leaders advised that the intelligentsia, as the group that could provide future leadership but was likely to suffer most under the Soviets,
should temporarily withdraw to the West.[16] Those who could
not leave were to seek safety with the partisans at home in order
to survive until the beginning of an armed conflict between the
victorious wartime allies. This day was believed to be near.

The explanation of this insightful but greatly oversimplified
interpretation of war and international settlement is found partly

in a psychological hope of deliverance that only captives can have and partly in the misunderstanding of the West and Lithuania's relation to it. The generation of Lithuanian intelligentsia that directed both the anti-German and later anti-Soviet underground had been educated in West European and Lithuanian universities during the years of Lithuania's independence (1918–40), when the nation's economic, political, and cultural life was directed toward Western Europe.[17] This intelligentsia regarded Lithuania as an integral part of the "Western" world. With small exceptions, this social group was anti-Soviet and disdainful of all things Russian.[18] Although during the twilight of Lithuania's independence (1938–40), representatives of this generation were emerging as intellectual and political leaders, they were denied leadership by the occupants, and thus assumed the direction of the nation from the underground. To these leaders it seemed preposterous to suggest that the Western powers, which meant the United States and Britain, would abandon Eastern Europe to the masters of the Kremlin. During the German occupation such views were denounced as German propaganda. Later they were dismissed as Soviet lies. Desperate and idealistic, this intelligentsia placed its trust in the Atlantic Charter[19] and in the United States and Britain, whose pressure was expected to force the restoration of Lithuanian independence in the San Francisco conference that founded the United Nations.[20] Dates marking the liquidation of Soviet rule were predicted.

This erroneous confidence in the West also underlay later misinterpretations of the policies of the Western powers. Generally, the policy of containment that the United States initiated in 1947 was confused with the policy of liberation for which the captive Lithuanians hoped. Winston Churchill's speech at Fulton, for example, was regarded as a call "to the entire world to begin the struggle against the Communist beast" and as a signal to start concrete preparations for war.[21] President Truman's speech on aid to Greece and Turkey was found to "give hope of liberation."[22] To the Lithuanians, then for the third year under Soviet oppression, such anti-Soviet declarations provided a tonic that was taken for a cure-all. It gave new encouragement to the partisans, inspired hope of help from abroad, and induced them fatally to exaggerate their long-term ability to resist the Soviets openly.

Another factor that encouraged the rise of anti-Soviet resistance was the momentum created by the anti-German underground, whose organizations now provided the initiative and nucleus for anti-Soviet resistance.[23] This anti-Nazi underground, brought to life largely by the leaders of the politically fruitless insurrection against the Soviets, was led by the Supreme Committee for Lithuania's Liberation (Vyriausias Lietuvos Išlaisvinimo Komitetas) and supported by a widespread and influential clandestine press. It maintained military formations but functioned differently from anti-German resistance groups in Western Europe.

The Lithuanians were caught between the Soviets and the Germans. Neither was their ally and both claimed Lithuanian land. Therefore the anti-German underground helped neither, but pursued its own policy of preserving the nation's manpower and resources, ready for the day they might be used to support purely nationalist objectives. Moreover, since there was no desire for the return of the Red Army, the underground did not sabotage the regular German military activity directed against the Soviets or Soviet partisans, but emphasized passive resistance, fought German propaganda, and sabotaged German plans for economic and military mobilization. Later this accumulated experience was used in an attempt to frustrate the re-establishment of Soviet rule and institutions. The tactics, significantly, this time were different. Now the underground resorted to open violence.

To the list of reasons that explain the rise of armed resistance it is important to add the Kremlin's relentless pace of sovietization, purges of unreliable elements, and the highhanded behavior of the regime's administrative authorities.[24] After Stalin's death, Lithuanian Communists themselves acknowledged the provocative nature of their conduct. One of the most resented Soviet policies was the forceful sovietization of agriculture, hastily decreed in August, 1944. This measure ordered a new land distribution that fragmented landholdings and inflicted economic punishment on "kulaks" and farmers singled out as German "collaborators."[25] A score of other harassing decrees, designed to tire the farmer into accepting collectivization, were passed during 1944–47. These measures invited violation, and prisons soon became overcrowded with ordinary villagers. Many of those still free rallied around the partisans, convinced that only the overthrow of the regime promised hope of salvation.

The vengeful purge of suspect and politically unacceptable inhabitants also incited people to take up arms against the regime. The purge, begun immediately after the return of Soviet security organs, was conducted very systematically and, though at first based only on individual arrests, actually continued the series of deportations that were started but not completed before the outbreak of the German-Soviet hostilities. The resumed screening was directed, as previously, against the potentially "counterrevolutionary" segments of the population. As captured NKVD-NKGB documents revealed,[26] in 1941 these segments included members of all non-Communist political parties; leaders of patriotic, religious, and youth organizations; former military officers; former law-enforcement officers; priests and ministers; and active workers of many specified organizations. The Soviets served themselves well by aiming to liquidate these people. The marked categories were citadels of militant Lithuanian nationalists who had led two successive nationalist movements against the Communist and Nazi occupations and in 1944 organized the first partisan groups.

The regime used two formal charges for arrests—"enemy of the people" and "war criminal."[27] Both charges were employed also against people considered socially alien to the regime (e.g., merchants, kulaks) and against former German "collaborators" (e.g., voluntary or involuntary soldiers in German uniform; local government officials during the German occupation). The arrests did not reach prewar proportions until February, 1946, when, because of intensified efforts to destroy armed resistance, the Soviets resumed the deportations of thousands of families and instituted mass reprisals against entire villages.

In addition to the feared collectivization and the purge, several other Soviet policies produced recruits for the partisans. One of these was mobilization for military service. To escape Soviet service, people resorted to draft dodging and desertion—tactics successfully employed against similar mobilizations by the Germans. These unwilling soldiers usually found refuge with the partisans. Similarly, violators of postwar labor regulations, such as the requirement of permission to change jobs, frequently sought refuge in the forests. Also, political prisoners freed by the NKVD on condition of serving as *sotrudniki* (informers), frequently chose to join the partisans. Finally, a general breakdown of postwar law enforcement encouraged partisan activity for protection in vigilante style. This usually happened in locations where authorities were either helpless or, as was mostly the case, unwilling to restrain civilian gangs or Soviet soldiers from looting farmsteads and attacking their inhabitants.

Although this Communist behavior was sufficiently oppressive to provoke violent native reaction, the Soviets never recognized the partisan movement as an indigenous force of opposition. At first, armed resistance was claimed to be German-inspired, and the guerrillas were denounced as "remnants of Lithuanian-German nationalists."[28] A decade later, this charge was refined to accuse "Hitlerite helpers," who were identified as "policemen, officers of the bourgeois army, active members of the bourgeois parties, priests."[29] At present, not only the Germans and their alleged collaborators are blamed for sponsoring the partisans, but the Western democracies as well. In a speech to the Twenty-second Party Congress, the first Secretary of the Lithuanian Communist Party, Antanas Sniečkus repeated the now standard charge that the partisan movement was "established by the Hitlerite occupant and supported by American and English intelligence."[30] However, data produced by the Soviets offer no convincing evidence to substantiate such broad contentions. These charges, in fact, are without foundation, initiated purely for propaganda purposes.*

* The extent of the alleged American and British involvement is discussed on pp. 100–101. The charge of German sponsorship and partisan collaboration must be taken up now, though available space does not allow a longer discussion. The Soviets have never produced evidence to show that armed resistance in Lithuania was German-inspired, because such a link never existed. The Soviet Union has fabricated the charge for political purposes, as a part of an extremely intensive Communist propaganda campaign in Lithuania, designed to create a pro-Nazi image of the partisans and to destroy existing nationalist influences by indiscriminately identifying all nationalists with the German occupation regime. Cf. B. Baranauskas, "Buržuaziniai Nacionalistai-Hitlerininkų Talkininkai," *Tarybinis Mokytojas* (Vilnius), December 21, 24, and 28, 1961. The few cases of "collaboration" among the partisans produced by the Soviets usually involve Lithuanian insurrectionists against the Soviet regime in 1941 and former soldiers in German uniform. For the latest case, tried in open court, see *Sovetskaia Litva,* June 17, 1962, p. 4. Interestingly enough, the Soviets have not produced specific collaborationist or war crime charges against any of the better known partisan leaders. It would be unrealistic to assume, of course, that among the more than 30,000 active partisans there were none of compromised personal or political integrity. However, such cases were not numerous, even on the basis of Soviet data, and hardly provide grounds for generalizations that impugn the nationalist character of partisan resistance.

It must be added that the Lithuanians did not consider all cooperation with the enemies of the Soviets, including the Germans, as infamous or treasonable. Ironically, although the German occupation was opposed by a strong nationalist underground, a minimum of cooperation with the Germans was regarded as useful for the purpose of keeping German armies fighting on the Soviet front. Thus, with the inevitable exceptions, neither the insurrectionists of 1941,

In retrospect, the Lithuanian Communists nevertheless conceded another point, namely, that the stern policies of the postwar period were at least partially responsible for the difficulties experienced in restoring Soviet rule. "Mistakes" were acknowledged but blamed on the Stalinist regime: the "cult of personality" and its disregard for "socialist legality,"[31] the "lack of attention for specific conditions."[32] Antanas Sniečkus in the quoted speech to the Twenty-second Party Congress, admitted that "breaches of socialist legality" had made it quite difficult for the Communists to win popular support.[33] "Illegally treating innocent people," the first secretary of the Lithuanian party said, "adventurers of Beria's type [possibly a reference to General Kruglov, former deputy of Beria, who conducted the suppression of the partisan movement] compromised the policies of the government, rendered more difficult the struggle against traitors, and on occasion made it possible for the real enemies of the people and socialism to escape unscathed." These anti-Stalinist phrases by a Communist with a Stalinist record dating back to 1936 may represent nothing else but Sniečkus' own effort to dissociate himself from the unpopular policies of the late 1940's. Yet voices heard in Soviet Lithuania of the 1960's suggest that, at least among the Lithuanian Communist leaders, there existed differences on the Party's agricultural policy and methods of collectivization.[34] These questions, of course, directly concerned the anti-Soviet resistance. The partisan movement, however, has not been recognized as a justifiable albeit improper reaction to the Stalinist regime. The chief of the KGB in Lithuania, A. Randakevičius, explained in a newspaper article that persons convicted for activities in the "bourgeois nationalist underground" did not fall into the category of victims of the "cult of personality."[35]

NATURE OF THE PARTISAN MOVEMENT

Organized primarily on the assumption that peaceful coexistence with the Communists was impossible and their rule only temporary, the Lithuanian partisans coalesced as a movement

---

the local administration officials during the occupation, nor soldiers in German uniform were regarded as collaborators. The exceptions were persons who worked for the Germans against the nationalist Lithuanian interests. Such cases were usually publicized by the anti-Nazi underground. See "Five Years of Lithuanian Underground Resistance, An Account of Activities of the Supreme Lithuanian Committee of Liberation," *Lithuanian Bulletin*, III, No. 3 (May–June, 1945), 5; Daumantas, *Partizanai Už Geležinės Uždangos*, p. 80.

under religious and nationalist symbols, and concentrated, by the use of violence, on resisting political and social changes that the Soviets, also by force of arms, were imposing. What sort of people combined under these universal symbols for such a seemingly hopeless resistance? What made them stand together? What were their concrete objectives? How did they pursue them and why by force? Several important characteristics of the partisan movement emerge from a discussion of these questions.

The membership of Lithuanian partisan groups reflected the national character of the anti-Soviet resistance.[36] It encompassed people from all walks of life and from diverse social and political backgrounds. High-school and college students rubbed shoulders with their teachers; farmhands and city workers fought together with the farmers; noncommissioned officers of the Lithuanian army were found side by side with their former superiors. Clergymen also participated. Usually they served as chaplains, though frequently they, too, carried guns. Women acted as nurses, fighters, and as liaison agents. Sometimes entire families, including teen-age children, were found among the ranks. Most partisans were young; the dominant social background was that of the worker and farmer with medium-sized holdings. As was the case in other countries, in Lithuania the poorer population strata were better represented among the partisans than the rich. At least one partisan paper, *Už Tėvų Žemę*, complained, furthermore, of a relative shortage of intellectuals, scholars, and artists.[37] Similarly, the same paper pointed out that independent Lithuania had educated a larger number of army officers than the proportion of those participating in the partisan movement.

Shades of political opinion and, at first, ethnic background were not important so long as a member's loyalty belonged exclusively to the partisan organization. A good number of freedom fighters and most of their chief leaders had borne arms against the Soviets in the insurrection of 1941 and later had worked against the Germans in the nationalist anti-German underground. A handful of them were persons originally parachuted as German intelligence agents; their joining the ranks had given partisan groups access to valuable German stores of munitions, weapons, and other needed materials.[38] Moreover, escaped German POW's and Russian Red Army deserters also were found among the ranks. These instances, needless to say, were seized upon by the Soviets as lending credence to the allegation that the armed resistance was of German origin. The partisans, however, from the beginning had disqualified those parachuted German agents who refused to subordinate themselves completely to partisan command and discipline. Furthermore, beginning in early 1945, membership was confined exclusively to ethnic Lithuanians, with an occasional exception made only for persons of Latvian origin.

The leadership was in the hands of the intelligentsia, educated and matured during the two decades of Lithuanian independence. However, contrary to the practice of the anti-German underground, commanding positions generally were entrusted to former officers of the Lithuanian army. Usually, these were of lower ranks (below full colonel); many of them were reserve rather than regular army officers. In many cases, partisan groups were organized by these officers.

The motives of these people were mixed. As suggested in the discussion of the causes of armed resistance, some sought personal safety (e.g., deserters from the Red Army or persons seeking protection against charges of "enemies of the people" or "war criminals"); others were dedicated to loftier nationalist ideals; some joined only when "legal" life became too uncomfortable, dangerous, and insecure; others chose partisan existence in preference to a life of accommodation to the Communists; still others were simply adventurers. Generally, however, under conditions of totalitarian rule, the instinct of self-preservation and some higher purpose overlap so much as motivational factors that classification of motives into "selfish" and "idealistic" seems to become somewhat unreal. Both result in dissent which, though of different origin, is likely to result in some form of resistance that under totalitarianism offers the protection (or its illusion) of both personal safety and group ideals. This at any rate seems to have been the case with the Lithuanian partisans.

Organizationally, partisan membership was structured like most underground groups; it resembled a floating iceberg. There were three layers to this iceberg.[39] Its visible part constituted the real underground of "active" fighters, armed with light weapons of German and Russian make and sometimes with light artillery.[40] These were "front-line" soldiers and lived in forests or farm shelters. Their ranks were continually changing, because the average life span of an active fighter was only two years.[41] This visible part of the iceberg also varied in size, especially during 1945–47. It expanded immediately after some repressive Soviet action and shrank when dangers in "legal" life tapered off. To the partisans this circumstance was very dangerous, as it permitted an easy infiltration of the groups by Soviet agents. The two other layers of the organizational iceberg were composed of "passive" fighters and "supporters." Members of the first group were armed but stayed at home on their jobs or at schools. They were called upon only occasionally for a variety of tasks. The supporters also lived legally. Although they did not bear arms, their contribution to the cause was no less important. They provided supplies and shelter, and they gathered intelligence.

The actual organizational structure of partisan groups varied from region to region, but everywhere individual organizations were built around two principles, conspiratorial secrecy and military discipline.[42] The groups were united into conspiratorial military formations under religious and nationalist symbols, which were helpful in maintaining both secrecy and disciplined standards of behavior. Partisan groups usually held prayer meetings and frequented sacraments of the Roman Catholic Church, to which the majority of the partisans belonged. The oath to new members was administered in a semireligious ceremony.[43] Whenever available, a priest, usually the group's chaplain, administered the oath, and the new partisans kissed a crucifix or the Bible, and often a gun as well. The leaders usually were required to sign this oath. Each partisan then chose a code name. Furthermore, fearing the NKVD methods of interrogation, the partisans agreed not to be taken alive. If no escape was possible, they usually committed suicide.[44] From about 1946 on, it seems, the partisans blew themselves up with grenades held close to the face, so that they could not be recognized. Such methods were used to protect their families and friends.

To identify themselves outwardly with Lithuanian nationalism and its military tradition, the partisans, though conspiratorial activists, wore uniforms of the old Lithuanian army with all the insignia of rank and merit.[45] This and decorations for courage, valor, or service that were occasionally conferred on individual fighters or supporters also emphasized the military nature of the organization and helped to maintain discipline. The primary partisan groups were small units composed of seven to ten men sharing two or three shelters. These groups were combined into companies, which in turn constituted regional organizations. Unity under a national command was achieved at the end of 1946, but only for a very brief period. National command, however, did not seem to be vital to the movement. Maintenance of discipline was more important. Where it was lacking, unnecessary losses resulted and behavior of individual partisans became needlessly brutal. Discipline faltered when there was a shortage of proper leadership. Yet in most cases commanding officers were elected. Leaders of primary groups were elected by the ranks; other commanders were elected by officers of subordinate groups. Only staff officers were appointed. Thus there was a close relationship between the leaders and the ranks; the quality of the ranks and the quality of the leadership tended to correspond, and the degree of discipline maintained varied accordingly. All of these factors varied somewhat from group to group, region to region.

Organized as conspiratorial military groups, the partisans were dedicated to the restoration of Lithuanian independence.[46] True to the tradition of previous underground nationalist movements,[47] the partisans maintained that according to international law, their country's independence had not been lost; the occupying power merely prevented the exercise of the nation's sovereignty. Consequently, the partisans not only refused to recognize the legality of Soviet actions but also maintained their own courts, issued credit papers, passed decrees, and enforced their regulations on that part of the population they could reach, and until 1951 or possibly 1952, maintained an underground government with a president and Council of the Republic.[48]

The blueprint of this new Republic is not available, though at least one was prepared and published in the papers of south Lithuanian partisans.[49] As a rule, partisans have no time for programs; they are people of action, not theory. Lithuanians were no exception. However, a glimpse into their political ideology can be had from a declaration of the founding conference that, in 1946, attempted to reorganize the partisan movement into the United Movement for Democratic Resistance.[50] In this very brief statement, a number of leading partisan groups proposed the creation of an international, democratic welfare state. They subscribed to the principles of Christian ethics and Western democracy; to charity, humanism, justice, tolerance, and freedom of conscience, speech, and thought. Law based on the principles of Christian morality was declared to be the only norm of personal and group behavior, and the use of force was held as a necessary evil. The declaration further rejected narrow-minded nationalism and envisioned a world government and a world economic community as the only guarantors of peace. It also spoke of the need for far-reaching social and economic reforms.

What were the partisans' concrete objectives? Dedicated to the restoration of a democratic Lithuanian state, they concentrated on obstructing the totalitarian Soviet regime. Though the methods of obstruction varied and different tactics were used in different regions, emphasis was laid on preventing the re-establishment of local soviets and on impeding the work of other Soviet institutions, especially the NKVD. Thus during the immediate postwar years (1944–47), the partisans made it impossible for the regime to recruit local government officials and very difficult to enforce the government's policies. Officials who endeavored seriously to cooperate with higher Soviet authorities were usually liquidated as punishment and as a warning to others. As a result, many districts and villages for months did not have responsible administrators.* The partisans also obstructed the implementation of the Bolshevik land reform and later impeded the collectivization of farms.[51] Peasants eligible for land were stopped from taking any that was confiscated from a farmer whose original holding did not exceed 40 hectares (99 acres). Organizational meetings for collective farms were dispersed; organizers and occasionally some farmers who joined were liquidated.[52] The partisans held up deliveries of agricultural products that the government requisitioned from many penalized farmers and punished the sellers of government credit bonds that the people were forced to buy.[53] On several occasions the partisans obstructed Soviet elections.[54] They disorganized local government in still other ways, frequently destroying smaller NKVD groups, cutting lines of communication, seizing government offices, and stealing documents, sometimes even attacking NKVD prisons in larger towns such as Kaunas.

Other partisan activities that served the same purpose of obstructing the re-establishment of Soviet rule may be divided into four categories: punishment of suspect collaborators with the Communists; dissemination of information; documentation of Soviet crimes and practices; protection of the lives and property of the civilian population.

In the view of the partisans, only native Lithuanians qualified as possible collaborators.[55] It was held that only Lithuanian citizens owed allegiance to the partisans. Russian and other non-Lithuanian civilians were generally safe, and the regular Soviet

---

* The shortage of local officials was so great that teen-agers were frequently recruited to serve as chairmen of local raion soviets; e.g., see *Tiesa*, February 22, 1962, p. 2.

military (as distinguished from the secret police) was not hampered, except in cases where partisans acted in self-defense. Lithuanians suspected of assisting the regime were punished by death, though occasionally the partisans employed less extreme measures and resorted to liquidation only after the demand to comply with partisan orders was disregarded. Sentences were passed and publicly announced by partisan courts, with the accused usually absent from the proceedings. A popular partisan leader, Žaliasis Velnias ("Green Devil," a code name for a former noncommissioned officer of the Lithuanian army), showed his responsibility for the sentence by attaching a calling card to the body of the executed person.[56] The list of liquidated persons was very long and included Party and Komsomol organizers, deputies of the Lithuanian Supreme Soviet and lowly administrators of collective farms or dairies, informers of state security agencies as well as teachers, and many others.[57] Such a policy of punishment struck terror among Communists and their sympathizers in the provinces unprotected by the shield of the Soviet military. Yet at the same time, the partisans' anger occasionally fell on persons who themselves were victims of circumstances or who lacked the power to change either the repressive Soviet policies or their administration.

Although partisan information services were not so well developed as the underground press during the German occupation, periodicals of every kind and quality appeared more or less regularly till the end of 1951, and their impact on the population greatly disturbed the Communist regime. The Soviets held these publications to be as destructive as the use of violence, because they sustained the hope of freedom and thus reduced the degree of cooperation the regime needed to restore local government and to fulfill economic plans. Juozas Žiugžda, the dean of Soviet Lithuanian historians, has eloquently acknowledged and aptly described the deep influence of the partisan press by writing that "while engaged in their homicidal activities, the enemies of the people [the partisans] in a variety of ways attempted to poison the consciousness of the working class as well. They disseminated lies and falsehoods about the Soviet state and spread rumors originated by the imperialist camp with the purpose of undermining the Soviet people's confidence in their state. Also, they supported bourgeois nationalist ideology and religious superstitions."[58]

Besides disseminating information, the partisans collected data pertaining to Soviet policies and their administration. Of these, the most important was the documentation of elections held in 1946.

Another important task of the freedom fighters was the protection of the civilian population.[59] This was necessary for the morale of their civilian supporters and for self-preservation. The partisans frequently assumed police functions and tracked down thieves and robbers, very numerous in the immediate postwar period. They restrained Soviet military and civilian officials from "confiscating" food and valuables. Furthermore, they punished those who looted the unoccupied homes of persons deported to Siberia. Partisan welfare officers and chaplains organized provisions for the needy supporters and relatives of the deported. Finally, on at least one occasion, the partisans in South Lithuania attempted to control mass behavior by issuing orders against drinking.[60] Since drinking unloosened tongues and made it easy for informers to learn too much, the partisans issued drinking regulations and enforced them for some time.

Why did the Lithuanian partisans choose the strategy of such frontal, offensive action that led to outright competition with the Soviet regime? Five reasons may be offered in explanation. First, the Soviet rule was assumed to be temporary, and the partisans therefore did not fear an open challenge to the regime. Second, in the partisan view, they, not the Soviets, exercised Lithuania's sovereignty, and thus it was their duty to restrain the Soviet rule wherever possible. Third, such tactics were chosen by leaders of military background who regarded any other method of resistance as impossible. Fourth, it was difficult to disregard Soviet provocations. And lastly, the key factor in the choice of tactics was the partisans' isolation from the West, which forced them to rely completely on local leadership and support.

Unlike the European anti-Nazi movements in World War II, the Lithuanian partisans sustained themselves without support and supplies from abroad, that is, from the Western powers. (The Soviets, however, have claimed differently; they contend that the partisans had contacts with Swedish, British, and American intelligence.)[61] It is true that liaison men sent from Western Europe penetrated the Lithuanian Iron Curtain in 1945 and 1946 and established contact with partisan leadership. The communication, however, was infrequent and did not produce material help. Early in 1948, representatives of the partisans themselves reached the West, but succeeded only in broadening partisan contacts. The Soviets reported that one of these representative groups returned in 1949, on a mission of gathering intelligence.[62] The other, the Soviets said, was parachuted by Americans in 1950, to be followed by reinforcements in 1951.[63] The leader of these groups, Juozas Lukša, the author of *Partizanai už geležinės uždangos* (*Partisans Behind the Iron Curtain*), was a prominent partisan leader sent to the West for help in early 1948. Justas Paleckis, Chairman of the Presidium of the Supreme Soviet of the Lithuanian Republic, claimed that this "degenerate, this beastly bandit Juozas Lukša" had graduated from an American intelligence school and then with the "consent and blessing" of Lithuanian nationalist leaders in exile had been "sent to Lithuania by American intelligence."[64] In Lithuania, according to another Soviet source, Lukša was appointed by the commander of the partisan Movement of Lithuania's Struggle for Freedom to the position of intelligence chief and liaison officer with the West.[65] All of these parachuted or landed groups perished within a year, their leader Lukša committing suicide under especially dramatic circumstances.[66] These contacts with the West did not represent help of any substance. They came too late and brought virtually no aid to partisan operations.

The isolation from the West during the crucial years of resistance (1944–48) clearly was the decisive factor in influencing the strategy of the partisan movement. Separated from the current of events in 1944 and 1945, the partisans were unfamiliar with the international situation, which was unfavorable to the use of aggressive tactics. Lacking a proper perspective, they overestimated the nationalist capacity to resist. Sometime in 1947, it is true, the partisans discovered that their appraisal of the international situation, particularly of the intentions of the Western powers, was wrong, but after several years of open warfare it was not only difficult but also quite impossible to change. Furthermore, without reliable and influential links with the West, they lacked experienced political leadership, and the military commanders acted as political leaders as well. A division between the military and political spheres did not really exist. The partisan movement was not a "home army" functioning merely as a military arm of a government abroad. Lithuanian *émigrés* did not have a government in exile. It must be said also that attempts to reorganize the anti-Soviet resistance on a home-army–government-in-exile pattern failed. The attempt was made in June, 1946, when a number of partisan groups, on the initiative of some *émigrés*, combined into the United Movement for Democratic

Resistance, which sought to induce the partisans to abandon violent tactics in order to achieve "more adequate and effective results in the struggle for the restoration of Lithuania's independence and for the realization of the great ideal of democracy."[67] A group of refugee political personalities in the West was invited to serve as a committee representing the partisan movement abroad. But the liaison established between the freedom fighters and the *émigrés* did not continue satisfactorily; attempts to organize the intended committee caused dissension among the *émigrés,* and ultimately the project was dropped.

In Lithuania itself, differences of opinion about organization and tactics continued, and on January 12, 1947, the national conference of partisan leaders rejected the organizational pattern and strategy that was proposed by the United Movement for Democratic Resistance. The differences seemed to center on the question of the "division of labor" and the use of force. The partisans refused to assume the role of a mere home army "without a direct influence on the future self-government of the country" and rejected a proposal to reorganize into a movement of nonviolent, "passive" resistance.[68]

SOVIET STRATEGY AGAINST THE PARTISANS

There is little doubt that the Kremlin, familiar with Lithuania's defection during the war, anticipated difficulties in reestablishing Soviet rule in the disloyal republic. To direct the restoration, Stalin chose a young but efficient man, Mikhail A. Suslov, then a rising star in the Party's Central Committee. Suslov's experience as wartime leader of Soviet partisans in the North Caucasus and as supervisor of the deportation of disloyal Chechen-Ingush and other North Caucasian nationalities eminently qualified him for the tasks in Lithuania. Suslov was named by the Central Committee to head the Organizational Bureau for the Lithuanian S.S.R. and given the formal task of rebuilding the Party and administrative apparatus and directing economic reconstruction.[69] Achievement of these goals, however, was successfully obstructed by the anti-Soviet partisans, then in the prime of their strength.

To combat the partisans, the Communists under Suslov's direction assumed a suitable ideological position and expertly employed tested Soviet tactics of force combined with persuasion. While concurrently blaming armed resistance on foreign sponsorship, Party ideologists explained it as a "kulak-nationalist underground"[70] supported by "reactionary priests."[71] This underground, the Communists said, sought to prevent collectivization by resisting measures designed to prepare the villages for it. Kulak reaction to these preparatory "softening-up" measures, Party ideologists continued, created conditions of class struggle, which found violent expression in armed conflict. Soviet suppression of the partisan movement, therefore, was justified not as a use of force to put down a nationally based rebellion (which would admit that the populace opposed the Communists) but as the proletariat's struggle against the exploiting class on the inevitable road to "socialism." In terms of this synthetic model, which the Party assiduously fostered and kept in popular focus, the partisan movement had to be destroyed before collectivization could be started. But like many ideological models of the Soviets, this one also did not correspond to social reality, and collectivization itself was speeded up for the purpose of undermining and destroying the partisans.[72]

During the summer of 1944, the Kremlin employed several divisions of border guards experienced in dealing with disloyal ethnic groups against the partisans. Thus, in June and July, troops that had just completed mass deportations of Kalmucks, Chechen-Ingush, and the Crimean Tatars, were thrown against the underground in Lithuania.[73] They, however, achieved no immediate results. Then, the Kremlin dispatched General Sergei N. Kruglov, Beria's deputy in the Commissariat of Internal Affairs, to Lithuania; he usually directed mopping up operations in areas recaptured by the Red Army. Kruglov was employed for this task because, as a deputy director of SMERSH, the Soviet counterintelligence agency, he proved himself "one of the most cruel and merciless" executioners in territories that had opposed the Soviets during the war.[74] Upon his arrival in September, 1944, Kruglov held a meeting of operational commanders of the NKVD, in which he demanded sterner measures against the partisans. Stalin and Beria, Kruglov said, entrusted the destruction of the partisans to the NKVD, and the security troops would brook no interference from any quarter in the performance of this task. Actions against the Lithuanian partisans should no longer be confined to military operations by Soviet troops, but should involve the local population and rely more on work and tactics of intelligence services combined with periodic combing of the forests (*gosudarstvennaia proverka*). The future successor of Beria decreed that in operations against the partisans regular procedures of arrest and investigation were to be suspended and any means employed that were considered efficient in extracting information or uncovering partisan hide-outs. "Enough of this [purely military] sentimental approach," he is reported to have said. In other words, Kruglov declared unrestricted war against the partisans.

Following Kruglov's orders, a special NKVD department for "bandit" affairs (OBO—Osobi Banditskii Otdel) was established to handle intelligence work, and units of local militia (*istrebiteli*) were authorized.[75] The OBO trained infiltrators into partisan ranks, printed nationalist newspapers to compete with the partisan press and to sow discord, and, for purposes of provocation, formed bands of agents posing as partisans or as foreign paratroopers. In 1945, these *provocateurs* masqueraded as Germans, later as Englishmen or Americans.[76] The units of native *istrebiteli* (in Lithuanian they were called "people's defenders") were formed in rural districts for local action against the partisans. Originally, the purpose of this militia was not clearly revealed, and it attracted many men of military age, because the "people's defenders" were absolved from military service during time of war. The partisans felt that this native force was an attempt by the Soviets to embroil Lithuanians in a civil war, and to prevent this, used pressure and force against individual "defenders" and their families to destroy this potentially dangerous formation. By the summer of 1945, this goal was largely achieved. Consequently, main operations against the partisans were conducted by the security troops (first the NKVD, later the MVD and MGB) and the regular Red Army divisions, sometimes with the help of the Air Force. On Kruglov's orders, these troops sought out the partisans for open battles and periodically combed villages and forests.

Furthermore, while with one hand wielding a club with a ruthlessness the Gestapo could envy, the Soviets extended the other hand in a gesture of peace. Ever since the summer of 1945, periodic declarations of amnesty had been made to persuade the partisans to come out of hiding and lay down their arms. To strengthen the appeal of these promises, the government in 1945 and 1946 sought to enlist the help of the Roman Catholic clergy. Priests were requested to ask the partisans to lay down arms. This procedure, however, failed. The Soviets then employed blackmail and intimidation. At the end of February, 1946, they suggested that a conference of the Roman Catholic episcopate be held to consider the question of banditism,[77] but to assure themselves of positive results, they arrested one of the bishops, Vincentas Borisevičius of Telšiai, on charges of aiding the partisans. The conference, however, refused to be intimidated, and no appeal of surrender was issued. Then the Soviets fabricated such appeals, and the Archbishop of Vilnius, Mečislovas Reinys, lost his life for daring to announce publicly in his cathedral that his signature had been faked.[78]

These amnesties nevertheless offered many young partisans a seemingly acceptable alternative to a cruel fate in the ranks of the "forest brothers," as the partisans became popularly known, and many active members surrendered to the authorities. Partisan leaders generally did not oppose this choice, especially since many partisan groups had grown too large for guerrilla-style warfare.[79]

The total-war tactics of General Kruglov began to yield fruit in a year's time. By the end of 1945 the regional organizations of the partisans were severely crippled by arrests of leaders, and the ranks thinned as a result of the ruthlessness of Soviet *proverki* and amnesty.[80] However, though critically disorganized, the underground was not broken, and the Soviets initiated a new concentrated campaign that continued without letup through 1949.

This new offensive, prepared by Suslov, was started in February, 1946, a month before the Kremlin's proconsul was reassigned to the Central Committee of the All-Union Communist Party. This was a year of great importance to Communist leaders. The Fourth Five-Year Plan was announced, and Lithuania's economy was to be integrated into this All-Union program.[81] Though collectivization of farms was not publicized as one of the goals of this plan, it was obvious that to participate in it effectively, the republic would need domestic tranquility and a measure of farm collectivization or socialization to provide the necessary funds for the scheduled industrial investment. Partisan resistance denied both of these conditions and thus had to be eliminated.

Suslov's attack on the partisans was therefore a furious frontal assault, combining the peace offensive with military action of increased cruelty and thoroughness. It was directed not only against active partisans, but especially against suspected supporters. The attack began on February 15 with an offer of amnesty, coupled with the threat of deportation. At about the same time, the Catholic hierarchy was called upon to help pacify the country according to Bolshevik dictates. Three days later, on February 18, the first postwar mass reprisals against the civilian population began. This date marked the beginning of the deportations of civilians, primarily those suspected of supporting the partisans. The February wave, ruthlessly carried out,[82] was followed by others and continued through 1949. Concurrently, the Soviet pacifiers increased the number of military *proverki* and intensified the infliction of cruelty, designed to provoke the partisans and their supporters. For example, they began to dump the bodies of murdered partisans in market places to be exhibited for weeks as a warning to all and as a possible bait for a relative or another patriot to come forward.[83]

However, they did not achieve the goal of eradicating organized resistance. The new Soviet measures of repression produced, at least temporarily, an effect contrary to the one expected. Civilian supporters and sympathizers, now fearing for their lives, became active partisans, and the numerical strength of the movement did not wane, as it had in 1945, when amnesty was not accompanied by mass deportations and by intensified cruelty. Furthermore, individual partisan groups now concentrated on reorganization, and by the end of 1946 united under a single national command. This ascendency of the partisan movement, however, did not long continue. The Soviet squeeze at home, and especially the pessimistic news from abroad which the couriers of South Lithuanian partisans brought in the summer of 1947, were responsible for the thinning of the ranks and a never-before-experienced attitude of despair.[84] The international situation was not changing as expected; help from the West was not in sight.

The gradual decline of the strength of the resistance may be graphically illustrated by the increase in the number of kolkhozes,[85] whose establishment the partisans unalterably opposed. By the end of 1947, there were only 20 kolkhozes, but in March, 1948, the Soviets, feeling that the village was now sufficiently softened, ordered mass collectivization, and by December the number of collective farms rose to 500. This pace was speeded up even more in preparation for the Sixth Conference of the Lithuanian Communist Party, which met in February, 1949; and during the coming two months (December and January), the number of kolkhozes was doubled. By the end of the next year, already 65 per cent of all private farms had become kolkhozes. This percentage rose to 90 in 1951, and by September, 1952, collectivization was virtually complete; 96 per cent of all individual farms were collectivized.

The success of Soviet efforts at mass collectivization indicated that the military strength of the organized movement had become impaired. After the end of 1948, the partisans could no longer effectively paralyze the functioning of local soviets or prevent the establishment of new kolkhozes. Open warfare could not be continued. Consequently, in February, 1949, the partisans reorganized into a new national formation, the Movement of Lithuania's Struggle for Freedom.[86] Tactics were changed from open resistance to sabotage. The Soviets reported that the partisans changed the "form of struggle" from open opposition to resistance by infiltration, so that they could obstruct the kolkhozes from within, frequently from the very offices of the farm chairmen.[87]

The use of violence, however, had not yet been abandoned. Partisan groups continued to restrain and liquidate local government officials and kolkhoz organizers.[88] Their punishing hand even reached the deputies of the Supreme Soviet of the Lithuanian S.S.R.[89] During the 1950–51 period the Soviets still maintained two divisions of security police to check on partisan activities, and in 1951 General Kruglov returned to take charge of the liquidation of partisan resistance that now was rekindled by groups parachuted from the West with promises of some tangible help.[90] Later, "mopping up" operations followed, and in 1952 organized resistance was completely destroyed.*

CONCLUSION: WHY THE PARTISANS FAILED

The reason for the defeat of the Lithuanian partisan movement is implicit in the story told in the previous pages. Two factors seem to have been crucial in determining the fate of the partisans. First, their leaders miscalculated partisan resources and the

* See Burlitski's testimony in the *Fourth Interim Report of the Select Committee on Communist Aggression*, pp. 1373–74. Amnesty was again declared on October 17, 1955, and March 22, 1959, and yielded some results. Arrests also continued. On March 11, 1961, for example, *Tiesa* reported the arrest of a former partisan posing as a specialist in a shop that repaired medical instruments; on June 17, 1962, several Soviet Lithuanian newspapers published reports of a public trial of three partisans held on June 12-15 in Rokiškis. The date of their capture, however, was not revealed.

chances of political victory. They misinterpreted international developments and the intentions of the Western powers and thus wrongly counted on support from the United States and Great Britain. Second, without support from abroad, a long guerrilla war against the total-war strategy of the Soviets became militarily impossible, especially under conditions of complete sovietization. Strong will, dedication, and support from the population in the long run were insufficient to prevent the destruction of organized partisan resistance. It is therefore not surprising that the partisans lost, after eight years of war. It is rather extraordinary that they were able to fight for such a long time.

It should be added that although the partisans failed to achieve their primarily political purpose—restoring Lithuania's independence—their resistance nevertheless was an event of deep significance in modern Lithuanian life. Partisan dedication to nationalist ideals and objectives seemed to have strengthened nationalist loyalties in Soviet Lithuania. Judging from propaganda initiated after the extraordinary conference of the Lithuanian Communist Party in 1958, the Lithuanian population holds an affectionately patriotic image of the movement, and the regime regards the destruction of this image a necessary prerequisite for sucessfully shaping the present generation of Lithuanians into Soviet patriots.

PART III

Under Soviet Rule: 1944-65

6. The Administration of Power: The Communist Party and the Soviet Government

THOMAS REMEIKIS

According to Soviet constitutional law, the Lithuanian Soviet Socialist Republic has a constitutionally guaranteed local autonomy and a share in the ruling of the entire Soviet Union. However, while the Soviet constitution provides for a federal system of state organization, at the same time it grants monopoly of power to a single political group, the Communist Party, which does not recognize this federal principle in its internal organization. Thus the federalist framework is dominated by a unitarily organized Communist Party that is centrally controlled from Moscow. Such control actually nullifies both the guaranteed local autonomy and the participation in the policy-making of the central government.

The purpose of the present chapter is to analyze one administrative subdivision of the Communist Party of the Soviet Union, the Communist Party and apparatus in Lithuania, to explain the federalist framework within which it executes centrally decided policies and to examine the patterns of control that it has developed.

THE COMMUNIST PARTY OF LITHUANIA: ORIGINS AND DEVELOPMENT

The Origins. An organized Lithuanian Socialist movement came into being in 1896.[1] The Lithuanian Socialists refused to join with the Russian Social Democrats, even though Lithuania then was ruled by the same Czar. The Lithuanian Social Democratic Party (LSDP) was separatist and nationalist, one of the first organized political movements to demand autonomy for Lithuania. Because of this nationalism and separatism, it never joined the Russian Social Democratic Labor Party (RSDLP) and did not experience a Bolshevik-Menshevik schism until after the October Revolution. Although within the LSDP both autonomist (or internationalist) and federalist (or separatist) factions existed, they in no way can be compared to Bolshevik and Menshevik factions in the RSDLP.

Lithuanian Bolshevism developed in Russia immediately preceding and following the October Revolution. Of the approximately 400,000 Lithuanian evacuees in Russia during World War I, about 2,000 joined the RSDLP(b).[2] The Lithuanian Bolsheviks belonged to the territorial Bolshevik groups, but at the same time were organized into Lithuanian sections, which were directed and coordinated by the Central Bureau of the Lithuanian Sections in the Central Committee, RSDLP(b). The Lithuanian Central Bureau, headed by the founders of Lithuanian Bolshevism, Vincas Mickevičius-Kapsukas and Zigmas Aleksa-Angarietis, organized Bolshevik activities among Lithuanian workers in Russia and brought about the Bolshevik-Menshevik split among the Lithuanian Socialist groups.

One of the main tasks of the Lithuanian Central Bureau was to facilitate a Communist movement, which did not yet exist in German-occupied Lithuania. The Second Conference of the Lithuanian Bolshevik sections in Moscow, held May 26–27, 1917, passed a resolution calling for the sending of revolutionaries into Lithuania for the explicit purpose of organizing Bolshevik groups there. This resolution may be considered the birth certificate of Lithuanian Communism. Many Lithuanian Communists returned to organize Bolshevik cells. The outcome of this activity was an organization of the Communist Party of Lithuania and Belorussia (CPL&B),* with some 800 members in its ranks. The First Congress of the Party met in Vilnius (October 1–3, 1917).[3]

---

* The Communist Party of Lithuania and Belorussia was so called because it was active in several districts of Belorussia adjacent to Vilnius territory. In February of 1919, the CPL&B merged with the Communist Party of Belorussia. The new binational party retained the CPL&B designation.

An Attempt at Socialist "Revolution." The purpose of the new Party became evident on December 8, 1918, when, on orders from Stalin and Sverdlov, the CPL&B announced the formation of the "Provisional Revolutionary Workers' Government of Lithuania."[4] At first faced by weak resistance, the Red Army easily won control over a good part of Lithuania, thus giving protection to the operations of this "provisional revolutionary government."[5] In February, 1919, again on orders from Sverdlov and to the displeasure of the Bolsheviks with nationalist sympathies, the Lithuanian Soviet Republic was merged with the Belorussian Republic into one Soviet Republic known as the Litbel.[6]

The Soviet intervention in Lithuania ended toward the summer of 1919, when the Red Army was pushed out of Lithuania by the armed forces of the independent Lithuanian republic. Thus the hopes of sovietizing Lithuania ended and the CPL&B disintegrated.

Twenty Years of Underground Training and Subversion. Slowly and painfully, the Communist Party of Lithuania was resurrected and organized for subversive and underground work during the next twenty years of Lithuanian independence. During this period, the CPL failed to develop into a significant political force. While the traditionalist, Catholic, nationalist, unindustrialized, rural nature of Lithuania was in the main responsible for the CPL's ineffectiveness, the constant policy reversals by the Comintern and Stalin drove the CPL almost to extinction. The CPL, according to official Communist sources, never had more than 2,000 members during its underground years.[7] The majority of the membership came from the ethnic and religious minorities—the Lithuanian Jews, the Russians, and the Poles.[8] Alone the national composition of the CPL testifies to the narrowness of the CPL's influence.

At least since 1921, the CPL has been formally a member of the Comintern. Its Political Bureau, and most of the Central Committee was in Moscow, while the Secretariat directed Party work in the Lithuanian underground. The principal members of the Political Bureau—Mickevičius-Kapsukas and Aleksa-Angarietis—were at the same time important officials in the Comintern apparatus. However, because the Political Bureau was located in Moscow, the CPL often was being controlled by the Russian CP. The CPL was affected by all events in the Comintern and in the RCP(b). When the Comintern took an ultra-left course after

its Sixth Congress, the CPL almost disappeared, its membership dwindling to about 400.[9] When Stalin purged his Russian
comrades, a purge was also carried out among Lithuanian Communists. Such prominent Lithuanian Communists as Aleksa-Angarietis, one of the founders of the CPL and the Secretary of the
International Control Commission of the Comintern, and two gen-
erals, Putna and Uborevičius (Uborevich), were executed. Since it
was difficult effectively to purge an underground party, Stalin
had to wait until the 1940 occupation and the merger of the CPL
with the All-Union Communist Party (Bolsheviks).[10]

Stalin had no intention of creating a mass revolutionary movement in Lithuania. His principal objective was to form an obedient instrument for limited political activity. In prespective, it is
possible to say that he succeeded. During the twenty years of
underground struggle, the CPL developed a group of professional revolutionaries, numbering perhaps not more than 100,
who were unquestionably committed to Moscow. They were *the*
Party. They were educated in the Sverdlov Communist University in Moscow, or else received their training from the revolutionary Communists in Lithuanian prisons. This middle level of
Party leadership, united by the camaraderie of common struggle,
turned out to be the basis on which the CPL developed after
Lithuania's forcible incorporation into the Soviet Union. As
late as 1960, the old revolutionaries still maintained the principal positions of power. Among them we find the present First
Secretary of the Central Committee, Antanas Sniečkus; the Chairman of the Council of Ministers, Motiejus Šumauskas; and a
number of Central Committee secretaries and ministers (Vladas
Niunka, Mečys Gedvilas, the late Kazys Preikšas, and others).

The CPL Under Stalin. When, in June of 1940, the Soviet Union
established a puppet People's Government in Lithuania, the
CPL was legalized. Soon after Lithuania's incorporation into the
Soviet Union was formalized by the Supreme Soviet in Moscow
on August 3, 1940, the CPL was merged with the Soviet Communist Party (October 8, 1940). Stalin then proceeded to purge
the CPL. When he had finished, in the spring of 1941, the CPL
had lost about 50 per cent of the underground revolutionaries.[11]

The CPL came out of its underground period with approximately 1,500 members.[12] For a short period it provided the necessary personnel for the transitional People's Government. When
Lithuania's annexation was completed and the sovietization of

the country began, the native Communists were displaced by officials from Moscow and relegated to secondary positions.

At the start of the German-Soviet hostilities, in June, 1941, the majority of the Lithuanian Communists and collaborators of the Soviet regime retreated with the Red Army. Those who remained in Lithuania were either liquidated or went into hiding. The Lithuanian Communists in Russia were organized for partisan activities in German-occupied Lithuania, and in a so-called Sixteenth Lithuanian Division of the Red Army. The partisan and military formations provided the source of Party members.[13] When the CPL emerged from the war, it had no more than 6,000 members,[14] the majority of whom were apparently old Lithuanian residents of Russia or belonged to other Soviet nationalities.

Such a Party organization, created in wartime conditions and from politically and ethnically diverse sources, could not be trusted to carry out the sociopolitical revolution that was required to re-establish the Soviet regime after the German withdrawal. The CPL in the postwar years played only a role of apprentice. All real power was concentrated in emissaries from the central organs of the All-Union Communist Party (Bolsheviks). Mikhail Suslov headed a special Central Committee Bureau for Lithuania until the spring of 1946. This special Bureau for Lithuania was the actual headquarters for policies of sovietization.[15] After Suslov assumed other duties in Moscow, his functions were taken over by a special Central Committee trouble shooter, Vladimir Vasilevich Shcherbakov,[16] and a host of other Moscow-appointed commissars and politicians. It is true that the native Communists occupied the nominal positions of power, but behind every one of them, including even the politically reliable First Secretary of the CPL, Antanas Sniečkus, there was a Second Secretary or an assistant from Moscow. Views of local Communists were stifled; the party was completely dominated by Russian *apparatchiki,* who molded the CPL on the All-Union pattern. Such strict political control and dominance by non-Lithuanian cadres in the CPL, as well as in the Soviet (Government) authorities, continued until the death of Stalin and the fall of Beria. In 1949, 50 per cent of the Lithuanian Party's Central Committee consisted of non-Lithuanians. It can be truly said that whatever individuality the CPL came to possess was acquired during the Khrushchev years.

THE COMMUNIST PARTY OF LITHUANIA UNDER KHRUSHCHEV

Patterns of Growth. To a considerable degree, the history of a Communist Party may be deduced from its membership data. This data suggests several significant generalizations on the nature of the CPL.

The CPL is one of the youngest and weakest of the Communist parties of the Soviet republics. Between 1952 and 1956, it had one of the lowest rates of growth. It had and still has practically the smallest percentage of Communists in the population, 2 per cent, as compared with about 4 per cent for the entire CPSU in 1960.[17] As if trying to catch up with the other republic Party organizations, the CPL has since 1956 accelerated its rate of growth very markedly. From 1956 to 1960, it increased over 40 per cent, while during the same time the entire CPSU grew by only about 26 per cent. However, even at that rapid growth rate, it will be at least a decade before the CPL can approach the All-Union percentage. In fact, this may never occur, since the CPSU in the last few years grew at a slightly higher rate than the CPL (see Table 1).

TABLE 1

Average Monthly Rate of Growth, CPSU and CPL, 1940–61

CPSU	Average Monthly Rate of Growth (Percentage)	CPL	Average Monthly Rate of Growth (Percentage)
Jan. 1, 1940–Jan. 1, 1945	1.15	Jan. 1, 1941–Jan. 1, 1945	1.91
Jan. 1, 1945–Sept. 1, 1952	.31	Jan. 1, 1945–Sept. 1, 1952	5.43
Sept. 1, 1952–Jan. 1, 1956	.12	Sept. 1, 1952–Jan. 1, 1956	.09
Jan. 1, 1956–Jan. 1, 1959	.15	Jan. 1, 1956–Jan. 1, 1959	.80
Jan. 1, 1959–Sept. 1, 1961	1.37	Jan. 1, 1959–Sept. 1, 1961	.95

Sources: Membership figures are derived from official announcements, usually made during Party congresses. It is assumed that the figures are for the first of the month in which the congress took place, or for the first of the year in other cases. Data for 1940 and 1952, *Bol'shaia Sovetskaia Entsiklopediia* (2d ed.), XXV, 262–63; for 1945 and 1949, *Sovetskaia Litva*, February 18 and 20, 1949; for 1957, *Ezhegodnik Bol'shoi Sovetskoi Entsiklopedii, 1957*, p. 155; for 1956 and 1958–61, *Tiesa*, January 26, 1956, p. 3; February 15, 1958, p. 3; January 17, 1959, p. 1; March 3, 1960, p. 3; September 30, 1961, p. 2.

Note: The average monthly rate of growth is calculated by dividing the known absolute increase in membership by the number of months in which the increase occurred. The resultant is calculated as a percentage of the membership figure at the beginning of the period concerned.

The fluctuations in the rate of growth of the CPL are roughly equivalent to those of the CPSU, except for the postwar years. Table 2 below suggests that during the war there was a fairly rapid growth of the CPSU and the CPL. The growth was almost arrested between 1953, the year of Stalin's death, and 1956, but again picked up after the onset of de-Stalinization. The impressive growth of the CPL in the postwar years may be easily explained. Since the CPL emerged from the war with only 6,000 members, it could not administer a government for two and a half million people. The CPSU sent in thousands of non-Lithuanian Communists to provide cadres from the lowest to the highest positions. It may be said that one reason for the dominance of the CPL by non-Lithuanians during the postwar years was the lack of a sufficient number of politically reliable native Communists.

A detailed examination of the membership figures for the CPL further outlines its development. From Table 2, we see that the CPL's membership increased nearly sixfold between 1945 and 1952. This increase was necessitated by the enormous revolutionary policies in Lithuania that were carried out during the postwar years. Between September 1, 1952, and January 1, 1956, a period of forty months, the CPL increased by only 1,394, or 0.09 per cent, a month. However, we know from Soviet sources that between January 1, 1953, and January 1, 1956, 2,834 people were admitted to candidacy in Lithuania's rural areas alone.[18] During the first nine months of 1955, more than 1,900 candidates were given full membership, which is 500 more than the absolute increase between 1952 and 1956.[19] During the same nine months, 2,800 individuals were admitted to candidacy.[20] In other words, contrary to the indication of the membership data, recruitment was not suspended during the 1952–56 period, but continued at approximately the same rate as before 1952.

This discrepancy between the absolute increase in CPL membership and the number admitted into the Party or to candidacy certainly suggests a purge. It is possible that two purges were carried out: one following the Nineteenth CPSU Congress, but before Stalin's death (November, 1952–March, 1953), and the other immediately following Beria's liquidation three months later. That a Stalinist purge was carried out in the city of Vilnius and surrounding districts was reported in *Tiesa* on March 26, 1953; possibly, it was associated with the last excesses of Stalin— the so-called doctors' plot and the vigilance campaign. That a possible purge connected with Beria's liquidation was carried

TABLE 2

Membership Growth Pattern of the CPL, 1940-64

Date of CPL Membership Census	Number of CPL Members		Total	Percentage of CPL Members in Total Population	Average Monthly Rate of Increase Since Previous Census (in per cent)	Number of Primary Cells	Average Number of Communists per Cell
	Members	Candidates					
June 1, 1940	*	*	1,741	.06	*	*	*
January 1, 1941	2,504	634	3,138	.10	13.40	*	*
January 1, 1945	*	*	6,000	.21	1.91	*	*
January 1, 1949	25,000	6,000	31,000	1.10	2.08	*	*
September 1, 1952	27,469	9,224	36,693	1.36	.41	2,669	13
January 1, 1956	*	*	38,087	1.40	.09	*	*
January 1, 1957	*	*	42,229	1.55	.90	3,436	12
January 1, 1958	38,372	6,449	44,821	1.65	.51	3,645	12
January 1, 1959	41,574	7,540	49,114	1.80	.79	3,885	12
January 1, 1960	46,381	7,943	54,324	2.00	.88	4,025	13
September 1, 1961	55,676	8,998	64,674	2.38	.95	4,434	14
January 1, 1964	69,522	7,696	77,218	2.68	.69	4,758	16

Sources: CPL membership—same as Table 1 and *Tiesa*, January 10, 1964. P. 3. For population—Tsentralnoe Statisticheskoe Uprevlenie pri Sovete Minstrov SSR, *Narodnoe Khoziaistvo SSR v 1958 Godu* (Moscow, 1959), p. 8; Centrine Statistikos Valdyba prie Lietuvos TSR Ministrų Tarybos, *Lietuvos TSR Skaičiais 1962 Metais* (Vilnius, 1963), p. 10. (The CPL membership percentages are based on the following population figures: 1940–49, 2.8 million; 1952–61, 2,713 million; 1963–, 2,879 million.

* No data available.

out is not only plausible but is also strongly suggested by a series of changes in the top personnel of the Lithuanian Soviet regime and the CPL, changes involving Ministries of Internal Affairs and State Security and a number of deputies of the Council of Ministers. These purges were distinctive in that they affected primarily the lower echelons of the Party hierarchy, and the non-Lithuanian deputies in the government and the Party, and so went almost unrecorded in the press and were scarcely noticed by Western observers.

Another factor may also have contributed to the near standstill in CPL growth during 1952–56. With the elimination of Beria and the consequent expansion of republic jurisdiction, there was, at least in Lithuania, a notable replacement of non-Lithuanian personnel by native Communists. The transfer of non-Lithuanian Communists, too, may have affected the absolute growth of the CPL. The purges, transfers, the succession, and natural causes, thus may be considered to be responsible for the slow increase in membership during this period.

A striking deviation from an apparent pattern is the noticeable decline of the rate of growth during 1957. Since 1955, the annual absolute increase in membership has been between 4,000 and 5,000, except in 1957, when the annual increase amounted to 2,592. No data is available to suggest a purge. The decrease may simply be a reflection of the intra-Party struggle for power and of de-Stalinization. Specifically, it appears to be a reflection of Khrushchev's struggle against the "anti-Party" group, which was eliminated in the middle of 1957.

The inevitable conclusion is that the growth pattern of the CPL faithfully reflects the major policy shifts as well as power struggles in the CPSU. They also suggest that the native leadership of the CPL managed to safeguard its position by instinctively following the dominant line in the Kremlin or by not committing itself too early.

The Clash of Generations in the CPL. The available data indicate that within the CPL there are at least four politically distinct groups of Communists. First, we find the old revolutionaries, who joined the CPL before 1940. Educated in Moscow's Communist University or in revolutionary circles and underground work in Lithuania, these Party members are highly committed to Moscow, violently antinationalist and pro-Russian. There are no more than 1,500 old revolutionaries in the CPL, but their influence is great since they still hold top posts in the CPL.

Second, there are between 6,000 and 10,000 Communists who joined the Party during the war. A third group, numbering about 20,000 and in many respects comparable to the second, is made up of persons who joined the Party during the violent postwar years. These two groups were indoctrinated by the gun, in the struggle against Germany and against the anti-Soviet guerrillas. Their ideological commitment to Communism and Moscow is strong, since they matured ideologically in a revolutionary situation and owe everything to Moscow. They are similar in many respects to the old revolutionaries—in their anti-nationalism and loyalty to Moscow. They differ from the old revolutionaries in that they never developed the sort of fighting camaraderie that sustained the early members in their darkest hours, and have not yet been admitted to the leadership of the Party. How this group would react in a crisis is unknown. Politically, they appear to be favored to succeed the old revolutionaries in the leadership of the Party. The leadership, however, will be challenged by the fourth group—the post-Stalin Communists, who surpass the wartime and postwar Communists in their technical competence.

The post-Stalin group of Communists may perhaps be best described as the "new class." In 1960, this group constituted at least 40 per cent of the entire Lithuanian Party membership. They are young people, mostly under forty, educated almost entirely by the Soviet regime. They matured in somewhat stabilized political circumstances and never had to fight for Communism. They grew up in a climate of resurging cultural nationalism and normalization of Party and government activity. These people have shown as much enthusiasm and concern for the Lithuanian cultural heritage as most of the intelligentsia. They did not have to be anti-Lithuanian, unlike the youth of the postwar years, who grew up during an intense struggle between Communism and nationalism, and for whom Communism and nationalism were mutually exclusive.

Seeking productivity and efficiency, the Soviet regime favored the educated technicians. As a result, the post-Stalin bureaucrats displaced many of the old revolutionaries and wartime Communists. The displacement was so great that marked friction arose among the cadres of various generations, and the First Secretary, Antanas Sniečkus, repeatedly had to admonish Party members to understand the situation and to keep peace.[21] To what extent the new class has gained power in the CPL is indicated by the Party standing of the delegates to the CPL congresses. Of the delegates to the 1949 Congress of the CPL, the old revolutionaries accounted for more than 60 per cent, the wartime Communists 18 per cent, and the postwar members 17 per cent; of the delegates to the 1960 CPL Congress, however, about 20 per cent were old revolutionaries, 40 per cent were the wartime and postwar Communists, and another 40 per cent were post-Stalin Communists.[22] In other words, the post-Stalin Communists gained as much as the old revolutionaries lost, while the war and postwar Communists just about kept their ground.

There are some significant political implications in these changes in the sociopolitical structure of the CPL, and in the shift of influence from group to group. The identifiable groups of Communists, with different backgrounds and ideological orientation, can be expected to react diversely to internal or external events. How each group would react to a particular event is, of course, a highly speculative matter. However, available information suggests that the possibility of diverse reactions by various groups to a particular event is real. In case of a crisis or of factionalism in the CPSU, the CPL may react along generation lines.

The Ethnic Composition of the CPL. The extent to which a republic Party organization has an ethnically homogeneous membership influences not only the political disposition of the Party but also the operation and autonomy of the organization. Perhaps this is a principal reason why the CPL has never publicized the ethnic distribution of its membership. However, a reasonable estimate of such differentiation may be obtained from the recently revealed ethnic composition of the CPSU and the nationality of the delegates to the CPL congresses. On July 1, 1961, there were 42,800 ethnic Lithuanians in the CPSU.[23] At approximately the same time, on October 1, 1961, there were about 65,000 members in the CPL.[24] Even assuming that almost all the ethnic Lithuanians in the CPSU are also on the roster of the CPL, we see that only about 65 per cent of the CPL membership are ethnic Lithuanians. The percentage actually is a little lower, since, no doubt, a number of Lithuanian Communists live outside Lithuania.

The above calculations are surprising because they are not

strictly compatible with the national representation in CPL congresses, the CPL Central Committee, or the Soviet regime in Lithuania in general. In the 1959 CPL Congress, 77 per cent of the delegates were Lithuanians, 16 per cent were Russians, and the remainder were Ukrainians, Belorussians, Poles, and others.[25] The situation was similar in the 1958 Congress.[26] Furthermore, nearly 75 per cent of the members of the CPL Central Committee elected in 1960 were ethnic Lithuanians, while the Lithuanian S.S.R. Council of Ministers was almost exclusively a Lithuanian body.[27] In other words, by 1961 the Lithuanian Communists assumed more responsibility or power than their absolute numerical strength in the CPL entitled them to. The promotion of native cadres evidently went further than the Kremlin expected. No wonder Sniečkus had to warn constantly against promoting cadres on a national basis alone.[28]

The non-Lithuanian Communists in the CPL, of course, provide a safety device that reacts automatically against actual or potential nationalist deviations.

The Leadership and Control of the CPL. The locus of power within the republic Party organization may be found in the Presidium (known as the "Bureau" until the end of 1962). The immediate lieutenants of the First Secretary, the members of the Presidium, represent the vital sectors of Party, governmental, and cultural activity and exercise political, economic, and social control.

To a very significant degree, the CPL is a political machine of Antanas Sniečkus.[29] He came to the CPL Secretariat in 1926, was appointed First Secretary in 1936, and has remained in this position to this day. Sniečkus, son of a well-to-do farmer and a devoutly religious mother who chose exile in the West, received most of his education in Russia and became a trusted professional revolutionary of the Kremlin. He is strongly committed to Moscow, a fanatical adherent to the Party line. Sniečkus' principal political characteristic is his willingness to obey anyone who happens to hold supreme power in the Kremlin. His flexibility and political loyalty to Moscow secured him the top leadership throughout the years of Stalin's reign, the succession struggle, and de-Stalinization. The CPL as such, together with Sniečkus, perhaps because of Sniečkus, also came out of all the intra-Party squabbles almost untouched. Another possible explanation for the long survival of Sniečkus might be that he was not a protegé of, or attached to, any one personality in power, but rather owes his allegiance to the politically powerful Party apparatus.[30] Since Stalin's death, Sniečkus and his native comrades have been able to evade much of the previous detailed surveillance and control from Moscow and have assumed a great many of the functions that were formerly carried out by Stalin's *apparatchiki*. Sniečkus now appears to be the real boss of the CPL; and throughout the long years of leadership, he has imprinted some of his political characteristics on the CPL.

The Presidium is, in a very real sense, a microcosm of the CPL. On it, we find the representatives of all the generations of the CPL as well as representatives of the non-Lithuanian Communists in the CPL.* Their influence, however, somewhat deviates from the interrelations of the various groups.

If we examine the composition of the CPL Presidium between 1949 and 1962, several obvious tendencies become apparent (see Table 3). First of all, the old revolutionaries, with First Secretary Sniečkus at their head, are still in control of the Presidium. However, as they retire or die, their influence is slowly declining. The CPL Presidium is being taken over by younger Communists, that is, representatives of the wartime and postwar generation together with the post-Stalin Communists, the men of the "new class." At present, the CPL leadership appears to be passing from the revolutionaries to the technicians-bureaucrats.

Secondly, the number of non-Lithuanian "watchdogs" on the Presidium declined from five, in 1949, to one, in 1961, while the marginal group of Party functionaries—the Russian-Lithuanians or the non-Lithuanians of Lithuania—have practically disap-

---

* The members of the CPL Bureau may be classified into old revolutionaries, wartime and postwar Communists, "watchdogs" (plenipotentiaries from the Kremlin), the marginal group of Russian Lithuanians or non-Lithuanians of Lithuanian origin, and the post-Stalin Communists (mainly the new class). The designations following the name are: (L) Lithuanian, (RL) Russian-Lithuanian, (NL) non-Lithuanian (mainly Russian), (J) Jew, (NU) nationality uncertain. The old revolutionaries: Sniečkus (L), Šumauskas (L), Gedvilas (L), Paleckis (L), Preikšas (L), Zimanas (J), Bieliauskas (L), Baranauskas (L). Wartime and postwar Communists: Maniušis (L), Barauskas (L), Barkauskas (L), Novickas (L), Raguotis (L), Petkevičius (L), Laurinaitis (L), Diržinskaitė (L), Matulis (L), Augustinaitis (L). The "watchdogs": Trofimov, Gusev, Pisarev, Chistiakov, Gorlinskov, Kondakov, Anushkin, Lutsenko, Meshchiarikov. The marginal group: Ozarskis (RL), Bartašiūnas (RL), Liaudis (NU), Kenevich (NU), Levitsky (NU). Post-Stalin Communists: Česnavičius (L). This classification is based on biographical data collected by the author from numerous sources.

TABLE 3

Members and Candidate Members of the Presidium of the Lithuanian Communist Party, 1949–64

Sixth Congress (1949)	Seventh Congress (1952)	Eighth Congress (1954)	Ninth Congress (1956)	Tenth Congress (1958)	Twelfth Congress (1960)	Thirteenth Congress (1961)	Fourteenth Congress (1964)
A. Sniečkus	A. Sniečkus	A. Sniečkus	A. Sniečkus	A. Sniečkus	A. Sniečkus	A. Sniečkus	A. Sniečkus
J. Paleckis	J. Paleckis	J. Paleckis	J. Paleckis	J. Paleckis	J. Paleckis	J. Paleckis	J. Paleckis
M. Gedvilas	M. Gedvilas	M. Gedvilas					
M. Šumauskas		M. Šumauskas	M. Šumauskas	M. Šumauskas	M. Šumauskas	M. Šumauskas	M. Šumauskas
V. Niunka	V. Niunka	V. Niunka	V. Niunka	V. Niunka	V. Niunka	A. Barkauskas	A. Barkauskas
E. Ozarskis		E. Ozarskis	E. Ozarskis	E. Ozarskis	K. Kairys	K. Kairys	R. Songaila
K. Liaudis		K. Liaudis	K. Liaudis	K. Liaudis		A. Randakevičius*	
						B. Popov	B. Popov
A. Trofimov	V. Aronov	M. Afonin	M. Afonin				
K. Preikšas	K. Preikšas		B. Sharkov	B. Sharkov	B. Sharkov		
	F. Bieliauskas	F. Bieliauskas	P. Levitski		F. Bieliauskas	F. Bieliauskas	
A. Chistiakov	P. Kondakov	M. Kenevich	M. Kenevich	M. Kenevich			
N. Gorlinskov	V. Pisarev	V. Augustinaitis	J. Maniušis	J. Maniušis	J. Maniušis	J. Maniušis	J. Maniušis
V. Pisarev	N. Gusev			A. B. Barauskas	A. B. Barauskas	A. B. Barauskas	A. B. Barauskas
D. Shupikov					J. Novickis	J. Novickas	
A. Anushkin*	A. Anushkin*	V. T. Lutsenko*	V. Meshchiarikov*	V. Meshchiarikov*	V. Meshchiarikov*	V. Meshchiarikov*	A. Česnavičius
G. Zimanas*	G. Zimanas*	G. Zimanas*	G. Zimanas*	G. Zimanas*	G. Zimanas	G. Zimanas	P. Dobrovolskis*
A. Raguotis*	A. Raguotis*	J. Petkevičius*	J. Petkevičius*	J. Petkevičius*	A. Česnavičius*	A. Česnavičius*	K. Mackevičius*
J. Bartašiūnas*			B. Baranauskas*	J. Laurinaitis*	L. Diržinskaitė*	L. Diržinskaitė*	
B. Baranauskas*				J. Matulis*			

Source: Compiled from Soviet announcements of "elections" at Party congresses.

* Candidate members.

peared. This is a significant indication of the changed role of the native Communists. During Stalin's reign, the non-Lithuanians were factually in charge of the Soviet regime, even though the Lithuanian Communists were assigned to formal leadership posts. In 1961, only a few "watchdogs" remained, with supervisory functions only. The Kremlin no longer tries to load every lower Party organ with its agents so that all practical decisions are made by the "watchdogs," as appears to have been the case before 1953. The Kremlin still maintains a few carefully placed functionaries for safety, but the "watchdog's" role now is to oversee, not rule. This change came about with Khrushchev's rise to power and with the changed attitude toward the native Communist bosses after the fall of Beria. Together with this changed role of the "watchdogs" and with the coming into dominance of native Communists, the influence of the old revolutionaries increased accordingly. Now they are checked, but not bossed to the extent they were during Stalin's reign.

The Kremlin has not, of course, abandoned control; it remains, though its character is different. The carefully placed watchdogs, the security organs, and the military power are still maintained. However, the Kremlin appears to place much more reliance on the political loyalty of the republic Party bosses. These bosses, feeling increased self-importance and influence, and having a larger voice in the management of the republic affairs, are ultimately more dependent upon the political leadership in the Kremlin than they were under Stalin's regime. The development known as the new class is an All-Union phenomenon, and it is apparent that the Lithuanian bureaucracies are well aware of their dependence upon the continued existence of the present regime. Thus, besides taking the usual safety precautions of any totalitarian state, the Kremlin recently has acquired several political integrating forces.

The Central Committee of the CPL is an expanded Presidium, having the same political groups, the same power relations, and the same tendencies as the CPL. For this reason, a few sentences suffice for the analysis of the Central Committee. The CPL Central Committee lacks the power that is vested in the members of the Presidium, though theoretically it is a superior organ. If on occasion the Central Committee of the CPSU does exercise real power, no such opportunity can be foreseen in the CPL. The leadership of the CPL is actually appointed by the Kremlin and any deviation or clash in the CPL will be resolved by the

Kremlin and not by the CPL Central Committee. Only in case of an extreme crisis in the Kremlin could the republic Central Committee be instrumental in deciding which faction to support. Such a possibility, however, is too remote to be considered seriously.

ORGANIZATION OF THE SOVIETS

The Constitutional Façade. Constitutionally, the Soviet Union is a federal state. Actually, behind the screen of federalism we find an extremely centralized system of government. Soviet federalism is nothing more than a limited degree of administrative decentralization.

The limits of administrative jurisdiction of union republics (Lithuania is one of fifteen such republics) have varied throughout Soviet history. After World War II, they reached the widest expanse of their discretion at some time after the Twentieth Party Congress in 1956. This expansion of republic autonomy, however, has been reflected neither in the All-Union nor republic constitutions. The constitution of the Lithuanian S.S.R., adopted in 1940 after Lithuania's forcible incorporation into the Soviet Union, has changed very little, except for some inconsequential amendments giving recognition to Lithuania's more advancing sovietization. It provides for all the familiar features of a Soviet government, namely, the Supreme Soviet, the Council of Ministers, the judicial system, the local soviets, the planned and centrally administered economy.

As of 1964, the constitutional status of the union republics, as defined in the constitution of the U.S.S.R., may be summarized in the following terms: First, the jurisdiction of the union republics is limited by Article 14, which reserves the principal powers of foreign affairs; defense; foreign trade; budgetary, industrial, and economic planning; culture; etc., to the authorities of the U.S.S.R., and places less significant functions of primary education, domestic trade, social security, construction, justice, road maintenance, forest preservation and exploitation within the concurrent (with the national) jurisdiction of the union republics. Second, the Council of Ministers of a union republic is subordinate not only to the Supreme Soviet of a union republic, but also to the Council of Ministers of the U.S.S.R. The individual union-republic ministries are subordinate to the republic Council of Ministers and to the corresponding ministries of the

U.S.S.R. Only the few republic ministries dealing with local matters are exclusively responsible to the Council of Ministers of the union republic.

However, apart from this highly centralized state structure, the constitution of the U.S.S.R. ascribes to the union republics three important powers that potentially could make the Soviet Union a truly federal state: (1) the right of secession from the Soviet Union, (2) the power to maintain foreign relations, and (3) the right to form national military formations. These constitutional provisions have been a dead letter from the very beginning.

The Soviet Regime Re-established, 1944–47. World War II destroyed the political and administrative apparatus that was built during the year of Soviet occupation, 1940–41. Around 1943, the vestiges of this apparatus in Russia were reassembled and the governmental institutions of the Lithuanian S.S.R. revived and staffed, though Lithuania still was under German occupation. In fact, as early as 1942, selected individuals were sent to training courses for workers in the judicial system.[31] More than a thousand people were trained in the Soviet Union for various governmental jobs, thus gaining practical experience before they were sent back to Lithuania toward the end of 1944.[32]

On January 25, 1944, at a time when the Red Army was still far away from Lithuanian borders, the formally functioning Council of People's Commissars of the Lithuanian S.S.R. adopted a decree "Concerning the renewal of people's commissariats and the central organs of the Lithuanian S.S.R. and the staffing of their *apparati*."[33] According to the decree, twelve people's commissariats and eight commissariat-level committees or commissions were reactivated. At the same time, preparations for re-establishing the Soviet regime on the local level were made. The Communist partisan groups or underground Party organizations that operated in various districts of Lithuania (most of them parachuted into German-held Lithuania) were given responsibility for the revival of Soviet administration in their areas of operation.[34] Also, a group of selected Party secretaries was sent into Lithuania together with the invading Red Army.[35]

Despite these preparations, local soviets were not fully established even as late as 1947, especially in rural areas. The principal reasons were the lack of a sufficient number of qualified and politically reliable personnel and the total, armed resistance of the Lithuanian people. The situation was aggravated by the vast program of sovietization, which the disliked and understaffed Soviet regime was incapable of accomplishing.

To stamp out the resistance movement as well as to carry out the principal sovietization policies, the Kremlin established the already mentioned Organizational Bureau, with Suslov as its head, and imported non-Lithuanian cadres to run the country. This Bureau in fact ruled Lithuania in the immediate postwar years; the CPL, the Council of Ministers, as well as the security forces, acted as the executors of its policies.[36] In addition, at least one third of the ministers and most of the deputy ministers and various "assistants" were also sent in from Moscow. The native Communists were not to be trusted with collectivization of agriculture, industrialization, deportation of scores of thousands of "enemies of the people," and the break-up of the resistance.

Furthermore, it must be noted that until 1947–48, governmental organization only partly conformed to formal constitutional requirements, although neither the All-Union nor the republic's constitution provides for an emergency suspension of regular constitutional procedures. Thus, the Presidium of the Lithuanian Supreme Soviet extended the term of the Soviet to 1947; its term actually expired in 1944.[37] Local soviets were not elected until January, 1948. The rule was arbitrary, even by Soviet standards. In addition, it was exercised by force and terror, as the Lithuanian Party's First Secretary, Sniečkus, admitted in 1961.[38]

On the local level, while elections of local soviets were delayed, the Presidium of the Supreme Soviet appointed district (*apskritis*) executive committees (ordinarily, these had to be chosen by district soviets), which, in turn, appointed county (*valsčius*) and local (*kaimas*) executive committees (also elective), on the recommendations of the city and district Party committees, of course. One of the most important functions of the local executive committees was "to organize the struggle against armed bourgeois nationalist bands and others."[39]

Since these local committees had to face violent opposition to the regime, former Communist partisans and demobilized soldiers were preferred for positions on them.[40] However, such loyal cadres were few, and the district executive committees had no choice but to appoint people who were at best neutrally or, more likely, even antagonistically disposed toward the regime.

Sabotage of the government's policies on the local level was thus inevitable. On August 17, 1945, just about a year after the establishment of executive committees on various levels, the CPL Bureau ordered the district executive committees to weed out "the enemies of the people" and to appoint new, loyal, and obedient local administrators.[41] Yet, even after drastic measures, a year later the local executive committees still were ineffectual.[42] Anti-Soviet partisans greatly contributed to their paralysis.

In an effort to justify the unconstitutional appointment of local executive committees and to create an impression of their dependence on the people's consent, the regime, in the spring of 1946, ordered public meetings on county and community levels to evaluate their work. In fact, these meetings were extensively used to "unmask the foreign element" in the local soviets.[43] Few people participated in these public "evaluations" and a propaganda failure had to be registered.

In order further to help the feeble county executive committees fulfill their functions, the regime, in April, 1947, provided for the appointment of county executive committee representatives for every ten households. These carried out the regime's policy on the lowest level of administration. In the postwar years there were more than 20,000 such representatives; they were the regime's front-line soldiers in the sovietization of Lithuania. For this reason, they came into violent conflict with the resistance movement. They were constantly threatened; the more ruthless agents were liquidated.[44] Many of these functionaries today are at the top of the Soviet hierarchy in Lithuania.

At this point, a note on the administrative division of Lithuania is relevant. This division, and therefore the organization of the Communist Party, differed until 1950 from that of the Soviet Union. Generally, during the period 1944–50, the regime continued the territorial subdivision of independent Lithuania. Thus, on January 1, 1950, there were 41 districts, subdivided into 320 counties and 2,774 communities. Each community usually consisted of several villages. Of course, the cities constituted another category of administrative units. Each administrative level was formally governed by an executive committee, but factually by a local Party committee and a committee bureau and secretariat at the district and city level.

On June 20, 1950, the Presidium of the Lithuanian Supreme Soviet adopted a new administrative scheme, consistent with the rest of the Soviet Union. Four oblasts, approximately 90 rural and city raions, and about 1,200 local soviets were established. The oblasts were abolished in May of 1953. By the end of 1962, there were only 41 rural raions and seven city raions left.

The Soviets After Stalin. Genrikas Zimanas, the editor of the Lithuanian counterpart of *Pravda,* writing in 1958 on the survival of nationalism in Lithuania, in retrospect recalled the cadres policies of Beria, "the enemy of the people." Zimanas wrote that "one of the chief forms of his subversion of national republics was opposing cadres of various nationalities to one another."[45] When Beria was liquidated, the discussions in Lithuania were concerned mainly with Beria's nationality policy, especially the enormous influence of the Kremlin's commissars in the Party and the government of the Lithuanian S.S.R.[46] The native Communists were enthusiastic in denouncing Beria for his alleged distrust of the native cadres. The CPL Central Committee, meeting in June, 1953, spelled out the claimed "distortions" in the nationality policy in Lithuania. "These distortions were especially manifested in the weak development of Lithuanian national cadres and their advancement to leading Party, Soviet, and economic work," the Committee said.[47]

Slowly, the influence (at least in terms of numbers) of non-Lithuanian cadres was greatly curtailed in the post-Stalin years, as is shown by the national composition of the leadership of the CPL, the Lithuanian SSR Council of Ministers, and the CPL in general. A single reference to the national composition of the Council of Ministers in 1949 and 1959 will suggest the magnitude of the change from non-Lithuanians to native cadres. The proportion of ethnic Lithuanians in the Council of Ministers rose from about 55 per cent to more than 90 per cent in ten years. In fact, the replacement became so chaotic that the non-Lithuanian bureaucrats began protesting and the CPL leadership had to warn repeatedly against promoting cadres strictly on an ethnic basis.[48]

The Expansion and Contraction of Republic Functions. While temporarily the promotion of native cadres was not considered a nationalistic deviation, Lithuania, like the other union republics, gradually acquired more functions and privileges. This was in large measure a reflection of the struggle for succession. Khrushchev shrewdly exploited local sentiments to advance himself. However, in 1957, when he ousted the anti-Party group and became the unchallenged ruler of the Soviet Union, he reasserted centralism over many vital functions that he had handed over to the republics during his rise to power.

During Khrushchev's rise and the de-Stalinization campaign, the republics acquired a number of privileges not granted under Stalin. In Lithuania a new state flag and anthem were adopted and state prizes for science and arts instituted. The national heritage could be cultivated to a degree that would have been considered a crime in Stalin's days, and intellectual and artistic activity took a significant step toward what could be called creativity. Recognition of national and territorial peculiarities was also emphasized in the permission granted to the republics to draft their individual codes of law, in accordance with centrally established principles. Khrushchev's rule also meant a step toward the normalization and regulation of governmental and Party activity. The norms of "socialist legality" became more meaningful to the Soviet citizen.

The decentralization of economic planning and industrial management was the most significant event by far for the expanding role of the Soviet republics. The republic Party organizations became responsible for most of the republic's economic activity. The sovnarkhoz (the Soviet economy was decentralized by introducing regional economic councils—sovnarkhozes) raised the local industrialists and economic planners to new heights of power and required the expansion of republic administrative and political bureaucracies.[49] At the same time, however, Khrushchev did not ease centralized Party control, and the new status of the Soviet republics was still far from the status of the satellites under the control of the Soviet Union.*

Most of the gains made by the Union republics before 1957 had been lost or had fallen into disuse by 1963. The intellectuals and the artists were returned to the Marxist straitjacket;[50] the emphasis on Soviet, as opposed to national, culture was reasserted. For example, a renewed campaign to rewrite Lithuanian history and integrate it into that of the Soviet Union was started in the Thirteenth Congress of the CPL (1961).[51] A new campaign to internationalize or Russify Lithuanian culture and customs

* The expansion of republic rights and functions was so noticeable that some Western sources began to speculate on the possibility of a satellite status for the Baltic republics. Needless to say, this was mere wishful thinking. The fact remains that separatist or revisionist tendencies did appear and had to be contained. At the 1958 CPL Congress, Sniečkus had to remind all dissident elements that "there is no third road." *Tiesa*, February 13, 1958, p. 4.

was undertaken by the ideologues of the regime.[52] The Lithuanian Republic failed to utilize the right to draft its own codes
of law. The judicial statute adopted by the Presidium of the
Lithuanian S.S.R. Supreme Soviet in June of 1960, is merely a
copy of the basic provisions of the U.S.S.R. court system, adopted
in 1958. This law does not spell out those aspects that are within
republic jurisdiction.[53]

In the economic sphere, industrial administration and planning are again being centralized and regionalized. Since 1961,
the Lithuanian S.S.R. sovnarkhoz has been a part of the Western
Economic Region, which also includes the Estonian S.S.R. and
Latvian S.S.R. Since the beginning of 1963, the East Prussian
part (Kaliningrad oblast) of the R.S.F.S.R. has been joined to
the Lithuanian S.S.R. for economic planning and administration
(but not for political control).[54] This means that the republic
economic bosses are losing their planning prerogatives to a larger
economic grouping, based more on regional boundaries than on
national ones. The Council of the Western Economic Region,
meeting regularly, resolves the essential problems of cooperation,
specialization, and planning of production for the entire region,
and the republic planners are bound by its policy decisions as
well as by the determination of the central planners in Moscow.
The limited authority of the republic planners is well illustrated
by the restrictions on capital for the development of the tool-
and-die industry in Lithuania. The chairman of the Lithuanian
sovnarkhoz, P. Kulvets, appealed to the Second Session of the
All-Union Supreme Soviet in December, 1962, to overrule the
directive of the Gosplan to cut the capital outlays for the development of the tool-and-die industry as planned by republic
planners.[55]

The republic's dependence on Moscow is especially apparent
in the budgetary appropriations. Of the 640.25 million rubles
budget of the Lithuanian S.S.R. for 1963, 629.95 million, or
more than 98 per cent, was appropriated by the Supreme Soviet
in Moscow.[56] This means that the republic is really a master of
only 10.3 million rubles. While the details of the budget are
worked out at the local level, in accordance with the general
policy directives from Gosplan in Moscow, the ultimate approval
and authority for alteration rests with Gosplan as well. The best
that the local planners can do is appeal to the All-Union authorities to reconsider policies devised by Moscow's planners, as the
just-cited appeal of Kulvets vividly demonstrates.

The Republic's Top Agencies. After the de-Stalinization Con- ' gress, there appeared also a tendency to revitalize the soviets and the ministerial organs. The Communist Party relinquished some of its explicit controls in order to involve a greater part of the citizenry in the administrative process, even though factually the Party still maintained its primacy. The most recent events, however, appear to have reversed this tendency. With the reorganization of agricultural production in the spring of 1962, and with the adoption of the production principle (industrial-agricultural) in the organization of the Communist Party and the establishment of a Party-State Control Committee after the November 1962 Plenum of the Central Committee of the CPSU, the merger of Party and governmental functions appears to be more complete than ever before.

In Lithuania there has been a pronounced intermeshing of Party and governmental bureaucracies, especially at the very top of the leadership. Although the Lithuanian Soviet regime in many respects was a personal political machine of Antanas Snieckus, a careful distinction between the Party* and the government has always been made. But this distinction has been almost obliterated by the recent organizational changes. This is best illustrated by the composition of the Presidium and the bureaus of the CPL. The Presidium, "elected" in the Fourth Plenum of the Lithuanian Party's Central Committee on December 7, 1962,[57] is presided over by Antanas Snieckus, who is also the head of the republic agricultural committee. The Presidium also includes the Chairman of the Council of Ministers, M. Šumauskas; the Chairman of the Presidium of the Lithuanian S.S.R. Supreme Soviet, J. Paleckis; the Second Secretary of the CPL, B. Popov; a Secretary of the Party and the Chairman of the Party-State Control Committee, A. Barauskas; the Secretary of the Party in charge of ideological and organizational affairs, A. Barkauskas; the long-time Secretary of the Party in charge of industry and Chairman of the CPL Central Committee Bureau for Industrial Production, J. Maniušis; a Secretary of the Party and the Chairman of the CPL Bureau for Agricultural Production, R. Songaila, who at the same time is the Minister of Agricultural Production; and the First Secretary of the Lithuanian Komsomol, A. Česnavičius.

* As of January 1, 1965, the production principle of Party organization was abandoned and the agricultural-industrial subdivisions abolished.

The CPL Central Committee Bureau for Industrial Production includes the chief of the CPL industry otdel, a Deputy Chairman of the Lithuanian Gosplan, a Deputy Chairman of the Council of Ministers, and the Chairman of the Economic Council.

The CPL Central Committee Bureau for Agricultural Production includes, besides the Chairman and the Minister of Agricultural Production, the head of the Party organs, the Deputy Minister of Agricultural Production, the head of Party otdel, the Chairman of Litselskhoztechnik, and others.

Even though the recent organizational moves tend to emphasize the renewed assertion of control by the Party, the top cadres of the Lithuanian Soviet regime have remained remarkably stable. The governmental bureaucrats were simply absorbed into the Party structure. For example, R. Songaila was only the First Deputy Chairman of the Council of Ministers and the Minister of Agricultural Production before the Plenum of December, 1962. After the December Plenum, Songaila was appointed to serve concurrently as Secretary of the CPL, member of the CPL Presidium, and Chairman of the Bureau for Agricultural Production.

The stability of the personnel of the republic's institutions is underscored by the fact that since 1940, there has been only one Chairman of the Presidium of the Lithuanian S.S.R. Supreme Soviet (J. Paleckis) and only two Premiers. M. Gedvilas was the Chairman of the Council of Ministers till 1956, when he was replaced mainly for his inability markedly to raise the agricultural production index.[58] In 1957, he was appointed Minister of Education, a post he still holds. Since 1956, M. Šumauskas has been the Chairman of the Council of Ministers. All these men—Paleckis, Gedvilas, Šumauskas—are colleagues of Antanas Sniečkus and were educated under Stalin and in the underground struggle. Other members of the Council of Ministers have equally impressive durability. The most unstable part of the Soviet regime in Lithuania has been the non-Lithuanian cadres, who were more subject to political purges in the CPSU and pushed out by native Communists after Khrushchev's rise.

In a very true sense the Council of Ministers is the executive arm of the CPL and, therefore, of the CPSU. There is almost a total overlapping of the Party and government leadership. The entire Council of Ministers is incorporated into the CPL Central Committee. Under Sniečkus' leadership, the Lithuanian Soviet regime is a highly unified political control system. The Council of Ministers as a decision-making body may be ignored.

Nevertheless, the republic Council of Ministers is an instrument of the U.S.S.R. Council of Ministers. The Lithuanian Council of Ministers has a permanent representative on the Council of Ministers in Moscow, a sort of "ambassador-lobbyist" in the Kremlin. K. Gabdank, a Communist of German descent, has served in this capacity at least since 1955. It is through him, as well as through the individual ministries and Party channels, that All-Union directives reach the Lithuanians. The Chairman of the Council of Ministers of a union republic is a constitutional member of the U.S.S.R. Council of Ministers. By the logic of its composition and its constitutional as well as political subordination, the Lithuanian Council of Ministers is not likely to assert autonomy, at least not in essentials. Any tendency in this direction is likely to be noted by the Kremlin immediately.*

The republic's Supreme Soviet (legislature) constitutionally has the most prestige, but actually the least power. Since 1940, its composition and role has varied insignificantly. It was and still is a completely subservient instrument of the Communist Party. The membership of the Supreme Soviet almost completely overlaps with that of the central or local organs of the Party. It therefore serves at best as a medium of transmission for Party policies and as a detector of the mood of the people. Finally, what has been said of the Supreme Soviet is even more true of its Presidium, which overlaps with the central organs of the Party and, furthermore, includes several non-Lithuanian "watchdogs."

The Republic in Foreign Relations and Defense. In February, 1944, the Supreme Soviet of the U.S.S.R. amended the Soviet constitution in order to grant the union republics authority to engage in foreign affairs and maintain military formations (Articles 18a and 18b).[59] The amendments were intended to give the union republics the lacking legal characteristics of statehood and thus to provide a basis for international recognition of individual republics. Such recognition, it was hoped, would

---

* This is exactly what happened in the case of the Latvian S.S.R. Council of Ministers. In 1959, Deputy Prime Minister Berklavs argued in favor of more rapid Latvian-based and Latvia-oriented industrial development. He was immediately purged. See the enlightening report on the situation in the Latvian Soviet regime and its nationalist tendencies in Vilis Hazners, "Latvia," in the Assembly of Captive European Nations publications, *A Survey of Recent Developments in Nine Captive Counties, October, 1959–March, 1960* (New York, 1960), pp. 115–22.

strengthen the Soviets in future peace conferences; it also was intended to pave the way for the Western recognition of the annexation of the Baltic states. It may be added that Stalin sought recognition for the Soviet regime in Lithuania by suggesting that Lithuania be made a member of the United Nations, together with the Ukraine and Belorussia, and that delegates of the Baltic republics be recognized in the Paris Peace Conference.[60]

In conformity with this constitutional change, a Lithuanian S.S.R. Ministry of Foreign Affairs was established in 1944. Its primary task was to continue the attempts for direct or indirect recognition of the Soviet rule in Lithuania as well as engage in propaganda activities for the Kremlin. A noted student of Soviet foreign affairs has described the functions of the republic Ministers of Foreign Affairs as "ceremonial, ornamental, and symbolic. They greet foreign dignitaries, attend diplomatic receptions and banquets, serve on various Soviet diplomatic or quasidiplomatic delegations to international conferences and meetings, and take part in the foreign policy 'discussion' in the Supreme Soviet or its Foreign Affairs Commission."[61] Since 1944, the Lithuanian Ministry of Foreign Affairs has been headed by three men, all experienced Lithuanian revolutionaries from the underground years, but only one with at least some diplomatic experience. This was Povilas Rotomskis, appointed in 1944, after serving in the Soviet Consulate in New York during World War II. In 1949, he was replaced by another professional revolutionary, Ignas Gaška, who had no previous experience for the position. Ten years later, the job was given to Kazimieras Preikšas, a Moscow-trained veteran of the Spanish Civil War. Preikšas died in December, 1961; the vacancy has not been filled. The functions of the Ministry of Foreign Affairs, however, have been taken over by the Society for Friendship and Cultural Ties with Foreign Countries, although there is no evidence that the Ministry has been abolished.

In addition, it has been a Soviet practice to appoint Lithuanians to Soviet embassies in countries with large numbers of Lithuanian immigrants. After Rotomskis' recall from the Consulate in New York, another old Lithuanian Bolshevik, Laurynas Kapočius, was attached to the Soviet Embassy in Washington. Kapočius was followed by A. Zenkevičius. The task of these officials is, apparently, to observe the political activities of Lithuanian *emigrés,* to maintain contact with pro-Communist elements among them, and, where possible, to present a favorable image of the Soviet regime not only among the Lithuanians in the United States but also among the American people in general. (The Soviet Embassy in Montevideo also has an accredited secretary of Lithuanian nationality, who performs the same functions in South America.)

Furthermore, Soviet delegations to the United Nations and other international organizations occasionally include Lithuanian officials, whose function is to promote the *de facto* recognition of the Soviet regime in Lithuania. J. Matulis, the President of the republic's Academy of Sciences, and I. Gaška, a former Minister of Foreign Affairs, have served on the Soviet delegation to the U.N. Chairman of the Presidium of the Lithuanian Supreme Soviet, Justas Paleckis, usually represents the Soviet Union in the Interparliamentary Union, to which the Soviet Union has belonged since 1955.

Lithuanian Communists are also involved in the Soviet program of "cultural exchanges." This program is administered not by the Ministry of Foreign Affairs but by the Society for Friendship and Cultural Ties with Foreign Countries. There is no doubt that not just since Preikšas' death, but for a long time, this Society, not the Ministry, has been the republic's actual instrument in foreign relations. Its importance is demonstrated by the quality of its leadership. Whereas in the 1950's the Ministry of Foreign Affairs was headed by people without diplomatic background, the Society was chaired by the former Minister Rotomskis. After his death in 1962, L. Kapočius, a secretary in the Soviet Embassy in Washington, was recalled to take over Rotomskis position. At the same time the Ministry of Foreign Affairs was left dormant.

The Society for Friendship and Cultural Ties with Foreign Countries is a front for the Agitprop, which arranges for exchanges of artists, scientists, tourists, publications, etc.[62] A front of this front—that is, a front for the Society—is the so-called Committee for the Return to the Fatherland and Cultural Ties with Compatriots Abroad. This Committee, in 1964 chaired by V. Karvelis, a former "bourgeois" general and later commander of the Sixteenth Lithuanian Communist division, organizes tours in Lithuania for Lithuanian emigrants, works for the return of Lithuanians from abroad, especially from South America, publishes a highly polemic newspaper, *Tėvynės Balsas* (*The Voice of the Fatherland*) for distribution overseas, and administers the

Lithuanian-language section of the Soviet counterpart of the Voice of America.

The case of the republic's military formation is different from that of foreign affairs, but even more enlightening in respect to the "sovereignty" claimed for the Soviet republics.

During World War II, Stalin utilized nationalism in the struggle against Nazi Germany and permitted the formation of Red Army units on an ethnic-republic basis. There was no constitutional provision for such units until the February, 1944, amendment. However, as early as in 1942, a so-called Sixteenth Lithuanian Division of the Red Army had been organized.[63] The Division, formed from various sources, was led by Lithuanian officers or Lithuanians from the ranks of the Red Army, and included a large number of Russian officers as well as Russian and other non-Lithuanian troops. This Lithuanian unit, perhaps composed largely of non-Lithuanians, participated in the Oriol front and later fought the Germans in the reconquest of Lithuanian territory. Although the Division was under reliable control, it nevertheless represented a potential threat to All-Union integrity. Therefore, by 1946, this division was disbanded. The only military institution surviving to this date on a republic level in Lithuania is the Military Commissariat, which deals with recruitment and mobilization and has offices in every region of the country. It is a branch of the Ministry of Defense in Moscow.

THE PROSPECTS OF AUTONOMY FOR OCCUPIED LITHUANIA

The short-lived expansion of republic functions in the 1950's gave rise to expectations among the Lithuanian Communists for greater independence from the Kremlin. Especially after de-Stalinization, many officials of the regime and the intelligentsia began to assert national interests. While the expression of national interests was most widespread in the cultural field, the liberal atmosphere of the thaw, the separate roads to socialism, and the economic decentralization became noticeable in other areas of life. By 1959, these tendencies had become too pervasive, and the Kremlin began to crack down on what it called "vestiges of bourgeois nationalism and tendencies toward revisionism." Two examples will demonstrate the rise and fall of this sort of nationalism.

First, let us consider the tendency toward economic separatism.

In the Soviet Union, the All-Union interests take precedence over the interests of any one republic. Economic planning is based on this premise. Consequently, no matter what a republic's production capacity is, its benefits to the local inhabitants are not proportionate to its output, since part of this must be contributed to other sections of the Soviet Union. A sense of exploitation inevitably arises among the people and even the officials of the regime.

Khrushchev's proposed decentralization of the economy was strongly supported by the Lithuanian Communists, since it promised greater autonomy and benefits for the republic. However, during the discussion of this reform in 1957, First Secretary Sniečkus found it necessary to warn the CPL in no uncertain terms of the dangers of decentralization. He said:

> Every development of the creative initiative must be attuned to the centralized elements. . . . Separate tendencies toward localism, attempts to create a closed economy and attempts to solve economic problems on the basis of limited local tasks may become evident. Such tendencies must be fought from the very beginning. . . . One should not forget that our enemies may try to exploit tendencies of this kind in order to inflict harm on us or to undermine our forces. Nobody will ever succeed in weakening the unbreakable force of friendship among the nations of the U.S.S.R. or in separating the Lithuanian nation from the great Russian nation and from other nations of the Soviet Union.[64]

Sniečkus succeeded in holding back Lithuanian economic nationalism. What could have happened had he not done so is illustrated by the experience of the Latvian soviet regime. In 1959, the Deputy Prime Minister of the Latvian S.S.R. and many lower Party and government officials were purged for the following deviations:

> Former Deputy Prime Minister Berklavs stood up openly against the general Party line, directed toward the development of heavy industry. . . . Berklavs opposed expanding production of railroad cars and diesel engines in Latvia, insisting that capital investments should rather be increased in consumer goods industries. Moreover, Berklavs proposed distribution of locally manufactured goods primarily within the Latvian Republic. These proposals meant in essence nothing but a striving toward autocracy and nationalistic tendencies. Thus, harm would have been brought to the general interests of the Soviet Union and likewise to the interests of the Latvian people.[65]

At about the same time that members of the Latvian regime were purged for economic nationalism, an extensive purge of the intelligentsia was carried out in Lithuania for cultural nationalism. The First Secretary of the CPL, in its Eleventh Congress (January, 1959), defined the deviation in the following terms:

> The most serious attention must be paid to the fact that among certain comrades, a one-sided view toward questions of nationality policy, toward the development of national culture, still manifests itself. Certain comrades tend to consider questions of nationalism as something unrelated to the class struggle and to the tasks of Communist construction. In certain statements concerning culture, nationalism is highly emphasized, without sufficient emphasis being placed on Socialist content and class viewpoint. These are dangerous tendencies, which may lead to nationalistic deviation if no fight is waged against them.[66]

Because of his espousal of such "uncritical" views on Lithuanian culture, because of the national "bias" shown in selecting scientific cadres, the Rector of the University of Vilnius was dismissed from his post, from the Central Committee of the CPL, and from the Party itself.[67] With him went a score of other top educators and professors.

These examples suggest that (1) even in the highest circles of the Party an awareness and a quest for the realization of national interests is strong and the Kremlin must exert constant pressure to contain such manifestations; (2) the recent purges in the Latvian regime and the Lithuanian intelligentsia make it clear that the Kremlin is not willing to tolerate nationalist deviations even in the interpretation of the national heritage, and takes ruthless measures to stamp out all autonomous tendencies; and (3) as the above examples indicate, there is a nationalist segment of the intelligentsia in the Communist Party itself, which actively strives for the enhancement of national values. A nationalist intelligentsia and the generally dissatisfied masses would provide the necessary elements for a political explosion if severe crisis arose, a fact of tremendous importance for the West and of ominous significance for the Communist bloc. Neither the Communist bloc nor the West can take the unity of the Soviet Union for granted, despite its façade of unitary centralism.

7. Lithuania's Economy: Introduction of the Soviet Pattern

PRANAS ZUNDĖ

Until World War II, Lithuania was regarded as an agricultural country. Its heavy industry was still in the stage of development and did not play a major role in the nation's economic life. Of greater importance were food-processing and light industry, which drew upon immediately available raw materials, primarily agricultural produce. The agricultural nature of Lithuania's pre-war economy was reflected in its population distribution: in 1939, the farming population comprised 77 per cent of the total.[1]

In a discussion of the changes brought about in Lithuanian economy during the Soviet occupation, agriculture would thus seem to be the proper starting point. Although the Soviet preference for industry reduced the relative importance of agriculture in the Lithuanian economy, it was not the extensive industrialization, but the sovietization of agricultural production that wrought the most important change in the country.

AGRICULTURE

First Preparation for Collectivization, 1940–41. Until the Soviet occupation in 1940, Lithuania was a country of small and medium-sized farms. Farm units not exceeding 75 acres constituted 90.2 per cent of the total number of farms and 66.2 per cent of the total area of cultivated land.[2] The agricultural labor force derived for the most part from the farm owners themselves. Thus, in 1939, farm owners and their families constituted 78.7 per cent of the total number of agricultural workers; the remaining 21.3 per cent were hired help.³ Wages of hired workers came to only 11–15 per cent of the total cost of agricultural production.⁴

Agriculture provided sufficient raw materials for the rapid development of the food-processing and light industries. Agricultural products such as butter, bacon, cured pork, eggs, poultry, and cattle ranked among the most important of export commodities. These products constituted 69.2 per cent of the total Lithuanian export value for the year 1939.⁵

Immediately after the Soviet seizure of power, the newly "elected" People's Diet adopted a "resolution declaring all land to be the property of the people, i.e., of the state."⁶ The declaration limited farm holdings to 75 acres. All land in excess of that amount was nationalized without compensation and distributed among the landless and the small landholders for their "perennial use." Moreover, the declaration expressed strong opposition to attempts at collectivization:

> *Any attempt to threaten the private ownership right of the peasants or to enforce collectivization upon the peasant workers against their will, shall be severely prosecuted as injurious to the interests of the people and of the state.* [Italics added.]

The Diet's insistence that there would be no involuntary collectivization of farms, however, was a mere tactical maneuver. It would have been naïve to expect that the Soviet Government would make an exception in the case of Lithuania and would tolerate private ownership of Lithuanian agriculture. "Socialization" of agriculture, or rather its nationalization, was at best a question of time. The real intentions of the Soviet regime were revealed by the pattern of land distribution ordered by the People's Diet. By such an agrarian reform, the new ruling body sought to atomize landholding and thus prepare "objective" conditions for collectivization. The results of this policy can be seen from the comparative table of landholdings (see p. 143).

As a consequence of this declaration by the People's Diet, a national land reserve was set up in the course of a few months consisting chiefly of the property confiscated from "landlords and kulaks," that is, farmers who had owned more than 75 acres. Part of this land reserve, about 393,000 hectares (980,000 acres) or 68.3 per cent of all confiscated land property, was subsequently distributed to previously landless peasants and small farmers for their "cost-free and perennial use." About 11 per cent of the land

TABLE 1

Classification of Farms According to Size
and Percentage of Total Arable Land Used by Each Class

| | Before the Soviet Occupation (*1940*) | | | |
Acres	*Number of Farms*	*Percentage*	*Total Acreage*	*Percentage*
Less than 12.5	97,310	27.4	586,910	5.3
12.5-25	91,290	25.7	1,730,360	15.3
25-50	104,890	29.6	3,692,610	33.2
50-75	38,630	10.9	2,318,960	20.8
Over 75	22,730	6.4	2,821,860	25.4

| | After the Soviet Land Reform (*1941*) | | | |
Acres	*Number of Farms*	*Percentage*	*Total Acreage*	*Percentage*
Less than 12.5	65,660	17.2	387,530	3.6
12.5-25	154,670	40.0	2,639,520	24.7
25-50	104,890	27.1	3,692,610	34.5
50-75	61,000	15.7	3,977,640	37.2
Over 75	—	—	—	—

Source: M. Gregorauskas, *Tarybų Lietuvos Žemės Ūkis 1940–1960* (Vilnius, 1960), p. 80.

in the reserve was consigned to the use of various public institutions.[7]

By no stretch of the imagination could such a reform be construed as an attempt by the new regime to strengthen agriculture and improve its efficiency. The real objective of the reform was to ruin the productive, self-sufficient Lithuanian farmer and to create a "class struggle" of the poor peasants against "kulaks." That this had been the purpose of the reform was publicly admitted by the First Secretary of the Lithuanian Communist Party, Antanas Sniečkus, not long after it was carried out, when there were no more farmers who possessed more than 75 acres.[8]

To achieve their objective of destroying independent farming, the Communists first of all made use of a taxation policy. On May 14, 1941, a new tax bill was enacted, levying discriminatory taxes on farmers and directed especially against those with larger holdings.[9] Within this new system, for example, a farmer with an annual income of 10,000 rubles had to pay nine times as much in taxes as a farmer with an income of 2,000 rubles. Even more important, taxes were estimated not in accordance with the actual annual income, but on the basis of a specified norm of income the farmer was arbitrarily allocated to receive from an acre of arable land or a particular breed of livestock. Thus, the yearly income from a hectare (about 2.5 acres) of arable land was estimated at 300 rubles (old currency); from a hectare of pasture, 120 rubles; from a hectare of orchard or berry culture, 380 rubles; from a single cow, 230 rubles; a hog, 160 rubles; a horse, 200 rubles.[10] For example, a farmer with the taxable income of 25 acres of land, 5 acres of orchard and berry culture, 10 cows, 3 horses, and 15 hogs was assessed 10,200 rubles, regardless of what his actual earnings may have been that year. Furthermore, the legislation provided that taxes of farmers with outside income could be increased by an additional 20–50 per cent levy.

A second measure of extortion and suppression imposed by the regime upon the independent farmer was the requisitioning of farm products by the state. The deliveries required from larger farms were out of all proportion to their productive capacity and to the amount of deliveries required from smaller farms. For example, from a 50-acre farm, a farmer had to deliver seven and one-half times the amount of meat required from a farmer with a 12-acre farm.[11] It did not matter whether the farmer was actually engaged in the production of the requisitioned items; he had to fulfill the norm, even if it meant that he had to buy the products for delivery. In this manner, the Communists sought to destroy the kulaks, a category comprising all farmers who worked 62.5–75 acres of land.

Another indication that the Communist Party was secretly engaged in preparing for collectivization was the installation of farm machinery and tractor stations. These were the necessary steps preliminary to collectivization, as Soviet practice earlier in Russia had shown. In the spring of 1941, 42 MTS's had already been set up, together with 283 rental stations for machine equipment and horses.[12] The government also established 60 state farms (sovkhozes), with a total of 115,000 acres. With this same idea in mind, the Party enjoined any further partition of villages into farmsteads, which had been an essential feature of the progressive land reform instituted in independent Lithuania in 1922. Early in 1941, the first signs of collectivization began to appear in the form of press articles on the subject and in the form of a "spontaneous sweeping movement of the working peasants into collective farming." Even the headlines of these articles and press notices, such as "Samogitians Demand Collective Farming," and similar items showed which way the wind was blowing.[13] The first collective farm (kolkhoz), named in honor of Lenin, was organized in January, 1941, in the district of Akmenė. In March, 1941, this farm was worked collectively by sixteen families and consisted of 625 acres of land, twenty horses, and sixty head of cattle.[14]

However, any further realization of the Soviet plans for collectivization, which was to alter completely the agricultural structure of Lithuanian economy, was cut short by the outbreak of the Soviet-German war in July, 1941, and the expulsion of the Soviets from Lithuania. During the subsequent German occupation, a small number of farmers regained the land that had been confiscated from them by the Soviet government, but otherwise the German occupation forces left in effect the Soviet-enacted legislation of land nationalization, and in most instances farms that had been nationalized by the Soviet regime were retained by the Germans as state property under government administration or were turned over to colonizing German nationals.

Second Preparation for Collectivization, 1944–47. When the Soviet forces returned to Lithuania in the summer of 1944, the land reform initiated in 1940 was continued for a time. However, in certain important respects it was modified to make it a better instrument in a "concerted attack against the kulaks." Essentially these modifications were contained in the "Ordinance Regarding the Liquidation of Effects upon Agriculture Left by the German Occupation,"[15] which was adopted by the Supreme Soviet of the Lithuanian S.S.R. on August 30, 1944. First of all, this law called for the use of more radical measures in putting the land reform into effect. Thus, the state land-reserve agency was empowered to appropriate all "land seized by German colonists, land that had previously belonged to those enemies of the people who had fled with the German occupation forces, and land left without claimants." In addition, certain restrictions were imposed in the matter of the amount of land permitted to remain in private possession, although nominally the maximum was kept at 75 acres. On this point, the ordinance directed that "taking into account the quality of the soil and the situation of the land, this allotment can be reduced to 20 hectares (50 acres), and in the case of farms whose owners had actively collaborated with the German occupation personnel, to 5 hectares (12.5 acres)." To the Soviet mind, the phrase "actively collaborated with German occupation personnel" allowed for very flexible interpretation. Thus farmers fell into this category if during the German occupation they had delivered the requisitions ordered by the occupation government on pain of being shot for failure to comply.

The state land reserve was used, in the first place, to provide land for Red Army personnel or their families, guerrilla fighters and other persons who had actively resisted the Germans, and peasants who had been deprived of their farms by the German occupation regime. Secondly, land from the reserve was assigned to sovkhozes, to MTS's, and to the state for other official uses.

By such redistribution of land the Communists sought to ingratiate themselves with the landless peasants and the small farmers. But their hopes in this respect were not fulfilled, for the peasant and farmer population understood the real Soviet motives. Even those peasants who had never owned land before and were "presented" by the regime with 25–32.5 acre farms quickly perceived that the Soviet land reform was in no way intended to help the small farmer or improve the general state of agriculture. Faced with a complete lack of farming equipment and livestock, they had very little use for the land they had received, while the regime, for the most part, seemed to ignore this matter. State subsidies for the acquisition of equipment and stock were negligible when compared to the need for such aid. The new owners found it impossible to finance farming operations with these small subsidies. Furthermore, there was a general disbelief that the regime intended to leave land in the farmers' private possession for any extended period of time. Under these circumstances, the land reform proceeded in very disorderly fashion. On December 22, 1944, in an outline of proposed measures for putting into effect the ordinance for the "Liquidation of Effects upon Agriculture Left by the German Occupation," the Council of People's Commissars and the Central Committee of the Lithuanian Communist Party observed:

Too many of the local Soviet and Party organs have underestimated the political significance of a swift re-establishment of the Soviet order of landholding; they have made insufficient use of the means at their disposal—the restoration of land rights in order to group the working peasants around the organs of the Soviet Government; they have shown neglect in enlisting the aid of agricultural workers, the landless, and the small peasant farmers in the work of putting the ordinance into effect; they have provided weak leadership for district and county land committees in their work; they have demonstrated laxity

in the appropriation of horses and stock surpluses from the farms of
the kulaks and in the mandatory purchase of cows; they have also
failed to take the necessary measure to suppress attempts at sabotage
and resistance to the ordinance by the kulaks, and to protect the
peasants who are being granted land from the threats and revenge of
the kulaks.[16]

According to the new regulations, the land reform was to be
brought to completion by February 1, 1945. Actually, the process
continued into 1948. Between 1944 and 1948, the regime confiscated and redistributed, or retained in its own immediate possession, about 341 million acres of land. The new redistribution of
land resulted in a diminution of farm size, even greater than that
accomplished by the 1940 reform, as is shown by the following
table.

TABLE 2

Distribution of Farms by Size

Acres	May 1, 1941		January 1, 1948	
	Number of Farms	Percentage	Number of Farms	Percentage
Less than 12.5	65,700	17.2	118,800	30.3
12.5–25	154,700	40.0	146,900	37.4
25–50	104,900	27.1	108,500	27.6
50–75	61,000	15.7	18,200	4.7
Over 75	—	—	—	—
Total	386,300	100.0	392,400	100.0

Source: M. Gregorauskas, *op. cit.*, p. 117.

It is evident that the objective of the "reform" was to create
an agricultural proletariat, heretofore practically nonexistent in
Lithuania. Needless to say, farms of less than 12.5 acres, which
constituted 30.3 per cent of all farms after the reform, could not
be operated even at cost under the existing conditions for agriculture in Lithuania, which have made grain and animal hus-
bandry the principal agricultural occupations. Besides, the new
landowners and small farmers lacked even the essentials for farming: seed for crops, livestock, machine equipment, fertilizer, and
countless other things. Circumstances such as these forced many
small farmers and new landowners to abandon the land that had
been given them and move to the cities in search of employment.
Later, it was not difficult to force those who had remained into

collective farms, which was what the Soviet regime had planned.

One point must be made, however, which is that in the early postwar years the Soviet Government did not embark on a general offensive against the average farmer and against private possession in agriculture. Likewise, the taxation of farmers was not as sharply differentiated as in 1941.[17] At present, Soviet spokesmen themselves admit that by this policy they sought chiefly to speed and encourage agricultural recovery after the war.

A similar policy was adopted in regard to the requisitions of agricultural products by the state. In the period following the war, the progression of these requisitions escalated according to farm size was not as steep as in 1941.[18]

The Soviet Government continued its lenient policies toward private ownership in agriculture until the end of 1947. Before that year, the government was content to propagate and support agricultural cooperation tending to demonstrate the "superiority of collective labor." Agricultural credit cooperation and consumers cooperatives had been widespread in Lithuania even before the war; all that the Soviet Government needed to do was to make use of the existing cooperative chain. But even these efforts by the regime met with reserve on the part of the farmers, who supected a possible trap. Credit and various consumer cooperatives, which in 1939 had had over 140,000 members, had only 39,450 in 1947, despite the considerable privileges they had to offer.[19] As for the new cooperatives for agricultural production instituted by the regime, they were entirely unsuccessful. In 1947, the units of these cooperatives had sown only 9,285 hectares (23,200 acres) for harvest, or about 0.4 per cent of the total acreage sown that year, although during that same year these production cooperatives had received 27 per cent of the total amount of agricultural loans.[20]

In late 1947, the Soviet regime began its onslaught on the so-called kulaks. On December 12, 1947, the Central Committee of the Lithuanian Communist Party issued regulations containing a definition of kulak. According to the terms of this decree, the following types of farms, among others, were classified as kulak farms:[21] (a) farms that, for compensation in either currency or produce, regularly employ hired agricultural workers or craftsmen; (b) farms that no longer regularly employed hired labor for compensation in currency or produce, but did so during and after the German occupation; (c) farms that engaged in "exploitation of outside labor in a concealed form," by claiming that the workers were relatives, or by taking into the household unpaid outside help under the pretense that they were members of the immediate family; (d) farms that systematically employed seasonal agricultural workers or craftsmen; (e) farms that under "slaverylike terms" supplied peasant farms with labor animals, seed, products, and farm machinery; (f) farms that owned complex farm machinery, mills, sawmills, or other equipment; and (g) farms that systematically purchased goods and agricultural products for resale, etc.

The kulak category, especially when used at the discretion of local Party units, could easily include practically every farm in Lithuania.

Kulak farms, needless to say, were subject to extremely high taxation. Although the regulations in question came out, as has been noted, on December 12, 1947, kulak taxes for the antecedent year of 1947 were increased by 75–250 per cent. In 1948, there was a further increase in taxation: In that year the kulaks were assessed an additional 150–500 per cent. Thus, for example, if a "nonkulak" farm with an income of 15,000 rubles paid 1,535 rubles in agricultural taxes, a "kulak" farm with the same income paid 7,957 rubles; if a "nonkulak" farm with an income of 22,000 rubles paid 4,075 rubles, a "kulak" farm paid as much as 18,425 rubles, or stated in another way, 84 per cent of its entire gross income. Naturally, many farmers found this tax burden unbearable and abandoned their farms.

Collectivization. The first collective farm in Lithuania after the war was organized on February 26, 1947, in the Dotnuva county, the district of Kėdainiai. In spite of the various exemptions and privileges granted by the government to collective farms, in spite of all the persuasion and propaganda, a "spontaneous" movement of farmers to join collective farms simply failed to take place. At the end of 1947, there were only twenty collective farms in all, which comprised only 0.08 per cent of the number of Lithuanian farm households then in existence and 0.09 per cent of all arable land. On the other hand, there had been action on all sides to promote the organization of collective farms. The taxes of a collective farm were insignificant compared with those of the self-sufficient farmer. The requisition norms for agricultural products were likewise considerably lower for collective farms than for "unsocialized" farms. For example, in 1947–48, the state required 44 lbs. of milk for each acre of cultivated land from the independent farmer and only 11 lbs. for every acre from a collective farm.

Although the number of Lithuanian farmers who joined collective farms amounted to less than one-tenth of one per cent of their total number, the Cabinet of Ministers of the republic and the Central Committee of the Lithuanian Communist Party unhesitatingly declared that, "inspired by the achievements of the farming proletariat in other fraternal republics within the Union, which had been accomplished on the basis of collective farming, under the leadership of the Communist Party a great many of the poor and middle-income peasants in a number of districts in Soviet Lithuania have begun to organize into agricultural artels —collective farms." In a joint session on March 20, 1948, the Ministers and the Party Committee issued a decree regarding the "organization of collective farms in the Lithuanian S.S.R."[22]

But regardless of this decree and of all the measures of economic pressure applied by the regime against the farmers, the number of collective farms continued to grow at a very slow rate throughout the first part of 1948. In the summer of that year, Lithuania had 150 small collective farms in all, organized largely from farms that had been completely unproductive. This prompted the regime to take more drastic measures. Besides taxation and other measures of economic coercion directed against independent farmers, various threats and physical repressions were brought into play. By these means, the number of collective farms during 1948 increased to 524 and included a little more than 12,000 previously independent farms, or 3 per cent of the total number of farm households. This was sufficient for the Sixth Congress of the Lithuanian Communist Party in 1949 "to affirm the manifest desire of Lithuanian farmers to organize into collective farms." In other words, the Congress had determined to abolish private farming in Lithuania.[23]

Persons who had been recently granted land by the Soviet Government were most easily coerced by the Party into collective farming, for their newly acquired land had failed to realize for them a means of subsistence.[24] But, in general, the resistance of farmers to collectivization was overwhelming and almost desperate. In the regime's effort to break this resistance, farmers who refused to join collective farms were placed in forced labor camps or deported to the Soviet Union en masse, where most of them were destined to perish. Although Soviet officials display a general reluctance to talk about this period of their rule in Lithuania, they are no longer able to prevent those facts from seeping out. Their own references to the use of coercion in the enforcement of collectivization, however, are very characteristic. Thus, in a Soviet publication issued to mark the twentieth anniversary of Soviet rule in Lithuania, appears the following:

> The process of reordering the village according to the socialist pattern intensified the class struggle and strengthened kulak resistance. An important weapon of the kulaks in their fight against collectivization was agitation directed against collective farming. The kulaks prattled a great deal about the gains in agriculture supposedly made during the period of the bourgeois government, alleging that the Soviet rule in Lithuania was merely temporary, and with all their strength reviling collective farms. Playing on the religious sentiment of the peasant believers, the kulaks used the church as a means, through its clergy, to contaminate the peasants with the poison of anti-collective farming and anti-Soviet agitation. By means of radio broadcasts, anti-collective farming and anti-Soviet propaganda was disseminated by those traitors to the Lithuanian nation who had fled abroad after serving the German occupation regime.
>
> Another important means that the kulaks used in their struggle against collectivization was the terrorization of Communists, members of the Communist Youth, village activists, and all other upright Soviet citizens who had been loyal in their support of the Soviet Government. In this campaign, the kulaks utilized the bourgeois nationalist underground in Lithuania, and themselves participated in and supported the bandit gangs.
>
> Again, another means the kulaks employed in their struggle against collectivization, particularly during the period when extensive collectivization was threatening to crush the existence of the bourgeoisie as a class, were their acts of malevolence and destruction directed at the productive-economic foundations of collective farms. The kulaks assumed false postures, disguising themselves as sympathizers of collective farming. Having wormed themselves into the collective farms, they would then set out to poison the environment and stir up strife; they tried to exaggerate every shortcoming, and in this manner, to break the spirit of the members within the collective farm, to sway the wavering, less committed ones; they sought to do positive harm, purposely damaging collective farm property and disrupting the internal harmony of the membership.
>
> *The Party and the government actively fought the kulaks and fought banditism. In 1948, the Soviet Government took repressive measures against the bandit element and its supporters.*[25] [Italics added.]

In this context, the Soviet scholar M. Gregorauskas shows even greater candor. He writes:

It definitely ought to be kept in mind that the exceedingly fierce class struggle and the kulak banditism, rampant in rural Lithuania during the period 1945–49, were very important factors, in certain instances resulting in violation of the principle of voluntary collectivization and of Soviet legality, and in many localities requiring the hastening of the collectivization process.[26]

Although guerrilla sacrifices could not save the entire country from eventual collectivization, in certain areas collectivization was greatly retarded by these activities. For example, although by early 1950 the task of collectivization had been practically accomplished in a number of districts, in the Varėna district the degree of collectivization reached was only about 3 per cent. The reason, as admitted by Soviet sources themselves, was that the "kulak nationalistic banditism and terror" (these terms are the Communist jargon for the guerrilla freedom fighters) were able to keep active in the forests of the Vilnius region.[27]

By such concentration of efforts, the Soviet regime succeeded in forcing almost 50 per cent of the farmers into collective farming by early 1950. By September of 1952, this number was raised to 96 per cent. At the end of 1952, collectivization had been practically completed.

Development After Stalin's Death. Collective farms organized in 1949–50 had been small, combining, on the average, fifty to eighty farmsteads. Most often, they were the same as a given village area. In early 1950, there were over 8,000 kolkhozes in Lithuania. That number was the highest ever reached. In the course of that same year, the Soviet regime began to enlarge their size. In 1951, Lithuania had only 2,939 kolkhozes, and in 1955 even fewer—1,795.[28] Evidently, there had been a strong movement to create the so-called agropolis (agrarograd) system. However, in June, 1955, at a conference of agricultural experts from the Baltic republics held in Riga, Nikita Khrushchev, the originator of the agropolis idea, declared that the expansion of the collective farms in Lithuania and in the Baltic area in general had been carried on with too much fervor, and as a result "many serious errors had been made." This served to arrest the campaign for the enlargement of collective farms, while the larger collective farms were again divided into smaller units. In 1958, the number of collective farms in Lithuania had increased to 2,185. It dropped to 1,867 in 1961, but this time for a different reason: many collective farms had been converted into sovkhozes (state farms).[29]

The first sovkhozes in Lithuania had been organized during the first Soviet occupation of 1940–41. After the war, these were re-established, while additional ones were also created. In 1948, Lithuania had 104 sovkhozes, which occupied 384,000 acres of land. Although by 1955 their number had been reduced by 87 (because of the expansion), the area of cultivated land in their use increased to 686,000 acres. During the period 1956–59, a number of the existing collective farms in Lithuania (a total of 434), primarily those whose operational level had dropped to a point where they could no longer be sustained, were converted into sovkhozes. Consequently, the number of sovkhozes in 1959 rose to 226, while their area of cultivated land approached 1.94 million acres. Of this, 1.53 million acres were arable—17 per cent of all arable land in the country.[30] The conversion of insolvent kolkhozes into sovkhozes served the interests, at least in part, of both the Party and the peasants who had worked those kolkhozes. The Party advanced a step toward transforming collective farming into "a higher form of ownership by the people," i.e., into state farms. And the workers on the kolkhozes converted into sovkhozes, previously often left destitute after an entire year's work, now could be assured at least a certain amount of remuneration. Sovkhozes in Lithuania as well as in the entire Soviet Union are under the particular protection of the government and generously subsidized by it, yet their production has been no more remarkable than that of the kolkhozes. In the same year (1959), the sovkhozes owned 22.4 per cent of all livestock in the "social sector" (that is, all kolkhozes and all types of sovkhozes), while their production measured a mere 20.0 per cent of the livestock production of that sector. In the same year, for every 100 hectares (about 250 acres) of arable land, the sovkhozes owned farm machinery of 62.2 horsepower units, while the kolkhozes *together* with the MTS's had a total of only 44 horsepower units in machinery. By 1959, 90 per cent of all sovkhozes, as compared to only 24 per cent of all kolkhozes, had been provided with electricity. In 1958, the sovkhozes utilized 16 kilowatt hours of electricity for every 100 hectares of arable land; the ratio for collective farms was 9.7 kilowatt hours.

The liquidation of the MTS's can be looked upon as another advance in the direction of the "sovietization" of collective farms. The liquidation was carried out in Lithuania after it had been ordered by the Central Committee of the Soviet Communist Party in its plenary session of February, 1958, and by a decree of the Supreme Soviet of the U.S.S.R. on March 31 of that year. Until then, only sovkhozes had heavy farm machinery at their immediate disposition. Following the liquidation of the MTS's, the tractors and farm equipment previously maintained by these stations were sold to the kolkhozes. Incidentally, this allowed the state to make a rather profitable deal at the expense of the kolkhozes: by late 1958, the kolkhozes had already bought from MTS's being liquidated tractors and farm machinery worth 213.7 million rubles, while the total amount spent that year by collective farms in the purchase of technical equipment was 313 million rubles. This sum amounted to more than 22 per cent of the total kolkhoz income for that year, and was only slightly less than the amount received by the kolkhozes from the government in exchange for agrarian products.

Consequences of Collectivization. A direct consequence of collectivization was the catastrophic decline of agricultural production, from which even to this day the country has not yet fully recovered.[31] Here are some relevant statistics.

TABLE 3

Agricultural Produce Computed in Tons per Acre

	1939	*1950*	*1955*
Rye	.58	.32	.22
Wheat	.59	.33	.25
Summer wheat	.45	.32	.14
Barley	.53	.33	.19
Oats	.50	.32	.12
Sugar beets	8.44	5.89	1.39
Flax	.14	.09	.08

Source: P. Zundė, *Die Landwirtschaft Sowjetlitauens* (Marburg, 1962), p. 34.

TABLE 4

Number of Heads of Productive Livestock

	1939	*1951*	*1955*
Cattle (including dairy cattle)	1,288,840	731,000	925,000
	848,800	504,000	531,000
Hogs	1,068,000	723,000	978,000
Sheep	611,000	378,000	434,000
Horses	546,000	381,000	272,000

Source: P. Zundė, *op. cit.*, p. 44.

Poverty and privation became permanent in the lives of farmers forced into collective farms. Collective-farm members work for contemptibly low wages, and the exploitation of the individual as a source of labor power in collective farming has reached proportions that are unknown elsewhere. As late as 1958, the average annual wage of the collective farmer in Lithuania was about 68.40 rubles (new currency) and 452 kilograms of cereal grain. To set this in comparison with prevailing 1963 prices, a few examples are given here: 2.8 rubles for a kilogram of sausage, 0.83 rubles for a kilogram of sugar, 20.2 rubles for a man's sweater, 980 rubles for a motorcycle.

Since the earnings of the average collective farmer are insufficient to provide him with even the minimum of a modest livelihood, the actual sources of sustenance for collective farmers are the plots of land on the farmstead, which have been allocated for their private use, and the few domestic animals in their private possession—one or two cows, several pigs, sheep, fowl, etc. And perhaps nothing goes to characterize the sorry state of the Soviet agricultural system and its faults so well as the fact that the productivity of this so-called private sector (the farmyard plots and the livestock in the possession of the collective farmers and others) surpasses by far the entire social sector—both the kolkhozes and sovkhozes. Although only 5.8 per cent of all arable land is used for these private plots, the comparative weight of the most important livestock products in production in 1959 was 65.4 for the private sector and only 34.6 for the collective and state farms. In the same year, the collective farmers raised 72.4 per cent of the total annual potato crop on their private plots, 86 per cent of the total vegetable produce, and 80 per cent of the total fruit yield.[32] At the same time the kolkhozes and sovkhozes, availing themselves of the extremely cheap labor provided by their members and workers and having at their disposal all the agricultural equipment, in most instances failed to produce even the remaining part of that year's production above cost.

INDUSTRY

While the sovietization of agriculture continued for several years, control over the remaining areas of economic life was achieved almost immediately. The nationalization of industrial, commercial, and other enterprises was begun in the first days following the Soviet annexation of Lithuania in 1940 and was practically brought to completion in that same year. Again, this posed no problem to the Soviet regime after the end of the war, either.

Emphasis on Industrial Development. Moscow is greatly concerned with the development of industry in Lithuania and the other Baltic republics. Naturally, the Kremlin has its own reasons for this concern. According to Communist dogma, the industrial proletariat is the mainstay of the regime. As has been pointed out, before the Soviet occupation Lithuania was essentially an agricultural country. Therefore, the industrialization of Lithuania from the Moscow viewpoint is equivalent to its "communization." But this is not the sole advantage anticipated by Moscow in its efforts to industrialize Lithuania, as well as Latvia and Estonia. Indeed, there would be no ground for quarrel if the industrial expansion were undertaken with the general welfare of the country primarily in view. As it is, the guiding motives of Moscow in the industrialization of these countries are by no means identical with the true interests of the countries involved.

In the postwar period, industry was developed at a much faster rate in Lithuania, Latvia, and Estonia than in the Soviet Union. In 1959, according to Soviet statistics, the volume of industrial production in Lithuania was 9.1 times that of the 1940 volume, while the equivalent ratio for the Soviet Union was only 4.8.[33] No such concern was being shown for the industry of the other republics. Industrial production from 1940 to 1959 rose only 3.8 times in the Belorussian republic, only 3.4 times in the Ukraine, 4.5 times in Soviet Russia, 3.8 times in Uzbekistan, and so forth. The only republic whose rate of industrial growth approached that of the Baltic republics was Moldavia, which was occupied by the Soviet Union at about the same time as Lithuania. During the period referred to above, Moldavian industrial production increased 8.3 times.

True, there may be grounds for doubting the credibility of Soviet statistics, particularly in the area of industry. It has been claimed that Soviet statistics comparing Lithuanian industrial production of a later period with that of 1940 are misleading on purpose; they are based not on the entire industrial output for 1940, but on production computed beginning with the annexation of Lithuania in July of that year; in other words, only the last five or six months are represented. Whatever the case may be with comparisons making use of figures for the year 1940, there is sufficient other data at hand to indicate that the rate of industrialization in Lithuania after the war outstripped that of the Soviet Union as a whole. For example, some Soviet sources state that the average annual rate of the growth of industrial production in Lithuania in 1946–50 was 37 per cent, whereas the same rate for the Soviet Union as a whole was only 21.8 per cent. From 1951 to 1955, the extent of total industrial production in Lithuania was increasing at a rate of 21 per cent a year, while in the Soviet Union it was increasing only 13.1 per cent a year.[34]

Effect of Sovietization on the Nature of Industry. The following table shows the progressively shifting relative volume of types of industry in Lithuania during the period 1939–58, computed against the total industrial output.

TABLE 5

Effect of Sovietization on the Nature of Industry

Industry	Percentage Showing Relative Volume (at Price Rates in Effect During Given Year)			
	1939	*1950*	*1955*	*1958*
Energy production	3.3	3.2	1.9	1.6
Fuel	0.6	0.8	1.2	1.0
Machinery, equipment, and metal-processing	4.8	9.2	12.1	12.4
Building materials	1.8	2.3	3.6	4.1
Timber-processing	11.7	16.8	9.7	7.5
Light industry	22.8	25.8	31.1	29.0
Food industry	47.6	36.2	37.2	41.5
Others	7.3	5.7	3.2	2.9

Source: K. Meškauskas, *Tarybų Lietuvos Industrializavimas* (Vilnius, 1960), pp. 129–30.

The Communists have always attached supreme importance to the development of heavy industry, or more accurately, to the manufacture of the means of production. The data in the preceding table indicate that they followed this policy in Lithuania, too: the most rapid growth is shown by the machinery, equipment, and metal-processing industries. But these are precisely those branches of industry whose usefulness to the Lithuanian economy is rather questionable, for only a small portion of the machinery and equipment manufactured in Lithuania is intended for domestic use, the greater part being shipped to the

Soviet Union. Whether it be the turbine factory *Pergalė* in Kaunas, or the metal-processing plant *Žalgiris* in Naujoji Vilnia, or the electronics-tube plant in Panevėžys, or a similar factory, their products will be found throughout the Soviet Union, but rarely within Lithuania itself.

The exploitative character of Soviet industrial policy reveals itself even more clearly when the types of industry that were intentionally neglected and prevented from further development are considered. First to attract our attention is the lag in the production of electrical energy when compared with over-all industrial expansion. As reported by Soviet statistics, in 1956, total industrial production increased 17 per cent, while the production of electrical energy increased 14.4 per cent. In 1957, total industrial production saw a 23 per cent increase, while the increase in the production of electrical energy was 14 per cent. The following table gives a summary comparison of the rates of increase in total production and in the production of electrical energy, with the year 1940 taken as a base.

TABLE 6

Comparative Figures for the Growth of Total Industrial
Production and the Production of Electrical Energy

(1940 = 100)

	1945	*1950*	*1955*	*1956*	*1957*	*1958*	*1959*	*1960*	*1961*
Total industrial production	40.2	190.1	494.1	577.9	701	800	910	1,030	1,120
Production of electrical energy	29.2	184.2	478.3	532.5	605	709	810	937	1,080

Sources: K. Meškauskas, *op. cit.*, p. 153; *SSR v tsifrakh v 1961 godu* (Moscow, 1962), p. 150.

This comparative lag in the production of electrical energy indicates, in the first place, a disregard for the general economic interest of the country, which requires that the rate at which energy production is developed be strictly consistent with the rate of over-all economic development. In the second place, data given below on the comparative utilization of electricity in various areas of the economy show that those branches of Lithuanian economy which should have been fostered to the greatest extent, such as light industry and food-processing, suffered most in this respect.

TABLE 7

Comparative Utilization of Electrical Energy, 1950–55

(1950 = 100)

Consumer	1955
Industry	
Peat	357
Electrotechnical	1,543
Machinery production	497
Building materials	1,219
Timber and paper	243
Light industry	256
Food-processing	214
Polygraph industry	187
Localized and cooperative	271
Railways	215
Agriculture	248
Communal economy	213
Various other consumers	174
Percentage increase of total consumption, 1950–55	262

Source: K. Meškauskas, *op. cit.*, p. 159.

As will be seen from Table 7, the increase in the utilization of electrical energy in light industry, food-processing, timber production, polygraph industry, railway transport, agriculture, and communal concerns was considerably lower than the average of the total increase in utilization for the 1950–55 period.

A closer look at the types of industry whose development was either partially or even wholly neglected would show that this comparative neglect was especially designed for industry conducive to agricultural growth and industry with sufficiently abundant raw materials in Lithuania. The mineral fertilizer industry, for example, has remained undeveloped to this day, despite the continued serious shortage of fertilizer in the land. In the estimate of Lithuanian economists themselves, 2 to 2.5 million tons of mineral fertilizer would be required annually for the soil to produce profitable returns.[35] However, the actual amounts of mineral fertilizer utilized were about 0.25 million tons in 1954 and about 0.48 million tons in 1958. Moreover, this mineral fertilizer must be obtained from other parts of the Soviet Union, despite the fact that all the conditions necessary for its manufacture are present in Lithuania. Characteristically, even the single fertilizer plant in operation before the war, during the period of Lithuanian independence, was closed down.

While agriculture to a great extent still retains its relative importance in Lithuania's economic structure, the production of agricultural machinery, equipment, and implements has also been denied opportunities for development. A few small factories, such as *Ūkmašina* and *Komunaras* (the latter engaged in production of farm machinery until 1959, when it was converted for other types of production), could in no way meet the demands of the agriculture. For the most part, the required machinery and equipment are imported from the Soviet Union, but in inadequate numbers. With this in view, the President of the Academy of Sciences of the occupied republic, Professor J. Matulis, who was also a delegate of the Supreme Soviet of the U.S.S.R., during a session of that body in December, 1960, pleaded with the Moscow officials that the kolkhozes and sovkhozes in Lithuania be assigned additional agricultural machinery.[36] Again, despite a recently-built large cement plant, Lithuanian economists admit that the building-materials industry is still underdeveloped, even though Lithuania is an excellent source of raw materials for this industry.

Characteristic Features and Underlying Motives of Economic Policy in Lithuania. It has been seen that efforts at industrial development in Lithuania have been concentrated primarily on those types of industry whose raw materials, such as metals, etc., must be brought in from Russia, the Ukraine, or elsewhere, and whose products are not intended for the Lithuanian market. Completely undeveloped or only slightly encouraged were fields of industry convergent with the actual economic structure of Lithuania, industries for which there is an abundant natural supply of raw materials, and which are essential to the development of the indigenous economy of the country. Nonetheless, while pursuing on the one hand a policy adverse to the nature of Lithuanian economy, the Soviet regime in Lithuania exports agricultural products to the other republics—products natural to the country but denied provision for development. This is seen from the import and export figures of 1960 for premanufactured and raw materials in Lithuania (see p. 161).

To be noted in these statistics is the extremely large relative volume of food products in the general structure of Lithuanian export. As has been seen, the food industry in Lithuania is

TABLE 8

Industrial Import and Export in the 1960's

Industry	Import	Export
	(Percentage of Total Volume)	
Fuel industry	49.2	—
Metallurgy	4.1	19.1
Chemicals industry	12.6	—
Machinery	2.2	2.2
Timber and paper	16.3	12.3
Light industry	0.8	3.6
Food industry	2.4	35.6
Agricultural and feed	12.4	10.6
	100.0	100.0

Source: *Liaudies Ūkis* (Vilnius), No. 11 (1961), pp. 338–39.

treated by Moscow as one of its stepchildren; it is allocated relatively little capital outlay, it is the worst-supplied where means of production and power are concerned, yet food products rank first on the scale of exports. The same policy of exploitation is followed by Moscow regarding the building-materials industry. Despite the shortage of construction materials in Lithuania, nearly the entire productive output of the Akmenė cement factory is shipped off for use in construction outside Lithuania, for Akmenė cement is far superior to ordinary Soviet cement.

Certain new objectives are discernible in the Soviet economic program of recent years. In line with the intensified industrialization of Lithuania, giant industrial plants are being built, designed to serve the production demands of all three Baltic republics and probably the entire western portion of the Soviet Union as well. Worth mentioning among these new projects is the thermodynamic power plant at Vievis, whose first turbine was put in operation in December, 1962, and the second in November, 1963. This plant will be the largest of its kind in the whole Soviet Union and, when finished, will have a 1.2 million kilowatt capacity. It will provide electricity for Latvia, the Kaliningrad area, and Belorussia.[37] Another large-scale construction is under way at Kėdainiai, where a chemical-industry plant was to be completed by 1964 (construction is behind schedule). Since the plant will need more water than can be provided by the Nevėžis River, a canal has been built joining the Nevėžis with the Dubysa River. The plant will supply a large area of the

Western Soviet Union with sulphuric acid, mineral fertilizer, anhydrous cement, and similar products. It will process concentrated apatite from the Kola Peninsula and sulphur from the Ukraine.[38] In the nearby town of Jonava, a liquid-fertilizer factory is under construction. Chief among its products will be ammonic and nitrogenous fertilizer. This will be the first plant of its kind in the Soviet Union. For production it will use natural gas, conducted through mains into Lithuania from Dashava in the Ukraine. This factory, to be finished in 1964, is ranked among the most important projects under construction in the Soviet Union. It will provide liquid fertilizer for the Baltic republics, White Russia, the Ukraine, and part of Soviet Russia.[39]

Other important projects include a synthetic-textile factory in Kaunas; a food-vending machine plant in Marijampolė, which will employ 5,000 workers and engineers; a metal-working factory outside Kaunas; the refrigerator plant *Vienybė* in Ukmergė; a furniture factory in Vilnius, which will be the largest in Lithuania; a glass factory in Panevėžys; and a meat-processing plant in Klaipėda.[40]

It may well be that when these projects are completed, the economic demands of Lithuania will be met somewhat more adequately than before. It might even be possible to view these undertakings as suggestive of the post-Stalin concessions of sorts granted to the occupied countries, if it were not for one revealing circumstance. The economic program forced upon Lithuania by the Soviet regime at the present time is such that it cannot possibly be met by the existing labor resources in Lithuania and, therefore, it is dependent for its execution on labor imported from other republics within the Soviet Union. This will become apparent from an analysis of the labor demand and supply in Lithuania.

The natural population increase in Lithuania for the period 1950–58 averaged 1.07 per cent a year.[41] Let us assume that until 1980, the annual natural increase in population will be 1.1 per cent. In view of the fact that on January 5, 1959, the population of Lithuania numbered 2.711 million, in 1979, the population of Lithuania, as a result merely of natural population growth and not of immigration, would be about 3.37 million.* On the basis of this estimate, the Lithuanian population will have increased about 33,000 a year.

* The Soviet estimate is 3,400,000. See *Švyturys* (Vilnius), No. 22 (1961).

To what extent will this natural population growth result in an increase in the labor force? In order to estimate this increase, let us first assume that all persons between the ages of sixteen and sixty are a potential source of labor. In 1959, the persons within this age group numbered 1.615 million, or 59.5 per cent of the total population.[42] If in succeeding years this ratio were to remain constant—and in any case it cannot vary too greatly— then the said age group (persons from sixteen to sixty years of age) would increase annually by an average of 19,600 persons (33,000 × 0.595 = 19,600). Let this be designated the reserve of the potential labor supply created by the natural increase in population. In late 1959, there were 1,084,000 employed persons in Lithuania. Of this number, about 490,000 persons worked on collective farms, while 594,000 were employed in industry, the administrative occupations, sovkhozes, construction, transportation, the educational system, etc.[43] It would be reasonable to assume that the majority of persons employed were of the sixteen to sixty age group. The above number of employed persons constitutes about 67 per cent of the total number of persons in that age group. The remaining 33 per cent is made up of the unemployed or those unavailable for employment, such as housewives, the disabled, full-time students, and others.

Understandably, the 19,600 persons described earlier as the labor-force reserve from the natural annual population increase will not all enter the labor force, either. Here, too, it may be assumed that the ratio of those who will enter the labor force and those who will not will correspond approximately to the present ratio in this age group. It is to be expected, then, that only 67 per cent of the potential annual increase in the labor supply will actually enter the labor force. Thus, the actual increase in the number of employed persons is to be estimated at about 13,100 per year (19,600 × 0.67 = 13,100).

Furthermore, of those persons who are capable of, and available for, employment, not all are going to remain in Lithuania. As is well known, constant pressure is being brought upon the Lithuanian population to leave their country for work in various parts of the Soviet Union, chiefly in the cultivation of the virgin lands and work in the far north. Also, after completing military service requirements, some Lithuanians do not return to their native land. Even by a conservative estimate, these developments will deprive Lithuania of 2,100 employable persons annually. This, then, would leave the annual natural increase of the labor force in Lithuania at only 11,000. Thus, if the only resource of new labor supply in Lithuania were the natural population increase of the nation, then in 1980, the number of workers (including collective-farm employees) and professionals would be 1,304 million (1,084 million + [20 × 11,000] = 1,304 million).

Next to be considered is the prospective labor demand during the period before 1980. A possible indication of this can be found in the existing rate of increase in the Lithuanian labor force and the correlation of this increase with the demands of the economic program foisted by Moscow upon Lithuania. Soviet statistics give the following information (the rapid expansion of industry resulted, of course, in an increase in industrial employment, as is shown by Table 9).

Thus, the number of workers and professionals in all fields of employment, excluding collective farming, was increased annu-

TABLE 9

The Increase of Industrial Employment

	Total Number of Workers and Professionals (Excluding Kolkhozniks)	Number of Workers and Professionals Employed on Sovkhozes and Other Agricultural Institutions (Excluding Kolkhozes)	Number of Workers and Professionals Employed in Industry
1945	187,300	16,500	42,200
1950	338,300	34,500	88,400
1951	370,000	*	*
1952	405,000	*	*
1953	415,000	*	*
1954	467,300	*	137,800
1955	490,900	73,200	146,900
1956	526,500	75,400	160,800
1957	577,700	88,900	178,000
1958	593,800	87,000	185,000
1959	646,600	96,500	191,200
1960	675,000	*	*
1961	725,000	*	*
1965 (planned)	770,000	*	*
1975 (planned)	*	*	400,000–444,000

Sources: *Tarybų Lietuvos Dvidešimtmetis* (Vilnius, 1960), pp. 282–83; *20 Metų Tarybų Lietuvos Liaudies Ūkiui* (Vilnius, 1960), pp. 268, 308; *Tiesa*, January 25, 1961.

* No data available.

ally by an average of 30,200 between 1945 and 1950, 30,500 between 1951 and 1955, and 36,800 between 1956 and 1960. Of course, these figures include the employees of state farms and other agricultural institutions (the kolkhozes excepted). Deducting their increase from the total, we have an average annual increase in the labor force of 26,600 for 1945–50, 23,800 for 1951–55, and 31,000 for 1956–60.

The number of collective-farm employees decreased by about 20,000–30,000 in the 1951–58 period.[44] The obvious explanation is that in recent years, a great number of collective farms have been converted into state farms. If employment on the collective farms and state farms is considered jointly, it is seen to have risen by about 60,000 during this period.

At this point, let us plot the development of the labor-force demand during the next twenty years or so. We shall begin with agriculture. Soviet economists claim that the agricultural labor force will diminish considerably during the next few years, but that agricultural production by 1980 will triple in volume.[45] This increase in production will be achieved not through increased agricultural employment, but by means of greater efficiency and growth in returns. Let us concede that, owing to mechanization and systematization of the agricultural occupation, the forecast increase in production will actually take place without an increase in agricultural employment. However, it is hardly possible to assume that this increase in production will be accompanied by a reduction in the agricultural labor force. Even at present, there is a severe shortage of labor in agriculture. During the harvest period, both manual and professional workers are transported from the cities to kolkhozes and sovkhozes to aid farm laborers who are too shorthanded to bring in the crops themselves. Therefore, it must be allowed that the size of agricultural employment will remain constant during the next ten to twenty years and that the entire natural increase in the labor force, which was earlier estimated, will be utilized in filling the employment needs of industry and other economic enterprises of the nation.

How large will the labor demand be in other economic fields, exclusive of agriculture? The following table is an attempted estimate, based on the average annual increase in the different fields of employment for the 1950–59 period, of the annual increase in the number of manual and professional workers during the period 1960–79.

It must be kept in mind that the estimated increase in the

TABLE 10

Average Annual Increase of Manual and Professional Employment
in Lithuania

	1950–59	*Estimated Increase During 1960–79*
Industry	11,400	15,600
Construction	5,200	6,000
Timber production	*	*
Railways	260	*
Shipping and maritime	*	*
Transportation and highway construction	2,260	2,000
Communications	220	200
Retail sales, deliveries to the state, supplies to factories, distribution	1,120	1,000
General nutrition	500	500
Education (schools and educational and cultural-educational institutions)	2,510	2,000
Science and scientific research institutions, geological research organizations, hydro-meteorological services	780	780
Health-service institutions	2,230	2,000
Credit and insurance units	*	*
Governmental, economic, and social organizational management	990	*
Other fields (capital repair, agricultural servicing, veterinary medicine, housing and communal services, press editing, publishing)	2,450	2,400
Total	27,940	32,480

Sources: For 1950–59, *Tarybų Lietuvos Dvidešimtmetis*, pp. 282–83; for 1960–79, cf. *20 Metų Tarybų Lietuvos Liaudies Ūkiui*, p. 308. The Soviets claim that in 1975 the number of industrial workers and employees in Lithuania will reach 444,000. This corresponds to the estimated annual average increase.
* No data available.

industrial labor force which is almost 50 per cent of the total estimated increase in the labor force, is based on predictions made by Soviet experts themselves. My estimate of the labor-force increases in other fields was made by taking the economic structure of each field as a basis and then plotting its course of development. For example, the Soviet regime is planning a large-scale expansion of the building industry and in 1960–79, hopes to erect many more residential and industrial buildings than during the 1950–59 period. For this reason, the estimated annual increase in the labor force during 1960–79 is somewhat higher than the annual increase during 1950–59. A summary of the figures shows that before 1980, the labor demand will be increasing by an average of 32,500 persons per year, while for the same period the natural increase in labor supply will be only about 11,000 persons per year. It would seem that the shortage of 21,500 workers each year will have to be filled from somewhere else. Since the labor situation in both of the other Baltic republics, Latvia and Estonia, is much the same or even worse than in Lithuania, there is no reason to believe that the labor force needed in Lithuania will be provided by these countries. Therefore, the only solution is the migration of laborers into Lithuania from other republics of the Soviet Union, in particular from Soviet Russia. It is, then, a very real prospect that until 1980, the government in Moscow will undertake to transfer and settle in Lithuania about 430,000 workers and professionals (21,500 $\times$ 20 = 430,000), most of whom will be Russian.

Naturally, this mass influx of foreign elements into Lithuania will cause significant changes in its national structure and conceptual climate. Obviously, the migration will bring not only single individuals, but workers and professionals with families and dependents. If, even on a low estimate, it is assumed that for every two employable immigrants there will be an additional family member who is unemployed or incapable of employment, then by 1980, the number of Russian and other non-Lithuanian settlers in Lithuania will have reached a total of 645,000. If this were to happen, the percentage of Lithuanians in the country would be reduced from 79.3 (1959) to about 66.3 by 1980. The effects of this on Lithuanian national culture would be even more disastrous than one can judge from these dry figures. A new influx of Russians into Lithuania would hasten the already intensive program of Russification. In effect, the time would not be far off when Lithuanians would be only a minority in their own country.

The above estimates have been made on the assumption that the industrialization of Lithuania will proceed at about the same rate as before 1960. This seems a well-founded assumption, and it is very likely that eventually the industrialization will be pushed ahead even more rapidly. With increasing vigor, Moscow is speeding up the industrialization of Lithuania and the other Baltic republics. By 1980, 700 new plants and factories are to be built in Lithuania.[46] It is asserted that in 1965 Lithuania will produce about 40 per cent of the Soviet Union's total production of precision metal frames.[47] The machine-drill factory in Vilnius will be expanded to become the largest of its kind in Europe. In general, an unparalleled expansion of the metal, machinery, and electrotechnical industries in Lithuania is to take place in the future. These are fields of industry that require comparatively little raw materials but a vast supply of qualified labor. What motives could be prompting Moscow to force these industrialization plans upon Lithuania? What are the economic or political considerations behind these plans?

With the exception of raw materials for the food, construction, and other light industries, Lithuania has no natural resources. Lithuania is unsuited for the development of metal, machinery, or other types of industry. As pointed out earlier, there also can be no question of an overabundant labor supply. Could it be said, then, that the geographical position of Lithuania is advantageous to industrialization at such a fast rate, if only from the standpoint of accessibility and transport facilities? Admittedly, Lithuania's geographical location is excellent in this respect, as a glance at a map will readily show. But from this point of view, the situation of those areas of Soviet Russia and Belorussia which border on the Baltic republics is no less suitable than that of Vilnius and Kaunas, the chief Lithuanian industrial centers. Moreover, the Russian and Belorussian areas have an added advantage: a much greater industrial labor reserve than is found in Lithuania, as is shown by the distribution of rural and urban population (see Table 11).

Thus it must be concluded that economic considerations play

TABLE 11

Urban and Rural Population in the Baltic Area
(Percentage of the Total Population)

	Urban	Rural
Lithuania	39	61
Latvia	56	44
Estonia	56	44
Pskov area (R.S.F.S.R.)	27	73
Vitebsk area	32	68
Gardinas (Grodna) area	23	77

Source: *Narodnoe khoziaistvo SSR v 1959 godu* (Moscow, 1960), pp. 27–33.

no part in Moscow's determination to industrialize Lithuania at a rate of speed out of all proportion to Lithuanian labor resources. The only inference to be drawn, then, is that the motives of Moscow are of a purely political nature. By its haste to industrialize Lithuania, Moscow aims to unite Lithuania permanently to the Russian sphere in an economic union and to colonize Lithuania demographically—in short, to Russify and assimilate it. These efforts are conducted under the pretext of improving the national economy, in order to escape giving the appearance of straightforward colonization.

Theoretically, the responsibility for Moscow's program of industrialization and simultaneous colonization would seem to lie with the Lithuanian Communist Party and the Soviet Government in Lithuania. It may be that motives of national security also played some role in these policies. Doubtless, Moscow is still mindful of the revolt against its rule during the first days of the Soviet-German war in 1941, which caused the Soviet front to break easily at that point and forced the Communists to flee headlong from the Baltic states. After the war, the mass deportations of Lithuanians were, of course, preventive measures against the recurrence of any similar threat in a case of eventual war. At this time, however, such measures of constraint in the hands of the Kremlin rulers are not nearly so expedient.

It is reasonable to expect that in Lithuania, perceptive individuals anticipate the direction of Moscow's policies and recognize its real objectives. This recognition, in time, may produce opposition, if the people should find their national existence threatened. Then the efforts to industrialize occupied Lithuania could bear fruit very different from that anticipated by Moscow.

8. Sovietized Education in Occupied Lithuania

VYTAUTAS VAITIEKŪNAS

The Soviet occupation of Lithuania did not only interrupt the exercise of Lithuanian sovereignty but also, to use the Soviet jargon, brought with it "a reorganization of the whole Lithuanian life" and "a cultural revolution."[1] This cultural revolution first affected the system of education—its administration, organization, and its ideology.

ALIGNMENT WITH THE SOVIET ADMINISTRATION SYSTEM

In independent Lithuania, all educational institutions except agriculture, forestry, police, and military schools were administered by the Ministry of Education in Kaunas. When the Red Army occupied Lithuania in 1940, however, Lithuania's educational system was incorporated into the highly centralized Soviet system directed from Moscow. Despite changes in the names of administrative institutions and in their internal relationships and jurisdictions, this basic centralism has remained.

Until the 1959–60 school year, the Lithuanian higher and specialized secondary schools were under the direct jurisdiction of the Kremlin. In 1959, it was decreed that such schools pass from All-Union to republic responsibility. The Council of Ministers of the occupied republic established a Committee on Higher and Specialized Secondary Education and gave it control of ten higher and sixty-nine specialized secondary schools.[2] The Committee consists of representatives of the Economic Council, the Ministry of Education, the Ministry of Culture, the Ministry of Health, the Ministry of Agriculture, and the University of Vilnius.[3] The administrative structure in 1962 is depicted in Chart A.

CHART A

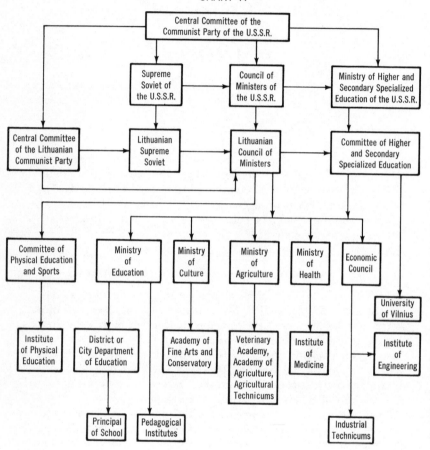

ALIGNMENT WITH THE SOVIET SCHOOL STRUCTURE

General Education. During 1940, the first year of occupation, only state schools were left open. All private schools, whether maintained by organizations, religious communities, or private individuals, were taken over by the government. Furthermore, the program in nontechnical schools was reduced. The six-year program of primary schools in independent Lithuania was reduced to four years. The Kremlin ruled that beginning with the 1940–41 school year, students would be admitted to secondary schools after four years of primary schooling. In this way, the educational program in general schools was reduced from thirteen years (six primary and seven secondary) to eleven.[4] Chart B depicts this situation; generally, such school organization survived until Khrushchev's reform in 1958.

Beginning with the 1956–57 school year, a new type of general school was established: the boarding school or *internat*. "The Communist system of peoples' education is based on the civic education of children," the Party program of 1961 declared.[5] In practice, this system eliminates parental educational influence and substitutes for it a total Party monopoly. It was discovered that boarding schools are best suited to maintain this monopoly. "*Internats* are educational institutions that increase the role of the state (i.e., Party) in the education of children," leaders of Soviet education declare.[6] Such schools provide much more than simply room and board. Their main task is to train Communist-indoctrinated technicians with the help of a "planned daily routine," directed and supervised by reliable educators.[7] The Kremlin considers these institutions "a prototype of Communist schools and the mass school of the future."[8] The Twenty-first Congress (January 27–February 4, 1959) of the Communist Party of the Soviet Union urged the establishment of such boarding schools as the best suited to accomplish the "tasks of preparing educated builders of Communism."[9] The Central Committee of the Party and Council of Ministers responded with a joint decree in June, 1959, which compelled administrators at all levels rapidly to increase the number of boarding schools.[10] In Lithuania, in the 1956–57 school year, there were only 3 such schools, with 760 students,[11] while in 1961–62, there were 41, with 9,500 pupils, and in 1962–63, 45 schools, with 12,700 students.[12]

Besides *internats,* Lithuania has numerous schools that main-

CHART B

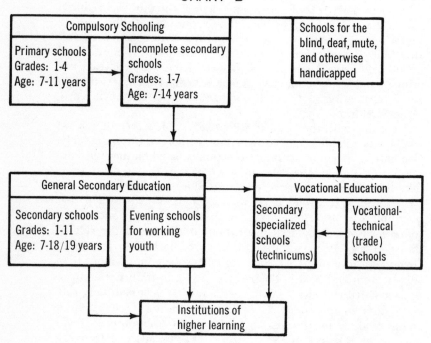

Compulsory Schooling		Schools for the blind, deaf, mute, and otherwise handicapped
Primary schools Grades: 1-4 Age: 7-11 years	Incomplete secondary schools Grades: 1-7 Age: 7-14 years	

General Secondary Education	
Secondary schools Grades: 1-11 Age: 7-18/19 years	Evening schools for working youth

Vocational Education	
Secondary specialized schools (technicums)	Vocational-technical (trade) schools

Institutions of higher learning

tain dormitories. In the 1960–61 school year, "some 17,000 students resided in the republic's 525 dormitories."[13]

The "extended day" school is another type now common but formerly unknown. In such schools, students from grades one to eight stay for several hours after attending their regular daily classes. Students in such schools are usually from homes in which both parents work and the children are too young to take care of themselves after school. In 1962–63, 23,000 students took advantage of such arrangements in 384 schools.[14]

Still another type of educational institution is the evening school. During World War II, the Kremlin drafted school-age youth to work in factories and on farms. To provide them with some sort of opportunity for study, the Soviet Government, in 1943, introduced evening schools for factory workers, and, in 1944, for workers on collective farms.[15] After the war, such schools were introduced in reoccupied Lithuania, and by 1956–57, there were 215; of these, 123 were operated for factory youths and 92 for the kolkhozniks. In the 1959–60 school year, the number of evening schools in rural areas dwindled to 50.[16] Generally, the number of such schools dropped to 127 in 1962.

After the introduction of Khrushchev's educational reform, correspondence schools of general education were established. Eight of these were in operation during the 1959–60 school year, and twelve in 1962–63.[17]

Secondary Specialized Schools. The sovietized economy of Lithuania required the teaching of a great number of specialties that the free-enterprise economy of independent Lithuania either did not need or did without aid from the state. The result of these needs of sovietized economy was the proliferation of specialized schools (technicums). Schools were established for the training not only of statisticians, budget clerks, personnel for state-banks, but also for waiters and cooks. Also, secondary schools were created to train medical assistants, midwives, pharmacist assistants. In independent Lithuania, these occupations were dying out as more highly trained specialists replaced these vocational trainees. On the other hand, while training in these specialties has been expanded, there has been a drastic decline in home economics courses. There were thirty schools of home economics in independent Lithuania;[18] by 1961–62, this specialization was offered by only one agricultural technicum.[19] The decline is an indirect result of forced collectivization. When a collective farmer's private plot is limited to one and one-half acres and his staple food is bread and potatoes, home economics becomes superfluous. Besides, the Kremlin has little interest in this field, for it serves personal, not Party, interests.

In Lithuania, as elsewhere in the U.S.S.R., students are admitted to secondary specialized schools on graduation from incomplete or complete secondary schools of general education. In the technicums, students without secondary-school diplomas as a rule study two years longer than those with diplomas. For example, students in the agricultural technicums with complete secondary schooling study for two years, those with incomplete schooling, four years. In general, the various technicum programs differ greatly. For example, store clerks, waiters, movie technicians, lathe operators, circular-saw operators, get ten to twelve months of training; locksmiths and machine repairmen, up to eighteen months; cooks and cement layers, two years; commodity experts, three years; students in technicums of applied art, five years.

Institutions of Higher Education. During the Czarist occupation (1795–1915), there were no institutions of higher education in Lithuania. The Vilnius University, founded in 1579, was closed in 1832. In independent Lithuania in 1939–40, there were two universities, a veterinary academy, an academy of agriculture, a conservatory, an academy of art, a pedagogical institute, a school of business administration and commerce, and a military academy. On July 16, 1940, the theological-philosophical faculty of Kaunas University was closed. The beginning of the 1940–41 school year saw the closing of the school of business administration and commerce, and the military academy. In 1951, Kaunas University was reorganized into a polytechnical institute. According to Soviet sources, in 1961–62 there was one university (Vilnius), one polytechnic institute, one medical institute, three pedagogical institutes, one art institute, one institute of physical education, one conservatory, one academy of agriculture, and one school of veterinary medicine.*

* Vilnius University has seven faculties (schools or departments): history-philology, political economy, law, physics-mathematics, chemistry, biology, and medicine. All faculties offer courses in physical education and military training. In all departments, the first state examinations are in the history of the CPSU.

The Kaunas Polytechnical (Engineering) Institute, established in 1951, has

All students in Lithuania are required to take courses in the history of the CPSU, political economy, or historical and dialectical materialism. On entering any institution of higher learning the student must present a variety of credentials: (1) a secondary-school diploma, (2) a biography, (3) a character evaluation by the Communist Party, Communist Youth, or other appropriate organization, (4) a certificate from his place of work, (5) a health certificate, (6) a birth certificate, (7) a certificate of military service (men), and (8) three to five photographs. Candidates take entrance examinations and are accepted competitively, except those sent by institutions or factories, who are accepted if they pass the examinations. Full-time students receiving a B in their entrance examinations are given scholarships.[20] Usually, a full-time candidate must be less than thirty-five years old, but there is no age limit for correspondence-school students.

Correspondence Courses and Evening Schools. In independent Lithuania, correspondence courses were organized only by private initiative and were limited to a general secondary education and foreign languages. In occupied Lithuania, such courses are offered by specialized secondary- and higher-education institutions. In the 1961–62 school year, all the institutions of higher education and 55.5 per cent of specialized secondary schools of-

five departments: electrotechnics, hydrotechnics, mechanics, construction, and technology. Two new faculties are planned. Common departments are those of industrial economics, physical education, and Russian and other foreign languages. The Institute has three extension centers.

The Medical Institute, founded in 1951, has three departments: medicine, dentistry, and pharmacy.

One pedagogical institute trains teachers for primary and pre-primary institutions; another for incomplete and complete secondary schools; and the third for schools conducted in languages other than Lithuanian.

The Institute of Art offers courses in painting, graphic arts, sculpture, ceramics, glass blowing, fashion and industrial design, urban planning, art education, and art theory and history. It has an extension center in Kaunas.

Independent Lithuania's Institute for Physical Education has been re-established and trains instructors for schools and sports organizations.

The Kaunas conservatory has been transferred to Vilnius and now has three departments: composition, performing arts, and theater. The performing arts faculty has classes in piano-organ, choral conducting, orchestra, voice. The theater faculty prepares film actors.

The Academy of Agriculture has been moved from Dotnuva to Kaunas. It has six departments: agronomy, agricultural economics and organization, agricultural mechanization, land surveying, land reclamation, and forestry.

The Academy of Veterinary Medicine, in Kaunas, has two departments: veterinary medicine and zootechnics.

fered correspondence programs; 22.8 per cent of the students enrolled in these institutions were correspondence students.[21] Examinations for correspondence students are scheduled throughout the school year, so that students of various specializations can take the necessary time off without inconvenience to their employers. Twenty-three so-called consultative centers have been established, where correspondence students "can get their most difficult problems explained . . . pass examinations, work in laboratories."[22] Since the 1959–60 school year, employers have had to give correspondence students additional paid vacations for study purposes. These vacations are given according to the following schedule: (1) freshmen and sophomores, for laboratory work and examinations—thirty days; juniors and seniors—forty days, (2) for state examinations—thirty days, (3) for diploma essays, students in specialized secondary schools—two months; students in institutions of higher education—four months. Furthermore, once each school year, employers have to pay half the expenses of a trip to the school for purposes of laboratory work or examinations.[23]

Evening schools have been set up within the schools offering correspondence courses. In 1961–62, 18.6 per cent of all students in specialized secondary schools and institutions of higher education were evening students.[24] Since the 1959–60 school year, employers have had to give evening students additional paid vacations. Freshmen and sophomores in institutions of higher education receive twenty days for laboratory work and examinations. Students in specialized secondary schools are given ten days. Juniors and seniors in institutions of higher education receive thirty days; in specialized secondary schools, twenty days. Students are also allowed time for state examinations and for diploma essays: students in institutions of higher education receive four months; students in secondary specialized schools, two months.[25]

AIMS OF SOVIETIZED SCHOOLS

Article 78 of the constitution of independent Lithuania held that the "education of children is the highest right of parents." The Communists deny this right. Soviet schools are founded on the Communist educational monopoly. The Party program asserts that "in the area of people's education, the Communist Party's main purpose is to complete the work of the October, 1917, revolution, transforming the school into an instrument of Communist education."[26]

The schools of occupied Lithuania have become such an instrument. The by-laws governing secondary schools of general education state that their aim is "to train Communistically educated people."[27] The guidelines to this goal are polytechnism, collectivism, a materialistic world view, atheistic and antireligious ideas, proletarian internationalism, Socialist patriotism, the friendship of Soviet peoples, love of the Socialist motherland, hate for the Kremlin's enemies, and Communist *printsipial'nost'*.[28]

Soviet polytechnism means the education of craftsmen and technicians for the Soviet economy, especially for the developing industry. Soviet collectivism implies the subordination of the individual's rights, aims, interests, convictions, and outlook to the decisions and directives of the Communist Party, the glorification and sanctification of Communist society, the justification of even the most extreme actions taken by the Party in the name of its goals.[29]

Soviet atheism is remarkable for its aggressiveness and intolerance of other ideologies and has become the official "religion" of the U.S.S.R. As such, it is supported and propagated with all the powers of a totalitarian state. The Soviet school is in turn the "church" of this new "religion." The Party demands that "children be trained atheistically in kindergarten"[30] and that "every teacher, whatever he teaches—literature or mathematics, natural science or music—must consider the Communist education of students a matter of honor"; this means that the teacher must "foster the students' materialistic world view and educate our youth as real atheists."[31] To make certain that all teachers propagate atheism, school administrators organize "scientific-methodological conferences on questions of atheistic education"; teachers must also attend "teachers' evenings on questions of atheistic work."[32]

But the duties of teachers do not end in the classroom. The Party demands that teachers organize "young atheists' circles," which aim "to propagate atheistic thought as extensively as possible among students and the society," to publish so-called *stengazetas* (wall newspapers) with an atheistic content, to visit atheistic museums, to organize theatrical programs furthering atheistic views. Teachers must also organize so-called atheistic seminars— weekend lectures on atheism. Another of their duties is to make use of special-interest clubs—in such subjects as folklore, literature, or natural sciences—for atheistic indoctrination. Students at the Vilnius Institute of Art must prepare special atheistic shows where only antireligious works are exhibited.[33]

Proletarian internationalism differs from the usual internationalism in that the latter signifies a principle of international cooperation for the common good, while the former implies the subordination of the interests of one's own nation and country to those of the Kremlin. Proletarian internationalism is the opposite of proletarian nationalism or national Communism, such as that of Yugoslavia, Albania, or China. Since the people of the constituent republics of the U.S.S.R. favor national Communism more than those of the satellites, who enjoy greater independence, the Soviet School is of particular interest to the Kremlin as an instrument for inoculating the younger generation with proletarian internationalism, i.e., Russian nationalism. The Kremlin's efforts sometimes become grotesque: Lithuania's youth are being told that Soviet man "sucks in the ideas of proletarian internationalism with his mother's milk."[34]

"Socialist patriotism," the twin of "proletarian internationalism," inculcates loyalty to the Kremlin alone, in contrast to the usual patriotism or loyalty to one's own nation. A "Socialist patriot" proclaims that Lithuania's occupation is liberation; economic exploitation, the "elder brother's" noble assistance; the destruction of Lithuanian national individuality, the progress of Communist culture.

The "friendship of Soviet peoples" is a device for subordinating all nations to the Russians and ensuring that the leading and deciding role be left exclusively for Russia (the Russian republic). To emphasize this Russian primacy, Russia is officially labeled the "elder brother."[35] Under the slogan of this type of "friendship," the youth are taught to understand that their fatherland is not ancestral Lithuania but the entire Russian-ruled Soviet Union.

In fact, all these "values" are merely aspects of the main "value" —Russification. To this end, the schools of occupied Lithuania use all available means. First of all, of course, Russian-language teaching begins in the second grade. The administrators of Lithuanian education admit that "from the first days, the Soviet school has given its main attention to the Russian language."[36] Like atheism, all subjects are used for Russification, especially classes in the history and geography of the U.S.S.R. Even the examples in drafting are exclusively Russian: Moscow's squares, the stars on the Kremlin, and the like.[37]

The curriculums of universities and the specialized secondary schools are filled with Russian subjects. For example, in the University of Vilnius, students specializing in Lithuanian language and literature must take 724 class hours in Russian subjects, i.e., 18.4 per cent of all classroom time. The following table shows the extent of Russification and Communist indoctrination.

TABLE 1

Required Subjects and Hours for Students Specializing in Journalism
at the University of Vilnius in 1957

	Hours		
Subject	*Theory*	*Practice*	*Term*
History of the CPSU	144	80	1, 2, 3, 4
Political economy	100	40	5, 6, 7, 8
Dialectical and historical materialism	80	60	6, 7, 8
History of philosophy	70	—	9
Modern history	84	—	6, 7
Logic	44	26	1
Basic introduction to linguistics	60	8	1, 2
Contemporary literary Lithuanian	108	200	1, 2, 3, 4
Russian language	—	270	1, 2, 3, 4, 5
Lithuanian stylistics	32	88	4, 5, 6
Literary theory	68	32	1, 2
History of Lithuanian literature	220	44	2, 3, 4, 5, 6, 7
History of Russian literature	220	44	2, 3, 4, 5, 6, 7
History of art	72	48	7, 8
Literary history of Soviet nations	100	—	8, 9
Foreign literary history	270	—	1, 2, 3, 4
History of journalism	114	16	3, 4, 5, 6
Marxist-Leninist esthetics	48	—	6
History of the Soviet Party press	114	36	5, 6, 7, 8
Theory and practice of the Soviet Party press	116	208	3, 4, 5, 6, 7, 8, 9
Technology of polygraphic production	36	32	3, 4
History of the foreign Party and workers' press	96	—	8, 9
Electives	130	100	7, 8, 9
Physical education	—	136	1, 2, 3, 4

Source: *Vilniaus Universiteto Žinynas* (Vilnius, 1957), p. 31.

Equally important instruments of Russification are Russian lecturers and students. Russian sources do not give statistics on the number of Russian lecturers in Lithuanian schools. In the 1956–57 school year, or immediately after the Twentieth Congress of the Party, and hence during de-Stalinization, 73.3 per cent of the lecturers in the University of Vilnius were Lithuanians.[38] In 1962, we have reason to believe, the percentage was smaller, since in 1958 "Stalinization" was reintroduced into Lithuanian education and in the 1959–60 school year, many Lithuanian lecturers were purged because of a lack of proletarian internationalism.[39] The same sources are also silent as to the number of Russian students in Lithuanian schools. But it is known, for example, that some of the courses in six specialized secondary schools are offered only in Russian, thirty schools teach in both languages, and one in Russian and Polish.[40] It is also known that schools of higher education have separate groups of Russian students with Russian as the language of instruction.[41] Quite obviously, the schools of occupied Lithuania are being transformed into bilingual institutions. In 1961, some American Lithuanian tourists found that large groups of Russians, sometimes up to 300 persons, were "imported" from Russia to Lithuanian specialized secondary schools, as well as to institutions of higher learning.[42] The effects of such "imports" on Russification should not be minimized.*

The Kremlin demands that Russification be carried on not only in the classroom, but also in outside activities. Teachers must encourage correspondence, and camping and hiking with Russian students; they must organize joint exhibitions, joint "friendship weeks," joint "brotherhood of peoples" evenings, as well as social gatherings with Soviet Army units. Student publications, libraries, and films must also serve the cause of Russification.

Among the "values" fostered by sovietized schools, Communist *printsipial'nost'* occupies an important place. The word, which has no English equivalent, means a mental habit of referring every matter, however trivial, to abstract Communist principles.

THE THREEFOLD PURGES

The sovietization of Lithuanian schools was followed by a threefold purge: of teachers, subjects taught, and materials used (textbooks, maps, etc.).

* In the past decade, the percentage of non-Lithuanian students in schools of higher learning has increased noticeably. In 1957, for example, the student body of Vilnius University was 76.3 per cent Lithuanian (*Vilniaus Universiteto Zinynas 1957* [Vilnius, 1958], p. 102). Five years later, this percentage dropped to 62.7 per cent in all schools of higher education (*Narodnoe khoziaistvo SSSR v 1962 godu* [Moscow, 1963], p. 573). According to this latter source, in 1962, Lithuanian students constituted only 61.4 per cent of the total student population in secondary specialized schools. It is also worthwhile noting that as a result of continued Russification, Lithuania's schools of higher learning—with the exception of the Institute of Medicine in Kaunas—have been practically deprived of the right to confer doctorates. Even in the fields of Lithuanian language and history, doctoral candidates have to write and defend their dissertations in the schools of Moscow or Leningrad.

Teachers. The purge of the teachers was extremely radical. Its extent is shown by Soviet statistics concerning the training of teachers, as well as the length of their service in Lithuania's schools of general education. Statistics of 1956 are used because more recent data have not been published.

TABLE 2

Training of Lithuanian Teachers

Grades	Number of Teachers	Higher (pedagogical Institute, University)		Specialized secondary (teachers' institutes)		General secondary		Incomplete General Secondary	
		Number	Percentage	Number	Percentage	Number	Percentage	Number	Percentage
1–4	5,710	17	0.3	108	1.9	5,714	90.6	411	7.2
5–7	7,430	684	9.2	2,430	32.7	4,257	57.3	59	0.8
8–11	2,946	1,385	47.0	943	32.0	612	20.8	6	0.2
Total	16,086	2,086	13.0	3,481	21.6	10,583	62.4	476	3.0

Source: *Kulturnoe stroitelstvo SSSR* (Moscow, 1956), p. 183.

Two facts are noteworthy in this table: (1) Ten years after the war only 13 per cent of teachers in Lithuanian schools of general education had higher education; and (2) 62.4 per cent had only general secondary, and sometimes only an incomplete general secondary education. In this respect, occupied Lithuania ranked with the lowest Soviet republics. Even the Tadzhik republic had a better percentage of teachers with higher education: 13.8 per cent.[43] The situation is even more striking if we note that in the 1939–40 school year, there were 8,417 qualified teachers working in Lithuanian schools.[44] After nearly twelve years of Soviet occupation, there were only 5,507 teachers with pedagogical training and 70–80 per cent of these were "made in Soviet-occupied Lithuania."

Table 3 shows that after some twelve years of Soviet occupation only 5.5 per cent of teachers were holdovers from independent Lithuania, if we assume that none of those with twenty-five years of service are Russian imports. Soviet statistics give the data for those with five to twenty-five years of service as one total and thus tend to hide the point, but if we note that ten years after the war, 41.4 per cent did not have more than five years of service and that only 5.5 per cent had more than twenty-five, we can draw con-

TABLE 3

Length of Service of Lithuanian Teachers

Grades	Number of Teachers	Length of Service					
		Less than Five Years		Between Five and Twenty-five Years		More than Twenty-five Years	
		Number	Percentage	Number	Percentage	Number	Percentage
1–4	5,710	2,000	35.0	3,259	57.1	451	7.9
5–7	7,430	3,485	46.9	3,693	49.7	252	3.4
8–11	2,946	1,167	39.6	1,596	54.2	183	6.2
Total	16,086	6,652	41.4	8,548	53.1	886	5.5

Source: *Kulturnoe stroitelstvo SSSR*, p. 183.

clusions concerning holdovers from independent Lithuania in the remaining 53.1 per cent. Their percentage is very small.

Subjects taught. Subject matter has been purged as thoroughly as the teachers teaching it. In the past as well as today, a six-day school week and a school year comprising from thirty-four to thirty-six weeks were and are in effect. In independent Lithuania, during six years of primary and seven years of secondary schooling, boys had to complete 13,736 classroom hours, and girls, 13,804. At the present time, there are 11,271 classroom hours during four years of primary and seven years of secondary schooling.

The purge of the curriculum is illustrated by the following table comparing curriculums of schools of general education in independent and in occupied Lithuania (see pp. 186–87).

The data of Table 4 show that in 1958–59, sovietized Lithuanian schools had 72.5 fewer total weekly hours for boys, and 74.5 fewer for girls. Latin, social studies, and religion classes were eliminated. Local history and geography were replaced by an additional 9.5 total weekly hours of the native language. Psychology was substituted for the introductory course in philosophy. The number of class hours in history, geography, physical education, drawing-drafting, singing-music, and handicrafts was decreased. Russian was made the first foreign language and instruction in it has been increased by 13 total weekly hours. The second foreign language has been increased by 3 weekly hours, and mathematics by 3.5. Added to the program were 6 weekly hours of shop work and 7 of practice in agriculture and electrical engineering, as well as familiarization with the principles of machine operation. The last two subjects represent the so-called "polytechnic profile" of schooling.

On the other hand, if we compare the present total hours per week in schools of occupied Lithuania with those of Russian schools in 1957–58 (the *desitiletka*), we find that for certain subjects the Lithuanian eleven-year school has fewer total hours per week than the ten-year Russian schools had. This is true of classes in the native language, which has 10 fewer hours per week; geography, 1; biology, 1; physics, 1.5; chemistry, 2.5. However, the number of hours was increased for the following subjects: mathematics, .5 hours per week; physical education, 5.5; singing, 3; drawing-drafting, 1; practice in agriculture, 1; foreign languages, 42. Because of the addition of the Russian language, certain other subjects have fewer hours devoted to them in Lithuanian schools than in Russian. This situation did not change much after the Khrushchev school reforms in 1958 and 1964.

Textbooks. No textbook, even if still pertinent, used in independent Lithuania is in use now. New textbooks in Lithuanian language, geography, and history textbooks were adapted, while the rest are translations of appropriate Russian textbooks. All the examples—problems in arithmetic, trigonometry, algebra, exercises in biology, physics, astronomy, drafting—are exclusively Russian. The primacy of the "elder brother" and Communist propaganda are also found in all the textbooks on Lithuanian linguistics. For example, the Lithuanian language text for the third grade has 224 exercises, and sentences like the following are used as illustrations: "The U.S.S.R. is our motherland"; "All the peoples of the Soviet Union are helped by the great Russian people"; "What do the warmongers want? They wish to enslave freedom-loving nations"; "Forward to the triumph of Communism"; "The children of workers in capitalist lands live very miserably"; "It's good for children to live in the land of the Soviets"; "Lenin has shown us the road to freedom and happiness"; "The capital of our motherland is Moscow."[45]

The sovietization of Lithuanian history and geography textbooks presented greater problems. They were published in 1957, during de-Stalinization. The geography text aims to denigrate Lithuania's independence and paints a glowing picture of occupied Lithuania. However, the very teaching of Lithuanian geography

TABLE 4 Comparisons of Curriculums in Schools of

Subject	1st Grade IL	1st Grade OL	2nd Grade IL	2nd Grade OL	3rd Grade IL	3rd Grade OL	4th Grade IL	4th Grade OL	5th Grade IL	5th Grade OL	6th Grade IL	6th Grade OL	7th Grade IL	7th Grade OL
Native language & literature	6	13	5	13/ 10	6	10	6	7	6	6	6	6	5	5
Local history & geography[a]	3	—	4	—	3	—	—	—	—	—	—	—	—	—
Religion[b]	2	—	2	—	2	—	2	—	2	—	2	—	2	—
Mathematics	5		5		6		6		6		6		4	
Arithmetic		6		6		6		6		6		4/0		—
Algebra		—		—		—		—		—		0/4		4
Geometry		—		—		—		—		—		2		2
Trigonometry		—		—		—		—		—		—		—
Geography	—	—	—	—	—	—	2	2	2	2	2	2	—	2
History	—	—	—	—	—	—	3	2	3	2	3	2	2	2
1st foreign language[c]	—	—	—	0/3	—	4	—	4	—	6/5	—	5	6	5
2nd foreign language	—	—	—	—	—	—	—	—	—	3	—	3	—	2
Latin	—	—	—	—	—	—	—	—	—	—	—	—	—	—
Natural sciences	—	—	—	—	3		3		3		3		4	
Biology	—	—	—	—		—		1		1/2		2		3
Physics	—	—	—	—		—		—		—		—		3
Chemistry	—	—	—	—		—		—		—		—		—
Astronomy	—	—	—	—		—		—		—		—		—
U.S.S.R. Constitution	—		—		—		—		—		—		—	
Physical Education														
Boys	2	2	2	2	2	2	2	2	2	2	2	2	4	2
Girls	2	2	2	2	2	2	2	2	2	2	2	2	3	
Drawing-drafting	2	1	2	1	2	1	2	1	2	1	2	1	3	
Handicrafts														
Boys	2	1	2	1	2	1	2	1	2		2	—	—	
Girls	2	1	2	1	2	1	2	1	2	—	2	—	1	
Singing-music	2	1	2	1	2	1	2	1	2	1	2	1	2	
Social studies	—	—	—	—	—	—	—	—	—	—	—	—	—	
Philosophy	—	—	—	—	—	—	—	—	—	—	—	—	—	
Psychology	—	—	—	—	—	—	—	—	—	—	—	—	—	
Shop work[d]	—	—	—	—	—	—	—	—	—	2	—	2	—	
Practice in agriculture & electrical engineering, introduction to principles of machine operation[e]	—	—	—	—	—	—	—	—	—	—	—	—	—	
TOTAL Boys	24	24	24	24	28	25	30	27	30	32	30	32	32	3
Girls	24	24	24	24	28	25	30	27	30	32	30	32	32	3

Sources: Data for independent Lithuania (IL) from V. Vaitiekunas, *Lietuva Okupacijoje* (New York, 1958) pp. 45–46; data for occupied Lithuania (OL) from T. Remeikis, *Lituanus* (New York), V, No. 2, 41–4.
[a] Since 1958, U.S.S.R. history and geography.
[b] The constitution of independent Lithuania made religious instruction mandatory, except in school set up for children of parents who did not belong to any religious group.
[c] In occupied Lithuania, the first foreign language is Russian.
[d] Introduced in 1954–55.

General Education in Independent and Occupied Lithuania

8th Grade		9th Grade		10th Grade		11th Grade		12th Grade		13th Grade		Total hours per week		Total hours per week in schools in Soviet Russia
IL	OL	IL	OL	IL	OL	IL	OL	IL	OL	IL	OL	IL	OL	
5	4	4	4	4	4	4	4	4	—	4	—	65	74.5	84.5
—	—	—	—	—	—	—	—	—	—	—	—	10	—	—
2	—	2	—	2	—	2	—	2	—	2	—	26	—	—
3		3		3		3		3		4		57	(60.5)	60
—												32		
2/3	2/3		2/3			1		2				14		
	2		2/1			2		1/2				11		
—			—			2		2/1				3.5		
2	2	2	3	2	—	2	—	2	—	—	—	16	13	14
2	3	2	4/3	2	3	3	4/5	3	—	3	—	26	22	20
6	4	4	4	3	4	3	4	3	—	3	—	28	41	20
—	3	—	3	5	4	5	3	5	—	3	—	18	21	—
—	—	4	—	4	—	4	—	3	—	3	—	18	—	—
3		2		3		3		3		4		34	(35)	(39)
	2		1/2		—		—					11	12	
	3		3		3		3					15	16	
	2		2		2		2					8	10.5	
	—		—		—		1					1	1	
—	—	—	—	—	—	—	1	—	—	—	—	—	1	1
4	3/2	4	3	4	3	4	3	4	—	4	—	40	25.5	20
3	3/2	3	3	2	3	2	3	2	—	3	—	30	25.5	20
2	1	2	1	2	1	1	1	2	—	2	—	26	11	10
—	—	—	—	—	—	—	—	—	—	—	—	12	4	4
2	—	2	—	2	—	2	—	3	—	—	—	24	4	4
2	1	2	1	2	—	2	—	—	—	—	—	22	9	6
—	—	—	—	—	—	—	—	—	—	2	—	2	—	—
—	—	—	—	—	—	—	—	2	—	2	—	4	—	—
—	—	—	—	1	—	—	—	—	—	—	—	—	1	1
—	—	—	—	—	—	—	—	—	—	—	—	—	6	6
—	2	—	1	—	2	—	2	—	—	—	—	—	7	6
31	34	31	34	36	32	36	33/34	36	—	36	—	404	331.5	293
32	34	32	34	36	32	36	33/34	37	—	35	—	406	331.5	293

[e] Introduced in 1956–57.

Note: Data for independent Lithuania are based on the 1939–40 academic year, those of occupied Lithuania on the 1958–59 year.

In independent Lithuania, mathematics was not subdivided into individual subjects. In 1964, the Soviet regime also discontinued the practice of subdividing mathematics.

Where two figures appear in one column, these apply to the two semesters of the school year.

is not acceptable to the Kremlin, and this course has therefore been made a part of the economic geography of the U.S.S.R.
Lithuanian history met the same fate. In falsifying Lithuania's
past, the history textbook is silent about the numerous Russian aggressions against Lithuania; the occupation in the late
eighteenth century, for example, is depicted as being useful to
Lithuania; the restoration of independence is treated as colonization by capitalist imperialists; the Kremlin's aggression and invasion in 1939–40 is, of course, labeled "liberation." Even so,
these falsifications were not regarded as sufficient. On October 8,
1959, a Moscow decree specified in detail which historical program should be studied in each school year, strongly emphasizing
that "the history program in secondary schools must . . . incul-
cate a conviction of the scientific historical development of society
leading to the downfall of capitalism and inevitable Communist
victory." In carrying out the decree, Lithuanian history became
a part of a "continuous U.S.S.R. history course."[46] In this way,
the Kremlin forced the Lithuanian schools to eliminate courses
in Lithuanian history and geography and to be satisfied with
sovietized economic geography courses and classes in the history
of the U.S.S.R.

THE IMPACT OF KHRUSHCHEV'S SCHOOL REFORM OF 1958 AND THE NEW PARTY PROGRAM OF 1961

The Kremlin vs. the Republic Reforms. An educational reform
in Lithuania was started by the local Communists before the
orders came from the Kremlin. As early as 1956, the Lithuanian
Communist regime had introduced obligatory agricultural labor
during summer vacations for ninth- and tenth-grade students in
schools of general education. In 1957–58, "production teaching"
was introduced into eighth-grade classes; that is, a certain part of
school time was spent on productive work. Since such work takes
up about one-third of school time, an additional year was granted
to schools with production teaching.[47] Furthermore, in May, 1958,
that is, before Khrushchev's reform, the administrators of education in occupied Lithuania had agreed on their own reform program. The plan proposed an obligatory eight-year primary school
and a four-year secondary school of general education. Part of the
student's time in the four-year program was to be devoted to
production in the school itself, or in a collective farm or factory.
The curriculums of secondary schools were to become more special-

ized; some schools were to emphasize the humanities, others mathematics, and still others science.[48] This program, however, did not receive the Kremlin's approval.

Khrushchev presented his thesis on school reform to the Central Committee of the Communist Party of the U.S.S.R. on November 12, 1958. He charged that Soviet schools were incapable of conducting even seven years of universal obligatory schooling and that graduates were unprepared for professional work. To correct this deficiency, Khrushchev suggested introducing an eight-year obligatory primary school of general education; graduates of this course (fifteen to sixteen years old) would be integrated into the productive system. For those seeking further education, Khrushchev proposed the establishment of additional evening and correspondence schools; furthermore, he suggested that higher education and specialized secondary schools be more oriented toward evening and correspondence teaching. (Significantly, the aims of Soviet education were not affected by Khrushchev's proposals.)

In Lithuania, there was little enthusiasm for these proposals, but since local Communists could not openly disagree with them, they at least tried to state certain reservations: (1) that if class time were to be devoted to productive work, there should be an additional school year; (2) that the language of instruction should be Lithuanian; (3) that besides evening and correspondence schools of secondary general education, regular secondary schools be retained.[49] The Kremlin paid heed only to the third request. The law of December 24, 1958, on the relation between school and life, retained normal secondary schools together with the newly established evening and correspondence schools. But the Kremlin ignored the other two points. It is true that a year was added to Russian schools with production teaching, so that the ten-year program was expanded to eleven years. But Lithuania did not receive the additional year. In effect, then, Lithuanian schools of general secondary education were made identical with Russian schools, although they have a different curriculum and for this reason, before this reform, had had one more year than their Russian counterparts. Lithuania also could not defend the principle that the native language be used in schools, although this practice is guaranteed by the Constitution of the U.S.S.R. Article 121 of that document—and Article 93 of the Lithuanian S.S.R. constitution—state that the citizens' right to education guarantees "instruction in schools conducted in the native language." Contrary to this paragraph, the new law stipulates that "parents have the right to decide in what language their children shall receive instruction" (Article 11). This provision enables the Kremlin to ignore the Lithuanian language and to pressure Lithuanian parents to choose schools in which Russian is the language of instruction. This provision seriously affects the principle of lingual autonomy so far enjoyed by Soviet republics.

Carrying Out the Reform. The Khrushchev plan was put into effect during the 1959–60 school year. In 1959–60 and 1960–61, instruction combined with productive labor was introduced into 403 classes with 10,003 pupils; however, only about 10 per cent of the students in the ninth, tenth, and eleventh grades were affected. This number nevertheless was claimed to be doubled in 1961–62 and tripled in 1962–63.[50]

The organization of the eight-year schools also proceeded at a slow pace. Administrators complained that in 1961–62, in the third year of the reform, only 50 per cent of seven-year schools were transformed into eight-year schools.[51] The process of transformation then quickened, and was claimed to be completed before September of 1962.[52]

Development of evening and correspondence schools at first lagged similarly. However, in 1962, the republic had twelve independent correspondence schools and eleven correspondence centers, maintained by regular schools.[53]

In the light of Khrushchev's reforms, greater changes in the plan of studies might have been expected. In fact, however, in 1959–60, grades six through eleven had the same program as in 1958–59. For grades one through four, the 1959–60 program differed from the previous year only in minor respects. In grades one through four, the time devoted to handicrafts was increased from one to two hours per week. In grades three through five, two hours per week were scheduled for so-called socially useful labor. Furthermore, two weeks of work experience on a collective or experimental farm or in a factory were added to the fifth-grade program.[54] (The course in basic political knowledge—somewhat like a civics course—introduced into the eleventh grade in 1961–62 has no connection with production teaching.)

Teaching is combined with production in the following way: Students in rural districts work one or two days a week on a sovkhoz or kolkhoz. This time is spent in learning how to "milk cows, measure and weigh them; prepare feed for pigs, feed and take care

CHART C

Organization of Schools After the Educational Reform

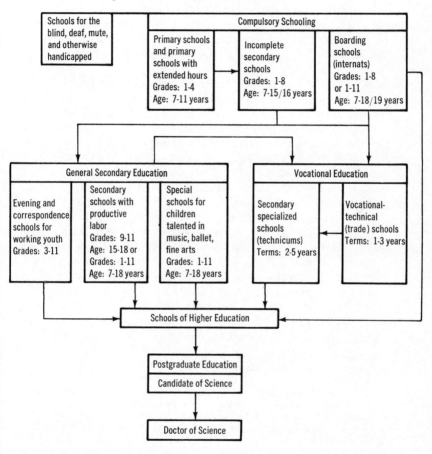

Schools for the blind, deaf, mute, and otherwise handicapped

Compulsory Schooling

Primary schools and primary schools with extended hours
Grades: 1-4
Age: 7-11 years

Incomplete secondary schools
Grades: 1-8
Age: 7-15/16 years

Boarding schools (internats)
Grades: 1-8 or 1-11
Age: 7-18/19 years

General Secondary Education

Evening and correspondence schools for working youth
Grades: 3-11

Secondary schools with productive labor
Grades: 9-11
Age: 15-18 or
Grades: 1-11
Age: 7-18 years

Special schools for children talented in music, ballet, fine arts
Grades: 1-11
Age: 7-18 years

Vocational Education

Secondary specialized schools (technicums)
Terms: 2-5 years

Vocational-technical (trade) schools
Terms: 1-3 years

Schools of Higher Education

Postgraduate Education

Candidate of Science

Doctor of Science

of them; graft trees and bind them; care for fruit trees; operate and service combines, tractors, and sowers." Urban students usually work one day a week in local shops: power stations, auto-repair shops, ship-building yards, textile mills, etc. Some schools maintain their own shops.[55] In general, such student labor practice does not yet have either a general plan or a common schedule. In this respect, each school is left to its own initiative. The Minister of Education of occupied Lithuania has asserted that "our [i.e., Russian] pedagogic science has not yet given a final and complete answer on how to combine, in practice, teaching and productive labor"[56]—a statement that questions the whole reform.*

Impact of the New Party Program. The new program is based upon the thesis that in the field of national relations the Communist Party of the U.S.S.R. will promote "the formation of the future single world-wide culture of Communist society."[57] In fact, this thesis means that the cultural individuality of captive nations must dissolve in the texture of Russian culture. As a consequence, Russification pressures have greatly increased in the schools. The Kremlin is forcing Lithuanian schools to pay particular attention to the Russian language and to the inculcation of love and respect for the "great Russian nation."[58] Furthermore, in the 1961–62 school year, the schools were instructed to devote part of the class time intended for other studies to the Party's new program. This was done as follows: in grades one through four, some class hours were taken from the native language, history, and natural science; in grades five and six, three class hours from history; in grades seven through ten, two from history, two from literature, and four from practical work in agriculture or factories; in grade eleven, thirty-four hours from a course in basic political theory.[59]

---

* Indeed, in August, 1964, Khrushchev again reformed education, reverting to ten years of secondary schooling. This new reform, of course, affected the curriculum.

For the transition period, Lithuania is to follow rules set up for the Russian Soviet Federated Socialist Republic. After the promulgation of the reform decree, Russia's Minister of Education explained that "beginning September 1, 1964, the existing curriculums and programs will be used in the teaching of the first eight grades in all types of schools. Students who will now enroll in the tenth and eleventh grades will be graduated from the eleven-year school, also according to the existing curriculums and programs. However, students now enrolling in the ninth grade will be graduated in two years [after a total of ten years], that is, in the spring of 1966. They will study according to a special transition curriculum." (*Tarybinis Mokytojas,* August 16, 1964, p. 1.)

ACHIEVEMENTS AND FAILURES

The Soviet Numbers Game. The Communists usually boast that only Soviet rule enabled the expansion of education in Lithuania. To demonstrate this thesis, they quote and compare present student and school figures with those of independent Lithuania of a quarter century ago. It is not surprising, of course, that progress in numbers has been registered in a twenty-five-year period (see Table 5 below). It is important to point out, however, that much of this numerical growth was due to the need of servicing the Soviet bureaucracy, not needed in non-Soviet conditions, and that the training of many of these Soviet "specialists" is very narrow and limited. For example, the agriculture of independent Lithuania was quite adequately serviced by some 3,000 agricultural specialists. According to the Party's monthly, *Komunistas*, occupied Lithuania's collectivized agriculture needs 50,000 specialists with secondary specialized and higher education.[60] This tremendous increase of agricultural technicians, however, has not contributed to agricultural productivity. Furthermore, the state-run industry, trade, transportation, health, recreational, and other establishments need even larger numbers of bureaucrats with specialized education. Moreover, some schools can never produce a sufficient number of specialists because these specialists leave their professions for more rewarding occupations. Thus, for example, there is a chronic shortage of teachers, because each year, about 8 per cent in this profession leave their jobs for work in other fields.[61] This explains why pedagogical institutes are pressured to graduate increasing numbers of students.

Soviet occupation has created several other pressures for large numbers of specialists with secondary or higher education. For example, Lithuanian schools have to train people not only for Lithuania's needs but also for those of the entire Soviet Union. Lithuanian engineers, physicians, and technicians are found throughout the Soviet empire. Furthermore, the number of schools and students has grown as a result of student influx from the other Soviet republics.

Taking these factors into consideration (and also the increase in size of the republic's territory), the comparative rate of growth of educational institutions and students becomes much less impressive than the Soviets would have us believe.

Detailed statistics, last published in 1956, reveal that the larg-

TABLE 5

Comparative Growth of Schools and Students in Lithuania, 1919–63

Year	Territory in sq. miles (in round figures)	Compulsory schooling schools and students		Secondary general schools and students		Professional and special schools and full-time students		Schools of higher learning and full-time students	
1919	20,000	1036	45,546	38	9,213	none		none	
1929	21,000	2431	171,384	118	19,614	13	627	4	4,852
1939	23,000	2713	338,319	96	26,662	143	14,040	8	6,701
1945	25,000	3151	279,379	92	26,085	37	7,986	10	5,541
1955	25,000	3389	353,418	386	54,291	66	19,033	12	14,669
1962	25,000	5007	509,000*	*	*	75	25,500	11	18,100

* The figures of 5007 and 509,000 include secondary schools and secondary-school students; separate data for 1962 are not available.

Sources: For 1919 and 1929, see V. Kemėžis, *Lietuva 1918–38* (Kaunas, 1938), pp. 272, 280, 294, 300; for 1939, see *Lietuvos Statistikos Metraštis 1939* (Vilnius, 1940), p. 72; for 1945 and 1955, see *Lietuvos TSR Liaudies Ūkis* (Vilnius, 1957), pp. 186, 188, 190; for 1962, see *Narodnoe khoziaistvo SSSR 1962 godu* (Moscow, 1963), pp. 558–59, 565–67.

est college student increase has occurred in pedagogical institutes, in the academies of agriculture and veterinary medicine, and in engineering and chemistry.[62] It is noteworthy that the number of students did not appreciably grow in music, art, and law—that is, in fields in which the Kremlin has no special interest.[63]

Failures and "Failures." For a long time, there was complete silence on the question of failures in Soviet education. But after Khrushchev pointed out certain shortcomings of Soviet schools, the curtain drawn over the failures of Lithuanian education was lifted somewhat. Recently, certain shortcomings in universal compulsory education have come to light. Previously, only one side of the picture was shown; it was simply claimed that with the beginning of the 1949–50 school year, "compulsory seven-year schooling has been enacted." Now we can see the other side; we are told that until 1961–62, "not a single city, not a single district [in Lithuania] had carried out compulsory seven-year schooling 100 per cent" (by law, eight years of compulsory schooling had to be in effect in 1962–63), and that "a significantly greater number [of children in the affected age group] do not attend school than is shown in official reports." This is because many children in the compulsory school-age group "are not even listed on student rolls."[64] Generally, we may ask whether seven-year schooling can be considered universal and compulsory if in many schools 13–17 per cent of all pupils drop out during the school year and if 75 per cent of those who enter in the first year drop out during the following seven years, and thus only 25 per cent graduate.[65] That a part of Lithuania's youth does not complete seven-year education is testified to by the fact that in 1959–60, the regime opened thirty evening schools to help working youth complete a seven-year education.[66]

The "repeating" problem points to the same difficulties. For instance, in 1960–61, between 20 and 30 per cent of all students in a number of districts had to repeat the school year. In some graduating classes, only 58.6 per cent of students passed their final exams.[67] There are many shortcomings in the so-called "production teaching," or the use of class time for productive labor. Many such classes combined with production have been established for professions that are not greatly needed by the economy. Not infrequently, students "arriving for production practice spend a greater part of the time without any work at all" or are assigned tasks "that have nothing in common with the teaching program." Again, we find classes combined with production in fields where no practical work is possible.[68] Neither is the plan executed in the higher and specialized secondary correspondence schools, on which Khrushchev put such emphasis. "Many correspondence students study badly," and hence "correspondence divisions graduate few specialists," the Lithuanian Minister of Education complains.[69]

Furthermore, there still exists a shortage of teachers. In 1959, a Western educator, after visiting the Soviet Union, concluded that "there is no teacher shortage in the Soviet Union. . . . There is no need in the Soviet Union for emergency certificates."[70] But in 1961, to alleviate this shortage, the Kremlin allowed the republics to establish "one-year pedagogical classes for the training of primary-school teachers"[71] in conjunction with secondary schools of general education. The extent of the shortage in Lithuania is testified by the fact that in 1961–62, the educational administration "was forced to appoint as teachers persons without any pedagogic training," while the First Secretary of the Communist Party warned district chairmen not to appoint former teachers to collective-farm chairmanships.[72]

There is also a great shortage of school buildings. In the period

1945–62, "only 127 school buildings were constructed or rebuilt," while 1,367 new schools were opened. Hence, even in 1961–62 there were "not a few schools established in unsuitable buildings," and even in the larger Lithuanian cities "more than 40,000 children are attending schools in two or three shifts."[73]

On the other hand, some of the failures of sovietized schools are failures only from the point of view of the Kremlin. One of the most conspicuous is the regime's inability completely to eliminate religious and nationalistic influences among school youth. Thus, the type of student who "after receiving an A in Marxism, runs to church to thank God"[74] is still representative. Similarly, secondary-school and college youth participate in demonstrations against the regime, like those that occurred in Kaunas and Vilnius during the Hungarian Revolution and in 1957, on February 16, the Lithuanian Independence Day. About the latter, a witness who fled to the West has written:

> Today, the noise there [in a student dormitory] is indescribable. . . .
> Old Lithuanian songs are sung again and again. Suddenly I am
> awakened by a loud commotion. It is midnight. The Lithuanian na-
> tional anthem is sung on Laisvės Alėja [Kaunas' main street]. I throw
> on an overcoat and, mindless of the danger, run to the street. In the
> darkness I see a moving mass. God, these are young people. . . . Sing-
> ing the national anthem [of independent Lithuania] they are moving
> on the town hall. . . . That night, in the old town, on the cathedral
> steeple and near the city hall, tricolor flags [of independent Lithuania]
> were raised.[75]

9. Literature and the Arts in Captive Lithuania

JONAS GRINIUS

Peace, freedom, national self-determination, progress, and culture are concepts that have one meaning in the West and another, quite different one, in the Communist East. When the Red Army had completed the occupation of Lithuania in June, 1940, official Soviet propaganda agents spoke unhesitatingly of liberation and self-determination, while at the same time the Soviet occupation regime was seizing control of all Lithuanian institutions, industry, and agriculture. The perverted meaning of culture and progress became clear to writers and artists more slowly perhaps than to the rest of the nation. But during the one year of the first Soviet occupation of Lithuania (June 15, 1940–June 22, 1941), they came to understand the Communist deception no less well than did Lithuanians of other professions. Thus, when the military forces of the Soviet Union made their second entry into Lithuania in 1944, more than half of the writers and artists left their native country and fled to the West; Germany, in flames and ruins by the rapidly nearing end of the war, seemed to them less perilous than Soviet liberation. One who is not familiar with the realities of Soviet life might want to ask why.

The answer is quite simple: From the professional and moral standpoint, the situation of the writer and the artist in Soviet-occupied countries is much more difficult and complicated than that of, say, an engineer. In the first place, the engineer's work does not entail public expression of his thoughts and feelings. If he is careful not to engage in any critical discussion of the Soviet regime in conversation with his friends, if at the official meetings he is content to remain quiet and merely applaud, he will not run too much danger of being blacklisted by Party officials. To writers and artists, however, these maneuvers of silence and applause as a means of personal safety are not possible. They have always been faced by a dilemma—either to relinquish their profession entirely (never to publish their works), or to become propagandists for the Soviet regime. No alternative is possible, for the Soviet regime exercises stricter control over writers and artists than the absolute monarchies of the past. They have to work under conditions of totalitarian encirclement.

THE ENCIRCLEMENT UNDER STALIN

How does this encirclement manifest itself? To begin with, it is made possible by material circumstances. The press and the publishing houses are owned and operated by the government, the Communist Party, or a Communist-controlled syndicate. A similar situation confronts the artist and the sculptor. Works of art are admitted for public display only after they have been judged and accepted by one or two special committees on which specially appointed Communist Party members hold the decisive vote. As a rule, exhibits are collective, and only in exceptional cases, when the artist has served the Soviet regime in some special way, is the right to present an individual display granted. These occasional individual displays are supervised by government museums (there are no others), while the collective exhibits are organized by the Communist-controlled artists syndicate, which alone has the right to arrange exhibits.

This material encirclement of the writers and artists is reinforced by Communist Party censorship and regulation, which is exercised in both negative and positive ways. Negative censorship and control is exerted by banning from public appearance any work that does not serve Party ideology or the political line of the Soviet Government. Lithuanian writers who inadvertently express views differing from those of the Party are listed as politically suspect, and in the recent past this has led to police arrest and deportation. The writer Antanas Venclova, a member of the Communist Party, gave unmistakable proof of this when he spoke at a congress of Soviet writers in Moscow on December 14–26, 1954:

> During the early postwar years, the young Soviet [Lithuanian] literature grew and developed in the fierce struggle against the still-undestroyed residue of bourgeois nationalism and chauvinism, against

the followers of "pure art," against the promoters of "aestheticism" and snobs worshiping the refuse of the Western bourgeoisie and mystics of various shades. The principal representatives of this fascistic-minded "literature" fled to the West with the retreating Hitlerist troops and now they are serving their new masters—the American warmongers. For some time after the war, their "ideological henchmen" tried to obstruct the development of our growing Soviet literature, but they were crushed and tossed onto the trash pile.[1]

What Antanas Venclova, then President of the Association of Soviet Lithuanian Writers, called the crushing and tossing of Lithuanian writers onto the trash pile really meant that certain writers had been silenced, imprisoned, or deported. As a matter of fact, as late as 1956–57, Juozas Keliuotis, Kazys Inčiūra, Antanas Miškinis, V. Drazdauskas, and other Lithuanian writers were still being held in Soviet concentration camps, while others, such as Kazys Boruta had been silenced (their names were not allowed to appear in the press). Similar measures have been imposed on artists: Some are still barred from participation in public exhibitions.

Although the Communist Party ideology is dogmatic, from time to time Soviet politics undergoes certain changes. At times this political oscillation becomes another source of real difficulty for writers. Sometimes they are forced by the Communist Party to retract and deplore ideas they have previously put forth. Before the death of Stalin, the following writers publicly acknowledged their ideas had been ideological errors and expressed their regret: Vincas Mykolaitis-Putinas (his works are classics of Lithuanian literature), Jonas Šimkus, Kostas Korsakas, Antanas Venclova. The admission made by Korsakas, a Communist poet and critic, is particularly typical, and his confession is highly interesting for its disclosure of the unconditional domination by the Communist Party to which writers are subjected. This can be inferred from the following passage:

> We, of the literary profession, should be deeply grateful to the Party for its constant guidance, for the criticism of our works in accordance with Bolshevik principles, for pointing out to us the proper way of correcting the errors we have committed.[2]

After the death of Stalin, it gradually became apparent that the instructions previously given the writers and artists by the Communist Party had been erroneous. Since the responsibility for these errors lay with the Party, individual writers were not obligated to make public confessions. At that time, the Communists contented themselves with general expressions of regret for the losses suffered. Little notice was taken of the damage done to the creative talent of writers, or of the faultiness of their works; the emphasis was placed on losses incurred by all. The weekly *Literatūra ir Menas* said in an editorial on December 1, 1956:

> There is nothing secret about the fact that during the time when the cult of personality was the prevailing practice, Soviet Lithuanian literature suffered great losses. Doubtless, there now exists a real necessity to speak about the damages that the cult of personality has worked, and its effects must be completely eradicated.

That earlier instructions by the Communist Party had had a damaging effect on literature can be seen from a statement by Kazys Boruta. At a meeting of the Association of Soviet Lithuanian Writers on February 1, 1957, this writer, who had previously been silenced by the Communists, said:

> The criticism to which the cult of personality and its consequences have been subjected has helped to extirpate in our literature and in creative practice the unhealthy manifestations of schematism and stereotypes, which were becoming rampant.[3]

Thus, by the admission of the Soviet press, directives issued by the Communist Party can be, and until 1956 clearly were, detrimental to writers. Nevertheless, at no time did the Communist Party have any intention of terminating its censorship and control of writers and artists. With the same unabashed boldness, the Party continues to make demands of them. Antanas Venclova, the previously quoted President of the Association of Soviet Lithuanian Writers, revealed this very clearly in a speech he made to Lithuanian writers in the early part of 1957:

> We Soviet Lithuanian writers are well aware of the love, the single-minded devotion, and the concern with which the Party has fostered our young Soviet literature, always encouraging it to serve our people. The Party has always taught us to be faithful to the best realistic traditions in the literature of our own and other nations; it has always fought and led writers to fight for a healthy realistic literature . . . literature that would educate men in the spirit of Communist ideology and morality. This spirit pervades all the pronouncements of the Party on literature and art, and these documents today are still the basic guidepost in our future work. We Soviet writers say this openly to all our friends and enemies: We are proud to be the helpers of our Party.[4]

From this speech and from a number of other articles it is evident that even after the so-called "thaw" in 1955–57 the relationship of the Communist Party to writers has remained unchanged. The Communist Party continues as before to play the role of principal critic and instructor of writers and artists. Socialist realism, as the aesthetic method officially established by the Party, remains mandatory for all. In the literary discussion of the West, socialist realism puts in an occasional appearance, but here it is not a matter of dogma—and sometimes a difficulty arises in comprehending just what the Communist Party seeks to achieve by means of it. In the Soviet Union and the countries occupied by it, however, socialist realism is nothing but a positive injunction to the writer and artist as to what and how he is to create.

Acting as another reinforcing link in the chain of material and intellectual controls placed around the writer, the method of socialist realism demands that the material for creative work shall be taken from real life, primarily from Soviet life, and that this material shall be interpreted according to the dialectical and historical materialism professed and preached by the Communist Party. In other words, through the material that the writer uses to depict life, he must always disclose some aspect of the class struggle, which is leading to Communist victory in Lithuania as well as in the entire world. Since this dogmatic thesis is too general, Communists Party officials find it necessary upon occasion to expound on other aspects of socialist realism as well. They indicate that the art and literature of socialist realism, which are required of Lithuanian writers and artists, must be didactic in character, i.e., art and literature of political indoctrination. At a congress of Soviet writers in Moscow, December 14–26, 1954, A. Surikov remarked: "Literature is a keen weapon in sociopolitical action. It is closely related to and subordinate to politics."[5] By reason of its educational character, the literature of socialist realism must be optimistic.

> Pessimism of any kind is repugnant to the literature of socialist realism, for "pessimism—mold and rust," [a phrase coined by Maxim Gorki], is a lack of faith, while the essence of socialist realism is the impregnable belief of our people in the ultimate victory of just social relationships.[6]

So said Konstantin Simonov, a well-known Russian writer, at the same meeting of Soviet writers.

In addition to these primary demands, socialist realism poses secondary requirements. These, for example, include the proscription of a purely humanistic admiration for natural beauty and demand that nature be shown transformed by technical civilization, i.e., subjected to the economic needs of man and controlled by man. Thus, in the literature of socialist realism even man himself cannot be portrayed freely in any way the writer might wish. In order to create an evil character, it is necessary to make him appear with all the supposed traits of the bourgeois—greed, an aversion to labor, and a propensity for exploiting the labor of others. In portraying a positive personality, on the other hand, love of work must be stressed.

Obviously, these dictates of socialist realism can be met only by fanatic Party hacks or official employees, who then produce a lifeless and barren literature. And in Lithuania, as in the Soviet Union as a whole, writers generally are employees of the state. They either hold official positions in the publishing houses and on newspaper editorial staffs, or are paid so well for their writings that their earnings are comparable to those of high government employees. Thus, the material rewards that the state extends to obedient writers provides one more means of controlling the literary situation, since the writers relinquish their intellectual freedom and integrity.

Thus far, how has this Communist encirclement of creative initiative affected literary and artistic achievement in Lithuania? Generally, Soviet control has significantly diminished the quantity and quality of Lithuanian literary and artistic achievement. In 1950, for example, when the Communists in Lithuania were celebrating the decennial of the first Soviet occupation. Lithuanian writers came out with nothing of importance or scope to mark the occasion. The only works published in observance of this anniversary were anthologies of Lithuanian prose and poetry. The Communist Party daily *Tiesa* commented on the prose anthology:

> In this anthology the Soviet reader will come across names that he never or seldom meets otherwise. It is common knowledge that such writers as Grušas, Simonaitytė, and Paukštelis have contributed very little or nothing at all to the development of Soviet prose, even though they enjoyed a wide reputation in their own time. . . . The collection shows that many of our writers write in very limited quantity, that their level of productivity is extremely low. . . . The anthology is a proof that our writers must struggle unceasingly in the attempt to improve the literary quality of their work.[7]

This anthology also revealed that Lithuanian writers have no taste for socialist realism. For this they were later reproached by the same newspaper:

> The role of the Communist Party is given very little attention, while that of the Communist leader is neglected altogether. Rarely is the Lithuanian working class portrayed. The achievements of collective farming are largely ignored; the exposure of bourgeois nationalists is rather weak.[8]

In a later review of the anthology of poetry, another critic, almost word for word, leveled these same accusations at Lithuanian poets. Clearly then, what Lithuanian writers were producing around 1950 was small in bulk and poor in quality. They were unable to conform to Communist standards. No work of any considerable scope was written during this period. This was affirmed by the same *Tiesa*:

> Readers are waiting expectantly for new and important works from the writers, but the literary balance of this year as yet shows no such contributions in either novels, epic prose, or poetical compositions.[9]

THE PERIOD OF THE THAW

The thaw that set in after the death of Stalin made the writers' situation somewhat more secure. This increased their productivity and made possible to some extent the practical application of the norms of socialist realism, but the literary value of their work remained low. The general estimate in which the Communists held the work of Lithuanian writers and poets in the period 1945–56 was at best skeptical. This is seen from a speech made by Antanas Venclova at a meeting of writers on February 2, 1957, in Vilnius:

> The main objective, which the Party time and again has emphasized to us, is to portray the life of our times, to engage actively in raising and studying those questions of the day which are the most timely and pressing in our socialist reality. . . . A great defect in our contemporary literature is its failure to reveal significantly those interesting and complex processes taking place in the consciousness of our people. The larger prose works so far give us no picture of collective farming with those involved processes by which the farm population proceeds from a primitive to a more progressive and better kind of life. As yet, our literature lacks any full-blooded portrayals of the really heroic personality—the dedicated socialist enthusiast. The life

and existence of the working class is still being given insufficient scope in literary writing; similiarly, our socialist intellectuals have not yet been depicted in literature with the breadth and depth due to them. . . . The long-abused genre of the sketch has shown effective development in recent years. The greatest obstacle to the intellectual and artistic growth of this genre was the pervasive view that the sketch should prove one or another political truth, to affirm one or another political slogan. In this way, literary characters came out artificially fragmented, artificial situations were set up, and in general there was a trend away from the reality of life.[10]

These, then, were the fruits produced by the Soviet encirclement of the literary world.

The pressure of this encirclement on Lithuanian writers during the period 1944–55 had a threefold effect. Some writers ceased writing completely or wrote very little and tried to preserve their personal security by declarations of loyalty at public meetings or by writing occasional poems. Others revised their earlier works to make them consistent with Communist ideology. Still others, if they continued to write, lost the creative individuality they had once possessed. From the Soviet Lithuanian press we know that among those who rewrote their earlier works to conform to Communist ideology were Teofilis Tilvytis, Kazys Jankauskas, and Jonas Marcinkevičius. However, these opportunistic "achievements" could earn no praise even from Soviet critics; this is shown by the reception given to the Soviet edition of *Nemunas patvino* (*The River Nemunas Has Risen*), an early novel by Marcinkevičius. "What has the author accomplished?" asked the critic and went on to comment:

> He took a crime novel he had written in the past, a book entirely lacking in intellectual content, and freely proceeded to "rework" it. The result has been a book that profanes and falsifies many aspects in the revolutionary struggle of the Lithuanian people (and that is not the worst), while our critics received this "work" as an acceptable contribution. . . . This is more a form of speculation than of literary creation, and that much more abhorrent for being an attempt to speculate in ideas, and in this manner serenely gain entrance from a bourgeois past into . . . socialism.[11]

An instance of the negative influence of Soviet pressure on those writers who, led by fear or other motives, tried to cope with the demands of socialist realism is to be found in a statement made by the critic J. Josadė about Jonas Paukštelis. In 1956, after careful examination of this writer's literary performance during the Soviet period, Josadė wrote:

> A very strange thing immediately meets the eye, namely, that the work appears as though it had come from the hand of some other person, not the writer; the means used are alien to the writer; it is as if J. Paukštelis renounced his own particular manner of dealing with the material of life, his own particular narrative style and tone. . . . To force oneself to perceive life and to interpret it in a language not one's own—this is impossible.[12]

Nevertheless, the Soviet system of control in effect demanded that Lithuanian writers accomplish these impossible tasks.

Similar impossible demands were made of Lithuanian artists, although their range of freedom could not be limited as severely as that of writers. Evidence of this fact is contained in comments made by the art critic J. Mackonis. Writing about the 1955 exhibition of Lithuanian art in Vilnius, he said:

> The narrow conception of socialist method and the dogmas of certain fellow-traveling critics have hindered artists in a freer use of the means of creative expression, have reduced to a common level their individuality, style, and temperament. Partly because of this, the state art exhibits in recent years have been unimpressive, poor not only from the standpoint of subject and genre, but lacking in creative imagination as well. This has been especially true of painting, which is beginning to look like color photography.[13]

The means by which this leveling of talents was brought about are discussed in greater detail by Antanas Gudaitis, an aged painter who had been educated in Paris. At a meeting of Lithuanian artists in April, 1957, he made the following complaint:

> For some time, under cover of opposition to formalism in painting, there was frequent opposition to form itself. It was desired to "create" a picture by administrative means, by dictating from above subject and manner of composition. All sorts of committees would advise the artist, while he was in the process of work, on a multitude of little corrections to be made, which essentially directed the work towards naturalism. Such "methods" have done our painting much harm, they weakened the creative activity of some artists; many of the works from the period in question appear depersonalized, monolithic, lacking in deeper emotional appeal. With such a narrow conception of the method of socialist realism, unpardonably little significance came to be attached to light, shadow, and lineal rhythm as means of expression.[14]

The statements by Soviet critics and complaints by painters about the damage done to creative talent, which have been quoted above, were made in Lithuania during the thaw (1955–57). Longing for greater creative freedom, Lithuanian artists and writers wished that the Communist Party and the Soviet state would at least allow public discussion of art and literature; until that time such discussion could be conducted only in private. In support of the need for public discussion of aesthetic matters, J. Mackonis wrote:

> It must be said that even when prescriptions were being forced down upon them and taste was dictated from above, our artists held on to a broader and deeper conception of art, although they may have avoided giving it public expression, for fear of being branded formalists. It is commonly known, by now at least, that certain of our painters acknowledged the nineteenth-century works of the Russian *peredvizhniki* [didactic realists] as the only artistic model to be followed, while backstage they were expressing admiration for the painting of Serov, Vrubel, Kontsalovsky, Matisse, and Renoir. Has not the time come for observations of this kind freely to make their way into the press and to be discussed with sincerity and without fear of a possible clash of opinion?[15]

The same freedom in regard to literary form was demanded by writers. As shown in an article by V. Kubilius, "On the Diversity of Soviet Lithuanian Literature,"[16] they tried to base their demands for new forms on actual changes within Soviet life itself, because new ideas and new phenomena in life, which literature must reflect, require "their own particular artistic expression." While accepting the basic thesis of Soviet realism—that literature must portray Soviet life—this critic argued that in the case at hand there could be only one question: "Is that which is new significant both intellectually and artistically?" But neither V. Kubilius nor the others succeeded in convincing the Communist Party on this point, although the hopes for creative freedom had risen high among Lithuanian intellectuals, writers, and artists during the 1955–57 period. These hopes were so high, that even the dogmas of socialist realism were being criticized in private discussion. At the same time the reading public started to coin slogans: "We don't want to be directed or led. We have heads of our own."[17]

Having seen that the demand for partial freedoms can lead to intellectual and creative independence, the Communists began to retaliate after the suppression of the Hungarian uprising. The first signs of this reaction appeared as early as December, 1956. In an editorial, the weekly *Literatūra ir Menas* asserted:

> We find it inexcusable that, under cover of the criticism directed against the cult of personality, attempts are made to negate the whole of Soviet Lithuanian literature. . . . Consciously or unconsciously, attempts of this kind seek to weaken the influence of our literature on the reader, on the masses of youth.[18]

These signs of reaction were followed by others. The threat of revisionism was purposely exaggerated, especially after Khrushchev's speech on art and literature in the summer of 1957. Amid cries that revisionism, which represents a threat to Communism, must be conquered, the period of the thaw in Lithuania drew to a close. The literary and artistic situation was summed up by a member of the Lithuanian Communist Party's Central Committee, Genrikas Zimanas, as follows:

> We all know that the disquieting wave of revisionism, which has risen recently and sought to wash away the foundations of Marxism-Leninism, succeeded in casting some of its poisonous spray on the Soviet people, particularly on some of our literary and artistic workers. . . . Let it be said to the credit of Lithuanian Soviet writers that they did not produce a Dudintsev in their midst. But the seed of the revisionist onslaught did make its way into our Republic and accomplished its harm. The year 1957 is the year in which this onslaught has been repulsed in our republic, the year of ideological formation for our literary and artistic workers.[19]

Regrettably, Zimanas did not have the courage to admit that what he termed "formation" would be more closely approximated by the term "Soviet reaction."

That reactionary activity was really taking place is borne out by a number of events in 1957 and early 1958. During this time, the Soviet Government blocked the performance of *Sukilėliai* (*The Rebels*), a new opera by Juozas Juozeliūnas. Juozas Bulavas, the Rector of the University of Vilnius, was relieved of his post; his supervision of the Department of Lithuanian Literature was declared incompetent because degree candidates in this department had been choosing non-Communist subjects for their theses (for example, only three of the thirty theses in Lithuanian literature submitted in 1957 were Communist in theme). Smilgevičius was dismissed as Minister of Culture because the desire to become emancipated from the dictates of the Communist Party had been noted in the Lithuanian theater and the state publishing house for *belles lettres*. The newly appointed Minister of Culture, Juozas Banaitis, addressing a meeting of writers and artists on January 17, 1958, in Vilnius, dashed all hopes for creative freedom that these people might still have held. Banaitis attacked writers, artists, musicians, and dramatists for their creative attempts in 1956–57, which had been characterized by a greater freedom and individuality. Communist Lithuanian officials laid part of the blame for the so-called revisionism on Lithuanians living in the West. At the Party convention in Vilnius, Antanas Sniečkus said: "The various revisionist tendencies received active support from the Lithuanian bourgeois nationalists who have fled abroad and hired themselves out to American imperialists." To this Sniečkus added a strong reminder that Lithuanians were to make no attempts to free themselves from Russian "liberation": "It is important for every member of the working class to know that anyone who would stir up antagonism toward the Russian nation, anyone who would tear the Lithuanian people away from the Russian people, would be digging a grave for the Lithuanian nation."[20]

Did the Lithuanians succeed in making any gains for their literature and art during the thaw? Although the original Communist system of control has continued to the present day, the thaw did have some lasting results, at least in matters of secondary importance. It made possible the rehabilitation of an important Lithuanian writer—Vincas Krėvė-Mickevičius, who had died in the United States in 1954; in 1956, his works were published in Lithuania (other Lithuanian writers living in the West are never mentioned in the Soviet Lithuanian press). From that time, the works of some Lithuanian writers no longer alive or advanced in age began to be published in series. But the works of a number of deceased writers (Vincas Pietaris, Vilius Storasta-Vydūnas, Šatrijos Ragana, J. Savickis, J. Baltrušaitis, and others) continue to be banned, while in the case of others only selected writings have been published and part of their works remain on the proscribed list (*Pragiedruliai* [*Flashes of Sunlight*] by Vaižgantas, *Klaida* [*Mistake*] by Lazdynų Pelėda, *Radvila Perkūnas* by Balys Sruoga, and others). Another feature has been the appearance of one or two new novels per year, while during the period 1944–55 only five novels in all were published.[21] During the thaw, those Lithuanian writers who had survived their imprisonment in Soviet concentration camps were released. After their return, these writers were allowed to pursue their occupation on the condition that they publicly renounce and deplore their past and declare their loyalty to the Soviet regime in Lithuania.

To some extent, the thaw was felt by Lithuanian artists, too. They succeeded in rehabilitating Mykolas K. Čiurlionis (1875–1911), the most important figure in Lithuanian art. Previously, no public discussion of this artist had been permitted, for the Communists considered his works the expression of individualism and symbolism, and hence, decadent art. As a result of the rehabilitation, a collection of thirty-two color reproductions of Ciurlionis' works was brought out in 1961, the fiftieth anniversary of the artist's death. Following the thaw, monographs on other Lithuanian artists with reproductions of their works were issued. The art exhibitions in Lithuania began to show greater variety and substance. The official publication *Pergalė* admitted that the 1957 exhibition, in which 230 artists participated, gave indication of worthwhile achievement by Lithuanian artsts. But at the same time it complained about the scarcity of Soviet themes in the art displayed at the exhibition. In an editorial entitled "Under the Flag of the Communist Party," *Pergalė* wrote:

> It cannot be left unsaid that a great number of the works are narrow and limited in theme and present a rather shallow treatment of the problems in contemporary life. Many artists still lack the courage to take up the issues of our time; the dominant motif in exhibitions is the landscape, not man. . . . All this points to the dire necessity for conscientious work by professional associations in the formation of our literary and artistic workers. This is true in the case of composers, of writers, of artists.[22]

This Communist publication seems to treat Lithuanian writers and artists as though they were children who have to be brought up. It does so for an obvious reason: Even the short duration of the thaw had given Lithuanians an opportunity for more definite and individual creative expression. Among the small gains made during this time was the chance to go on foreign tours with Russian groups. In 1956, permission was given Lithuanian theaters to work in collaboration with their Baltic neighbors—Latvians and Estonians. While the evaluation of these joint theater performances depended mostly on the opinions of the Russians commissioned from Moscow, nevertheless this represented at least a certain measure of freedom to the repressed Baltic nations. Lithuanian singers and actors were permitted to tour Poland, while Polish actors could visit Lithuania. In 1957, the state established annual awards for the best works in Lithuanian literature and the other arts. Of course, the first recipients of these prizes were Communists, but one or two of the awards went to non-Communist writers. However, these state awards, which carried with them a sum of money, were given for only three years. The last award was made in 1959. The Lithuanian encyclopaedia, which the Communists planned to publish in 1957, has not yet appeared and probably never will, for the Russian Communists have increased their nationalistic pressure on the small non-Russian nations within the Soviet Union.

THE SITUATION IN THE EARLY 1960's

The wretched condition of literature in occupied Lithuania is brought out even more sharply when the literary achievements of 1960 are contrasted with comparable Lithuanian works written in the West during that time. Since they must earn their living by means other than writing, Lithuanian writers in the West can devote only their spare time and energy to literary composition. They usually receive no pay for what they publish, let alone financial support from the state. Yet in 1960, these writers produced nine new novels. In the same year, only two novels appeared inside Lithuania, and even these were printed only in serial form by the literary journal *Pergalė*. Moreover, after 1959, there was a drop in the number of all other types of books printed in Lithuania.

Efforts to submerge all nationalities under the cultural hegemony of Russia were intensified after the Twenty-second Congress of the CPSU, and their impact is being felt in Lithuania. The Communist press issues frequent statements against national traditions, even when they are not admixed with Christianity—which is still being fought as radically as in the time of Stalin. (An incident in Vėžaičiai, during the early part of 1963, is typical: a picture of St. Casimir was hacked out with axes by the police from the altar of a Catholic Church). The general population is urged to learn the Russian language, and writers are expected to set the example in this case. To ease the renunciation of the native tongue in favor of the Russian, various means are tried. In 1962, Moscow gave one of the Lenin Prizes in literature to a Lithuanian, E. Mieželaitis, because his collected poems, *Žmogus*, first appeared in Russian translation. (Only several months after the presentation of the award were they printed in Lithuanian.) A reading of the rhetoric that passes for poetry in this collection clearly shows that the award was made on the basis of something other than the aesthetic value of the poetry.

Although the sovietization of Lithuania is carried on with added strength, Lithuanians have not yet relinquished all of their hopes: They are still struggling for conditions that will assure creative freedom to the writer and the artist. However, with the passing of the thaw, they have become more cautious. They avoid any public expression of personal thoughts and feelings, and all discussion of contemporary philosophy and art is held within private groups of friends. The story *Pušis, kuri juokėsi (The Pine-tree That Laughed)* by Justinas Marcinkevičius, published in 1962, gives evidence of this renewed caution. The author uses the story to denounce the pessimistic philosophy of the West, abstract art, and all other novel artistic experiments that have found their way into the private circles of Lithuanian writers and artists. In 1963, this story was published in Russian by a Moscow publishing house.

Such private discussion groups of writers and artists can be found throughout the Soviet Union, not only in Lithuania, as was disclosed by the CPSU Secretary Leonid Ilychev on December 17, 1962. Ilychev, speaking in Moscow to the writers and artists assembled from the entire Soviet Union, declared:

> When literary and artistic matters are discussed in our meetings, an atmosphere is created in which any defense of legitimate Party claims is considered unfashionable and out of place; one runs the risk, so to say, of being branded a retrograde and conservative, or being charged with dogmatism, sectarianism, narrowmindedness, obduracy, Stalinism, etc. Recently, the well-known film director Sergei Gerasimov, very much perturbed, declared at a conference of film workers that nowadays it requires a certain amount of courage to remain committed to socialist realism.[23]

A month later, in a desire to imitate the reactionary displays of Moscow, CPL Secretary Antanas Barkauskas delivered a rebuke to Lithuanian writers. He made the following charges:

> Some artists, aping certainly not the best models of Western art, have taken to producing work that is lacking in content and unacceptable in form. . . . Formalistic tendencies have appeared to a certain extent not only in art, but in music, literature, cinematography. . . . Some critics and theoreticians have been vociferous in their praise of formalist works, which they consider examples of innovation with an

exclusive right to existence. These works are set above the best of realistic art. In some cases formalism, and even its extreme expression, abstractionism, have been held out as the principal course for socialist art to follow. Alongside this, there has come into prominence a certain liberalism and concessions to views that are alien to Marxist aesthetics.

Having noted that many artists and writers had interpreted the freer climate after Stalin's death to mean the advent of liberalism, Barkauskas continued:

Using the pretext of creative freedom, they began to attack the leadership prerogative of the Party. These people declare: "Let us be free to create as we like, we want no directives, no restrictions, and no interference." But if the Party were to lose its ties with the intellectuals, it would lose the strongest foundation on which its role as educator and builder of Communism rests.[24]

The speeches of these Party officials contained nothing original; they were simply the reiterations of reactionary ideas clearly defined by L. Ilychev. Speaking in Moscow to writers and artists, he said:

Without any equivocation, let the following be stated: There never was and there never can be a peaceful coexistence of socialist and bourgeois ideologies. The Party has always fought and will continue to fight the bourgeois ideology in all of its aspects.[25]

On March 8, 1963, in a long speech to writers and Soviet artists in general, Khrushchev merely repeated Ilychev's statements while presumably making an evaluation of certain writers and artists. The reactionary character of Khrushchev's speech is best revealed by his injunction to writers—that the Stalinist period was not to be criticized in its totality, for Stalin had been a Marxist-Socialist and had made considerable contributions to the spread of Communism in the world. Lithuania's Soviet press showered the same approval on this speech by Khrushchev that it had given all other similar speeches in the past. On the other hand, an unofficial estimate of the artistic situation in Lithuania runs as follows:

At this time Soviet artists find themselves standing at a crossroads. There is general confusion as to what is advocated and what is being disparaged. The attacks on abstractionism were suddenly halted when it was seen that they had provided the necessary cover for the legions of pseudo artists who had dominated the scene and flourished in the time of Stalin to come to the fore again, with their usual impertinence. . . . Between these two extremes, nothing of any worth or significance is produced. The artists keep on at their work, each according to his own knowledge and ability; usually they imitate aspects of past epochs and styles, and are unable in any way to achieve a creative grasp of the present. The existing situation is best characterized by a saying that has recently come into vogue here: A donkey's tail should not be used in painting, but then neither should the donkey's hoof be used in criticism.[26]

The last sentence quoted obviously refers to Khrushchev's lack of critical competence, since his denunciation of abstractionism contained mention of the donkey's tail.

From these statements by Moscow Communist officials, made in the years 1962–63, it can be seen that the Party and the Soviet Government have no intention whatsoever of lifting their encirclement of the writers and the artists. For this reason, the situation of Lithuanian literature and art remains unchanged. The small margin of freedom that had been granted during the thaw has again been narrowed and diminished to accord better with the purposes of the Communist Party and Russian nationalism.

10. Soviet Policy Toward Religion in Lithuania: The Case of Roman Catholicism

VITTORIO VIGNIERI

Roman Catholicism is the traditional religion of Lithuania. It has deep historical roots and commands strong, almost universal support. In 1940, 94 per cent of all ethnic Lithuanians were Catholic, and nearly all of these were formally affiliated with the Church. Of the total population of the country, 85 per cent was Catholic and only 8 per cent Protestant and Greek Orthodox. Therefore, to speak about religion in Lithuania means primarily to discuss Catholicism.

THE CHURCH IN INDEPENDENT LITHUANIA

The Lithuanian Church was very well organized. In 1940, there were two archdioceses and four dioceses, with three archbishops and nine bishops. The Church was served by 1,439 priests, 708 churches, 314 chapels, 37 religious houses for men with 580 monks, and 85 religious houses for women with 950 nuns. The four seminaries accommodated 425 students of theology.

Although religious instruction in all faiths was provided in the public schools, the Catholic Church maintained eighteen private secondary schools and an equal number of primary schools. The nuns operated thirty-five kindergartens, ten orphanages, and twenty-five homes for the aged; in addition, they served two hospitals, a home for delinquent girls and an institution for deaf-mutes. The State University of Vytautas the Great in Kaunas included a Catholic-run faculty of philosophy, social science, and

Catholic theology (Teologijos-Filosofijos Fakultetas). A department of Protestant theology, too, was maintained as a part of the same university. Catholic chaplains were attached to the armed forces and served in hospitals and other public institutions.

The constitution of independent Lithuania guaranteed freedom of religion and conscience, allowing all religious communities to govern themselves. A concordat signed with the Holy See in 1927 formally guaranteed rights to the Catholic community. Clergymen were exempt from military duty; they also received salaries and pensions from the government, in part as a recompense for former church property then held by the state.

Within this framework, Roman Catholicism (and other denominations too) could develop freely and fully. The faithful could belong to a variety of Church organizations and religious brotherhoods, and it is estimated that such organizations had a membership of 800,000. In addition to these associations, the Catholics operated several publishing houses for the publication and distribution of Catholic literature. These had their own modern printing shops, libraries, bookstores, and agencies. In 1935, the twenty-eight Catholic newspapers and journals published in Lithuania had a circulation of 7 million copies annually. Learning was encouraged and supported by the previously mentioned school of philosophy, social science and theology, and by the Lithuanian Catholic Academy of Learning. In 1939, Pope Pius XII, while greeting the Lithuanian representatives to the Holy See, rightly called Lithuania the outpost of Catholicism in northern Europe.

THE FIRST SOVIET OCCUPATION: JUNE, 1940–JUNE, 1941

To destroy this northern outpost of the Church, Moscow used all its powers. Following the occupation of June, 1940, the Russians attempted to sovietize Lithuania as quickly as possible. The destruction of the Church, it soon became apparent, was an important part of sovietization. On June 25, 1940, even before the election of the "people's" *seimas,* the regime decreed an absolute separation of church and state. Five days later, the concordat of 1927 was repudiated and the Papal Nuncio, L. Centoz, was ordered to leave the country.

Church property was confiscated; the law nationalizing land allowed individual owners to retain control of not more than seventy-five acres, but parishes could retain only seven and one-half acres, including land occupied by buildings and cemeteries.

In this manner, 93,025 acres were taken from 690 churches and 3,775 acres from 28 monasteries. In addition, salaries and pensions paid to clergymen were discontinued and Church funds in banks and savings institutions were confiscated. Catholic printing shops and bookstores were expropriated by the Act of August 6, 1940, nationalizing all trading and manufacturing establishments, and their stocks of religious publications were destroyed.

Further decrees especially affecting Church property followed. The decree of October 31 nationalized all private buildings larger than 720 sq. ft. in cities, and 550 sq. ft. in villages. However, these exemptions did not apply to Church holdings; the clergy was deprived of all housing and had to rent it back from the state. They paid "capitalist" rent of three rubles per square meter, while the "workers" paid only one ruble. Single persons could occupy only nine square meters; for anything over that double rent was required. Many Church buildings, monasteries and rectories included, were taken over for the use of the Red Army, thus automatically becoming state property.

As a result of these acts and decrees, the Church lost all its property, capital, and sources of income. Only donations by the faithful supported it, but even these had to decrease as the country was pauperized by the introduction of the ruble at par value with the litas (the unit of Lithuanian currency), though its actual purchasing power was only 25 per cent of the latter.

The Communists gave particular attention to the education of youth. On June 28, 1940, the Party banned religious education and prayers from public schools; crosses and other religious symbols were ordered removed from all classrooms. The Catholic-run school of philosophy, social science, and theology was closed, and all private schools were nationalized. Chaplains were removed from their positions in the army and in hospitals and prisons. When it was discovered, in the spring of 1941, that certain priests, following the orders of their bishops, were giving religious lessons in churches, sacristies, or their own homes, they were immediately ordered to discontinue all instruction, and in some areas they were forced to pledge formally in writing not to teach religion.[1] Complete enforcement of this prohibition was prevented, however, by the outbreak of the Soviet-German war.

Furthermore, during this first occupation (1940–41) the Communists exerted every effort to isolate the Church from public life, hoping that even adults would "forget their religion." At first, the usual propaganda techniques were employed in the press, but after these failed to produce the desired results, new methods were adopted. Local government officials began a program of intensive surveillance to prevent any civil servants, especially teachers, from attending religious services or associating with clergymen. Persons seen in church frequently were summoned to local Party headquarters and threatened.

The battle against the "mass superstition" of religion also included the abolition of religious holy days: Corpus Christi processions in the streets were banned; Christmas and Easter were declared work days and those failing to report to work were punished. During Lent and Advent, in violation of old religious traditions, the Party organized dances and other amusements. Sundays were often declared workdays, especially if a Communist feast day had been celebrated during the week.

Furthermore, the new regime confiscated the buildings of theological seminaries, hoping thus to prevent the education of new priests. The Catholic hierarchy attempted to keep at least one seminary going, and in fact received permission to operate the seminary at Kaunas, though the confiscated school buildings were not returned. Despite this apparent concession, Soviet intentions soon became apparent. When Bishop Vincentas Brizgys visited V. G. Dekanazov, the Deputy People's Commissar for Foreign Affairs, who was sent to preside over Lithuania's sovietization, the Russian explained that the Catholic clergy must understand the situation and display positive loyalty to the new order. There was no need for "illusions," he made clear; a colossus with twenty years' experience had fallen upon tiny Lithuania, and what was achieved in Russia in twenty years would be accomplished in Lithuania in two or three. A seminary, Dekanazov explained, was really not needed: Why deceive the young men, who when they became priests would have nothing to do? Even the Bishop himself should give some thought to what he would do when no one any longer obeyed him.[2]

The Communists hoped that as a result of their decrees and other measures at least half of the priests would voluntarily abandon the priesthood and become available for "positive work." Efforts were made to persuade them to abandon their vocation and take secular jobs, but none were converted. Threats forced some to remain inactive, but the large majority carried on their work with even greater perseverance and energy. The Party was also unsuccessful in its attempt to recruit informers among the clergy and to introduce distrust and dissension into its ranks. Those who refused such "job" offers either fled to Germany or went to prison.

After the abolition of all national and religious organizations, the church was the only place left where men of good will could gather. Noting this, the Party organized the surveillance of priests, choosing informers from among those close to the clergy. In addition, many measures were taken to discredit the clergy: in the press, priests were cursed as "enemies of the people" and "exploiters of the working class"; Communist Party meetings resolved to destroy these enemies at any price.

In fact, the Communists, almost from the moment they occupied Lithuania, realized that because of education, influence, and prestige, the clergy—"the servants of the cult"—were the most conspicuous Soviet enemy. The Communist attitude may be seen from a secret directive sent out from Moscow on October 2, 1940, by Gladkov, the Soviet Deputy Commissar for State Security, to all regional NKVD chiefs. This directive ordered organization of a drive against the "oppositional activity of the clergy." Agents, recruited from the ranks of the clergy and church employees, were to be employed in spying on priests, deans, and members of the diocesan curiae. Files and dossiers were to be built up showing which priests still maintained contacts with the laity, especially with students and prominent Catholics. Older high-school students also were to be recruited as spies and troublemakers. Information collected was to be relayed to the headquarters of the NKVD by October 10, 1940.[3] The directive ended by stressing that "some priests are not economically provided for and waver in their ideology"; the Soviets apparently hoped that economic hardship would be a particularly strong inducement to potential agents and defectors.

Several months later, on January 21, 1941, the same Gladkov demanded that regional NKVD chiefs supply him with the names of clergymen of all faiths by January 30, noting their influence among the masses and upon the political life of the country.[4] This information, we now know, was one step in the plan, then being formulated, for the annihilation of the clergy. However, because of unfavorable public opinion, the physical destruction of the clergy was delayed until after the country itself was purged of all "antirevolutionary" elements. This massive purge began on June 14–15, 1941. (Further about deportations see pp. 87, 91.) The first transport included nine Lithuanian priests; in addition, another fifteen priests were slain by the Communists, who, as they retreated from Lithuania, massacred political prisoners. Eighteen priests whom the Russians had imprisoned were freed from prisons as the routed Russians were forced to withdraw.

THE SECOND RUSSIAN OCCUPATION

We discussed the events of the first occupation at some length because they clarified Soviet policy toward religion. They provided ample reasons to fear that if the Soviets reoccupied Lithuania, the persecution of religion would be carried on with even greater intensity.* This new persecution—from 1944 on—can be divided into three stages: the war and postwar years (1944–54); the years of the thaw (1954–56); the period of intense attack (1957–).

The War and Postwar Years (1944–54). This period was characterized by the moral and physical terrorization of the faithful. If during the first postwar years (roughly until 1946), because of the intense anti-Soviet partisan movement throughout the country, the Soviets felt insecure and were unable to introduce mass terror, by late 1945 and early 1946, they were able to mount an intensive campaign against the partisans and to commence mass deportations, which continued in waves until 1950. Terrorization of the clergy began at the same time. Members of the clergy were

* The Catholic Church did not have an easy time during the German occupation (1941–44). Lithuanian bishops reopened the seminaries in Kaunas, Telšiai, Vilkaviškis, and, somewhat later, in Vilnius, not because of any favors from Germany, but because the insurgent Lithuanian government in power during the first weeks of the war had abolished all the laws and directives of the Soviet regime. In the fall of 1941, the School of Theology-Philosophy reopened its doors. The teaching of religion was reintroduced into schools, and chaplains were appointed to prisons and hospitals. However, the German occupational authorities deposed the insurgent government and retained the Russian laws; hence Catholics could not reopen their schools and did not have their own press. Churches and all church and monastery property remained under German control. In the winter of 1942, the Germans began to close churches, ostensibly because of an epidemic, though movie houses, theaters, and other gathering places remained open. Early in 1942, the Nazis closed the Vilnius seminary and deported 50 of its students to Germany; about 30 priests were jailed, monasteries were dispersed and their buildings confiscated, and the wearing of religious habits by nuns was banned. These were purportedly anti-Polish measures. In the course of the war, tens of thousands of Lithuanians were deported for work in Germany. In 1944–45, however, 50–60,000 Lithuanians, including 3 bishops and 250 priests, fled to Germany to escape the second Soviet occupation.

charged with having contact with the underground (the so-called nationalist bandits) or at least with being sympathetic to them. Such charges were a pretext for annihilating the clergy. Priests were arrested and deported, churches closed, and the faithful mocked and persecuted. During 1946–49, 180 priests were deported to hard-labor camps in the interior of Russia.

During those early years, the Bolsheviks even tried to use the bishops for the regime's political ends. When, in 1946, the NKVD could no longer cope with the underground, the Lithuanian Commissar for Internal Affairs demanded that the bishops condemn the resistance and urge the partisans to surrender. When the bishops refused, the NKVD, after threatening, took severe measures. The first victim was Bishop Vincentas Borisevičius of Telšiai, who was arrested on February 3, 1946, and condemned to death by a secret court in Vilnius. His auxiliary, Bishop Pranas Ramanauskas, was arrested late in 1946, tried, and deported. About the same time, Bishop Teofilius Matulionis of Kaišiadorys and Archbishop Mečys Reinys of Vilnius were deported to hard-labor camps. (Archbishop Reinys died on November 8, 1953, in Vladimir prison.) By 1947, only one bishop, K. Paltarokas of Panevėžys, remained in Lithuania.

As the number of clergymen declined, many churches could no longer be served and were taken over by the state. In 1940, there were 708 parish churches and 314 chapels; in 1962, only 575 churches remained and all the chapels were closed. Churches in larger cities suffered most: of 37 churches in Vilnius (1940) only 12 remain open; in Kaunas, only 8 of the former 29 churches and chapels remain open. Churches have been turned into museums, storehouses, and so on.

After June, 1941, the seminaries in Telšiai, Vilkaviškis, and Vilnius had been reopened. The Soviets closed them a second time, leaving open only the one in Kaunas, but limiting the number of its students at first to 150, later to 75, 60, 45, and in 1963, to 25. Nor has this "approved" seminary been left in peace. One after another, members of the administration and faculty were arrested and deported. The Party interfered with the internal rules, created various obstacles, conducted ceaseless searches, and so on. Students wishing to enter the seminary were discouraged in various ways; government permission (necessary for entering the seminary) is obtained only with great difficulty. Among those receiving permission, the government tries to introduce agents and informers to destroy the seminary from within.

About 1947, all religious houses for men and women were finally closed, their members dispersed and many deported. Members had to sign affidavits that they no longer belonged to a religious community. Membership in such communities was declared a crime, subject to punishment.

The Years of the Thaw (1954–57). Stalin's death brought new developments in the war against religion. Physical terror began to abate. Khrushchev created a sensation with his declaration of November 10, 1954,[5] to the Central Committee of the Communist Party of the U.S.S.R., in which he acknowledged that in many parts of the Soviet Union antireligious attacks had been made, priests cursed and insulted, and the feelings of the faithful hurt, while antireligious topics had been handled by incompetents. The Central Committee demanded a change. In the future, it was decreed, religion must be fought by strengthened ideological means. Leaders must be specially trained for these tasks.

The organ of the CPL, *Tiesa,* analyzed this new development as follows:

> Many collective farmers and workers, while active in production and conscientious in performance of civic duties to the fatherland, are still under the influence of religious ideas. The Party teaches us to treat them with feeling and attention. It would be stupid to consider these or other Soviet citizens unreliable in the political sense because of their religious beliefs. In the human consciousness, religious superstitions are only a relic of the past. Therefore, the battle against religious superstitions must be seen as an ideological battle between a scientific, materialistic *Weltanschauung* and an antiscientific, religious one.[6]

Khrushchev, in order to strengthen his control of the government, used demagogic slogans. One of them—the idea that the war against religion should be only ideological—confused the Lithuanian Communists, who for some time could not determine what line they were expected to follow. As a consequence, discussions of religious topics appeared in the Soviet Lithuanian press in 1956; even the faithful could publicly if cautiously express their views. Statements defending religion began to appear. For example, A. Vengrys, a doctoral candidate and member of the Lithuanian Academy of Sciences, wrote:

> Religion does not make people bad collective farmers, bad workers, or in general bad citizens of our socialist fatherland. Each of us is probably acquainted with some believers who are industrious, conscien-

tious, and efficient in the performance of their duties. These people would undoubtedly achieve even better results, greater victories, if they did not poison their minds with religious superstitions.[7]

Possibly the most daring article defending religion and attacking atheistic propaganda was written by L. Drotvinas, a candidate for an advanced degree in Vilnius University. The article is of special interest because it was written by a man educated under the Soviet system and thus to some extent reflects the position of the new Lithuanian intellectual. Drotvinas wrote:

To an enlightened person religion is not a barrier. Present-day religion has become so modernized, has made so many concessions to modern life, that we cannot say it impedes the development of science, technology, art. Technological and scientific progress is noticeable even where religion has rights in the state, where scientists are religious. In contrast, twentieth-century art, especially painting, is inferior to the art of previous ages, although the twentieth century is much more atheistic. Religion does not shackle the initiative of either workers or collective farmers, for it does not encourage men to work badly, or to cease working. On the other hand, religion cannot be replaced by cultural entertainment. Services, splendor, music, hymns, ceremonies, holy days—these appeal strongly to people, especially people of the older generation. Films and other cultural amusements have not replaced religious ceremonies and cannot replace them, as there are not enough of these new amusements and they are not always on a high cultural level. In the old days, in Lithuania, atheists led exemplary personal lives; they were few and had to oppose clericalism, which was defended by the state. Among present-day atheists we find many hypocrites and we cannot say who is better, he who goes to church, or he who goes to a tavern. In general, this problem is too extensive, too deep, to be easily solved. . . . But the religious bigot and antireligious fanatic are both comically stupid: one believes in superstitions while the other attacks them; it is not clear what the one believes or why; neither is it clear what the other is attacking nor why he becomes so excited about religion if God and the rest is all a fiction.[8]

This unusual discussion was the last relatively free statement on religion. The Party soon realized that too much freedom had been granted and, on Moscow's instructions, the press once more returned to attacking and mocking religion, the faithful, and the clergy.

The thaw brought relief to many who had survived the deportations: on February 27, 1953, and on September 17, 1955, amnesties were decreed allowing deportees, except those in certain categories, to return home. However, only about one-tenth of the deported, about 35,000 persons, returned to Lithuania. Others, though not permitted to return, were freed from forced-labor camps; they were required to settle in designated areas, usually in Asian Russia. About 130 priests returned to Lithuania at this time. A small number voluntarily remained in Russia to minister to the spiritual needs of the exiles. Bishops Matulionis and Ramanauskas were permitted to return but were not allowed to resume control of their dioceses. (Those who returned, it must be emphasized, were not rehabilitated, but only amnestied; they remained "criminals" and their "guilt" was constantly pounced on in the press.)

The thaw was marked by yet another important change in policy: On September 11, 1955, the regime permitted the consecration of two new Bishops. Julijonas Steponavičius and Petras Maželis were appointed by the Holy See to govern the dioceses of Vilnius, Panevėžys, and Telšiai. In addition, permission was granted to renovate several churches and even to build new ones in Klaipėda and in Švenčionėliai.

The Period of Intense Attack, 1957–. The thaw did not last very long, for Communist leaders soon were frightened by the dynamic manifestations of religion. So they resolved to deal the final blow to religion and the Church in Lithuania.

The Party now uses all its powers in this massive new drive, the like of which has not been seen in the history of occupied Lithuania. Mass physical terror is not employed, primarily because the regime does not find conditions favorable for it. The use of moral terror, however, knows no limit. The Communists, convinced that a complete ban on religion only serves the Church, and that persecution and terror harden the faithful and increase their number, now seek to break up the Church from within.

Nor is it only for ideological reasons that the Party has engaged in such a campaign. With the liquidation of active armed resistance and the collectivization of farms, the Church has become the sole center of spiritual and national resistance. It therefore must bear the brunt of the attack.

This attack pursues four main lines: antireligious propaganda, war against the clergy, obstacles to worship, and formal restraints on religious practice. The war against the clergy, the obstacles, and the restraints on worship are carried out by police methods.

Antireligious Propaganda: In the present period, the attention of the Party is concentrated on "scientific" atheistic propaganda. As early as 1956, *Tiesa* wrote:

> The battle against religious superstitions is an essential, indispensable part of the Party's work and of the people's education in the spirit of Communism. The Party, the professional and youth organizations, and the cultural and educational institutions must all use energetic means to correct the situation.
>
> In the expanded scientific-atheistic propaganda, it is important to employ all the means of ideological-political work: lectures, announcements, interviews, the press, radio, television, films, theater. The best propagandists of the Party and the Communist Youth as well as scientists, the Soviet intelligentsia, and agricultural specialists must take part in this especially important work. It is vital that lectures be given in every factory, every collective farm, MTS, state farm, brigade, and construction gang, so that the immortal ideas of Marxism-Leninism, the light of science, may reach the working people.[9]

A "scientific" education program designed to destroy "religious superstition" was rapidly formulated. To carry on atheistic propaganda, professors, scientists, writers, artists, actors formed special agitprop groups; 779 such groups existed in 1960. Their activities are directed by the Society for the Propagation of Political and Scientific Information, which is aided, according to Soviet boasts, by more than 15,000 lecturers in the various disciplines. In 1960, these speakers gave 80,000 lectures throughout Lithuania.

Members of the Communist Youth are required to display particular energy in this educational program. Their task is atheistically to explain natural phenomena to the workers and to popularize information about astronomy, biology, chemistry, physics, and medicine. They must create "Soviet traditions," organize solemn Communist marriages, and the like.

"Schools of atheism" have been established in Lithuania's cities and towns, where teachers, youths, and workers are informed about the alleged harm of religion and the reputed crimes of the clergy. In some cases, two-year "universities of atheism" have been founded. Graduates receive certificates of atheism.

In the cities, the work is coordinated by "atheist houses." All the city's atheists belong to such houses. Members are formed into squads that give lectures, distribute atheistic literature, write articles, organize evenings with question-and-answer periods, form atheist clubs in schools, train new propagandists, maintain contact with similar institutions in other Soviet cities, organize atheistic mock-trials, and so on.

Special attention has been directed at the younger generation. The Seventh Plenary Session of the Central Committee of the Lithuanian Communist Party, on December 3–4, 1958, had only one point on its agenda: the strengthening of political-ideological work among high-school students. New directions for antireligious propaganda in the schools were drawn up, which all educators had to follow. The Party and the Communist Youth were entrusted with its supervision. Shortly after the session, *Tarybinis Mokytojas* noted that

> the formation of a materialistic world view among high school students, scientific atheistic education, is an important field of ideological work for all educators. Teachers of biology, physics, chemistry, history, and literature can be especially effective here. . . . Even teachers of physical education cannot stand aside.[10]

Upon the reception of these directives, the press was flooded with questions from individual teachers asking how to conduct lessons. Teachers complained that such education was not easy. They raised many specific problems. Even though fully in accord with the views of the regime, a teacher faces great difficulty, they pointed out. After an exhaustive lecture, for example, a student may ask: "Why is religion persecuted here?" The teacher must then go over everything again from the beginning. It is particularly difficult, teachers pointed out, to explain why people for ages have believed in the existence of the soul, its immortality, etc.

The troubles of teachers are not solved by the antireligious literature, for it is scarcely read by the students. Difficulties are increased by the Party's insistence that high-school students must not remain mere passive listeners but must become active fighters for atheism. To this end, teachers find it necessary to organize special atheistic seminars and special lectures in addition to the regular lessons. Teachers organize "atheistic corners" in schools and assign themes on atheistic topics; they encourage students to read atheistic writers. Furthermore, to prevent any slackening of the teachers' efforts, functionaries of the Party's Central Committee travel throughout Lithuania inquiring of teachers what they have done for the cause of atheism. Advice on better educational methods is generously given.

Where can the student find support, subjected as he is to such "enlightenment" from all sources? At church? Hardly, for church attendance is considered a crime, and those caught attending are punished, sometimes even expelled from school and deprived of any further education. Teachers have been publicly warned that believing students, being "superstitious," cannot receive high marks. Until very recently, younger students were quite willing to serve at Mass and other services. Now, however, they are forbidden to do so; if caught, they are punished and moreover, the priest who has allowed them to serve is also punished.

Clearly, the Church can give but little support to the student. What about the home? Religious parents try to counteract school influences, but by doing so they risk the loss of their children, for it has happened that children whose parents "spoiled" them and obstructed their "growth" as good Communists and atheists, were taken from their parents by court decision. The education of such children has been entrusted to state institutions. Thus, parents are intimidated.

The Communists are quite aware of the strength of parental influence and very recently have devised new means to separate children from their parents. Boarding schools have been established for children who, for one reason or another, cannot live home while attending a regular school. Even when visiting, parents cannot talk freely with their children, since staff members are always present. Boarding-school students cannot return home even during vacations; they are kept busy with camps, outings, and work on collective farms.

But the Party wants the active support of parents, and to gain this end it has established a special night school—a "university"—in Vilnius to give parents an understanding of Communist education. Classes are held twice a month, with lectures, antireligious movies, and visits to atheistic museums.

Schools of higher education have even greater responsibilities than the high schools in furthering atheism. These must train their students not only to be convinced atheists but propagandists as well. In the course of their studies, students take part in various atheistic propaganda exercises; those who refuse to make such practical application of their study lose their scholarships and must leave the university.

In addition to teachers and parents, medical men have been given an important propaganda role. In 1959, Professor V. Girdzijauskas asserted that

the function of medical lectures is not only to supply information on the medical sciences, but also to aid in forming a materialistic *Weltanschauung*. As a branch of biological science, medicine is a strong weapon against obscurantism and superstition. It is hence not surprising that the best Russian doctors . . . were materialists. . . . In every medical lecture, the lecturer encounters religion. He must lay bare antiscientific idealistic views, demonstrate the incompatibility of religion with medical science, in explaining natural phenomena.[11]

Such directives forced medical bacteriologists to attempt experiments proving that Church attendance, use of consecrated water, and kissing the cross are harmful. It was claimed that many infectious diseases were caused by the practice of such "superstitions."

In sovietized Lithuania, it is not enough merely to attend antireligious lectures. All civil servants, teachers, and doctors must publicly attack religion. It is therefore not surprising to find in the press "confessions" of conversion to atheism by persons nobody could possibly expect to become atheists. Few escape the atheistic organizations: one must become a propagandist, sign up for a seminar, or join a discussion group. Each faces the same dilemma: either he declares himself an atheist and convinces others that he is, or he loses his job and risks reprisals. The instinct of self-preservation, desire to protect one's livelihood, and hopes for the future force people to join the ranks of atheists. However, such public confessions and participation do not yet reveal the true spiritual state of these coerced individuals. On May 29, 1961, Vilnius radio indulged in some speculation:

> It is really strange that frequently even atheists baptize their children in church. They surrender to the influence of devotees, bow before superstitions. . . . This allows the people to think that atheists only pretend to be such and really think differently, since they baptize their children and so on.[12]

Especially active in atheistic propaganda work are former priests. There are several of these (about a dozen), the most active of whom is J. Ragauskas, an author of numerous atheistic tracts. They go on lecture tours, speak on the radio, and perform other functions. These unhappy victims of Communism are regarded by the people more with pity than with hate.

All media of mass communication are used in this propaganda work. In 1957, a journal called *Mokslas ir Gyvenimas* was established to further antireligious education. It frequently publishes "confessions" by those who have renounced religion and have become atheists. Furthermore, this propaganda is served by specially produced books and pamphlets, both original works and translations. As early as 1949, A. Sniečkus announced the printing of

650,000 copies of periodicals to disclose "the reactionary activities of Catholic clergymen." In four years, 1,500 antireligious books and pamphlets were published. According to *Sovetskaia Litva*, 3 million copies of Russian books have been imported. A group of translators is at work in Vilnius, translating Russian works into Lithuanian. Many of these translations are popularly written pamphlets that spread atheism by "uncovering" many alleged crimes of the clergy. In recent years, this production has been stepped up considerably.

Radio is frequently used as a propaganda instrument. Radio Vilnius has scheduled regular hours of atheistic education. The atheist club broadcasts answers to questions on religious topics.

Atheistic films such as *The Creation of the World, The Essence of Life,* and others have been produced to further antireligious propaganda. A film called *Turkeys* mocks the saints and miracles, and *In the Shadow of the Cross,* to cite the Communist press, is a visual "act indicting religious morality and its defenders." It shows Juozas Skvireckas, Archbishop of Kaunas, allegedly thanking the Nazis "for the massacre of thousands, for the burning of towns and villages." This film, as much of the other Soviet propaganda, seeks to prove that priests not only collaborated with the Nazis and other bandits, but that they are bloodthirsty themselves. They are pictured as heirs to the Teutonic Knights and the Nazis.

Besides the media of mass communications, other means have been devised for propaganda purposes. The chief of these are museums of atheism and the introduction of new ceremonial symbols to replace religious ones. Up to now, antireligious museums could be found only in isolated areas and were not noted for the number of their exhibits. Early in 1962, however, Vilnius radio announced the creation of a central atheistic museum in the closed Church of St. Casimir in Vilnius. Its aim is to organize traveling exhibits and generally to propagate atheism. It will include an atheistic library. The former priest Markonis has been appointed director of the museum.

The Communists, furthermore, seek to change religious loyalties by changing the meaning of Catholic holy days. For a long time, the Party hammered away at the theme that religious feasts are only relics of paganism and hence meaningless inventions of the priests. However, this interpretation did not deter the faithful from attending church on feast days. The only way to eliminate feast days was to "paganize" them by destroying their religious character and using them for Communist ends. Thus, Easter has been transformed into a spring festival; Pentecost, into a day celebrating the shepherd and his herds; St. John's Day, into a summer solstice festival. Christmas poses greater problems, and a suitable alternative has not been found. New Year's Day, however, has already become a festival of the Russian "Old Man Frost." When no substitutes for a feast day can be found, as in the case of St. Peter's or St. Michael's, some other festivities are arranged on those days. Young people are required to participate and are thus prevented from attending church. Usually, such celebrations are noisy; it is carefully arranged that they take place near churches when services are being held. To keep children from attending religious services on ordinary Sundays, athletic games or other recreational activities are organized.

To counterbalance the ceremonial effect of baptism, confirmation, and religious marriages and funerals, civil rites have been substituted for religious ones. "Civil traditions"—in reality new ceremonials—are thus being created. Specially established "soviets for the introduction of new traditions" are to see that baptismal ceremonies are replaced by the "name-giving" ritual, etc. Such efforts to replace the religious rites were particularly stepped up during the first months of 1963.

Several well-known Marian shrines, visited by thousands during special festivities of the Church, are located in Lithuania. Hundreds of priests used to attend these shrines. At present, however, priests are barred from visiting these sites, and pilgrims are intimidated and discouraged: roads are blocked, transportation is refused, visitors are searched and arrested, and so on.

Churches that remain open in Lithuania are now state property and must be rented by the parishes. Since they are considered places of entertainment, rents are extremely high. Before 1960, rents varied from 10,000 to 15,000 rubles (in old currency). Since parishioners had to contribute this sum, it was hoped by the regime that inability to pay such high rents would bring about the closing of the churches. Until recently, however, the required sums were raised and the churches were kept open. Recently, rents were increased threefold and even fourfold, in a bold attempt by the government to coerce the faithful, who they hope will tire of this financial burden and at last surrender.

Latest reports indicate that the regime has dropped all pretense and has been freely turning churches into museums, warehouses, and so on. The beautiful church in Klaipėda, which the Soviets permitted to be built in 1956 during the post-Stalin thaw, has had its tower razed and been converted into a music hall. Many beautiful Lithuanian churches, which in the past had been classified as architectural monuments and hence cared for and renovated by the government, lost this protection on Moscow's orders, delivered by Khrushchev himself. Worse still, proposals have been made to raze them as relics of a feudal age.

War Against the Clergy: The campaign against religion has so far not brought the desired results; people still hold on to their "superstitions" and the Party charges that this is the priests' fault. They are the guilty ones: "The Church and priests through long centuries have entangled the people in religious cobwebs, which now are not easy to break."[13]

After the regime pushed the Church off the mountain, the Church descended to the valleys and continues its sermons. It seems that these "sermons from the valley" are a great thorn in the side of the regime, for the press suggests that the "preachers" be stopped by police measures.

What are these "preachers" accused of? They have closed their eyes, the Communist indictment runs, and refuse to recognize the new morality and ethics that are blossoming in Lithuania. From their pulpits, they moan about the decline of virtue, about sins such as theft, drinking, adultery. Even worse, the priests slander the regime and try to frighten the people. They have directed all their artillery at the hearts of the youth, especially of young girls. Mothers are warned how loosely their daughters will behave once they lose their faith. In this way, these preachers openly condemn Soviet society. The clergy, the Communists say, is particularly worried about the younger generation. At times, priests do not even bother to ask if the children and their parents want any religion at all; they lure or force them to attend classes in religious instruction. From the pulpit, mothers are encouraged to teach catechism at home. Many priests exert every effort to draw away children from Soviet educational institutions.[14] The clergy is also accused of visiting the faithful and encouraging them to fulfill their religious duties. Priests who "disturb freedom of conscience" are threatened with imprisonment. Even the press in Moscow has found that the inhabitants of Lithuania are still quite religious and conscientiously attend church on holy days.[15] The priests, the Communists say, have invented a new way of maintaining contact with the faithful: They organize sports clubs, dances, and reading circles. Also, they have found ways of producing and distributing religious articles, the Communists claim. In 1963, two Jesuits were arrested for "speculating" in such articles.

The Communists, aware of the popular respect for the clergy, have recently developed a special campaign of slander against them. Priests are charged with having collaborated with "bandits" (Lithuanian guerrilla freedom fighters) and German fascists. According to the regime, there is no crime against morality, humanity, or existing laws that priests have not committed. The accused, however, have no opportunity to defend themselves. No newspaper will print a priest's answer, no court will accept his defense. And if sometimes the priest defends himself in a sermon, he is punished for "hooliganism," for daring to oppose Communist "truth."

Police Methods: Besides propaganda measures and direct harassment, the Communists have decreed a whole series of prohibitions aimed at destroying religion in Lithuania. It is important for the Communists to disrupt the structure of the Church, to separate the clergy from Rome; hence communication with the Vatican is discouraged and made as difficult as possible.* The Apostolic Administrator of the dioceses of Vilnius and Panevėžys, Bishop Julijonas Steponavičius, has been deposed and deported to the remote village of Žagarė. T. Matulionis, the recently deceased Bishop of Kaišiadorys (elevated to the archbishopry by the Pope), suffered a similar fate: He was exiled from his diocese to the small town of Šeduva, and his auxiliary, Bishop V. Slatkevičius, was deported to Nemunėlio Radviliškis (near the Latvian border). The recently appointed Apostolic Administrator for the diocese of Panevėžys has been deposed and exiled to Merkinė. These officials are not allowed to have any ties with the faithful or fulfill their duties. Hence, in the whole of Lithuania, only one Bishop, P. Maželis of Telšiai, remains free, and even he is constantly badgered in the press.

The Church is, in fact, administered to the last detail by the Commissar for Affairs of the Cult. He even specifies when and how long church bells can ring. Without his permission, no priest can fulfill his duties or occupy any position. There are priests who have been refused his permission. The appointment of priests to parishes and their transfer is also within the commissar's juris-

---

* The regime allowed delegations of Lithuanian priests to attend the Vatican Ecumenical Council; however, none of the bishops was permitted to travel to Rome.

diction. He himself endeavors to fill vacancies. He also seeks to promote priests faithful to the government.

The only theological seminary in the country (in Kaunas) is permitted to have only 25 students and it is also supervised by the commissar, who appoints and dismisses teachers and controls admission. Recently, admission has been restricted even further and it seems that the seminary will be slowly throttled. Since more priests die each year than are ordained, the time is nearing when the regime will be able to close many churches for lack of pastors.

The clergy is not allowed to teach the catechism to children. Previously, they could at least examine children taught by their parents, but even this is no longer permitted. If it is discovered that some old lady has been teaching a group of children, she is brought to court and sentenced for keeping a "secret school." The parents are punished, as is the priest in whose parish the "school" was discovered. Although no law forbids parents to teach the catechism to their own children, parents found doing so are persecuted and punished for "injuring the children's conscience."

Priests cannot visit their flocks, solicit donations to support their church, visit the sick in hospitals (even if the sick person requests his presence in writing). Similarly, those who are in contact with the priests are subject to much unpleasantness. In this way the clergy is gradually being isolated from the faithful. It has happened that priests were sentenced and deported because they organized excursions for their altar boys or distributed candy and hence were "enticing" persons to attend church.

Without official permission a priest cannot visit other parishes for religious services or in general leave the place of his residence. Priests must pay heavy taxes. During the thaw some priests were allowed to build rectories, but these have now been declared illegally built and have been confiscated. In 1956, permission was granted to build a church in Klaipėda, and material was released for this purpose by the government. People gave money with enthusiasm, and the church was completed. But permission to use it was never given; instead, the priests who built it were brought to trial in 1962 on charges of having illegally used materials and having speculated in foreign currency (some donations were received from Lithuanians in the U.S.). The building became state property; its builders received sentences from four to eight years. The 1962 trial of the Klaipėda priests was also used to impugn the personal and vocational integrity of the entire Lithuanian clergy.

In Lithuania today there are no religious publications. Anyone discovered circulating handwritten material is punished for "circulating illegal literature, disseminating superstitions." No religious publications or religious articles (rosaries, medals, pictures) can be imported from abroad.

Church attendance is not illegal, but schools, offices, and factories apply their own sanctions. Those attending are carefully watched and controlled. The faithful, to avoid persecution, fulfill their religious duties away from home, where they are not known. Those who have their children baptized, or who marry or bury their dead with benefit of clergy, can expect various unpleasant consequences. Thus, even such things as these must be done in secret.

Results

What are the results of such intensive propaganda, terror and persecution, carried out by the whole apparatus of Party and state? Although the Communist press likes to boast that most people are already free of "superstitions," the constant complaints lead us to believe that results are not easy to achieve, that "religious superstition" has deep roots. The regime publicly admitted this during the Plenum of the Central Committee of the Lithuanian Party early in 1963. The Plenum, it is worth noting, dealt solely with the topic of antireligious propaganda. Often, we find complaints in the press that antireligious literature is not being read; it has to be forced into people's hands and reading groups then have to be organized. People herded into meetings, lectures, and seminars remain passive or ask questions that the speakers themselves cannot answer. Another complaint is that not only high-school, but even university students, publicly draw attention to their presence in church. Of course not all do, only some—the more daring ones.

Informed sources have stated that in Lithuania almost 100 per cent of the children are baptized, that 80 per cent of all funerals are religious, and that 60 per cent of all marriages are performed in churches (many others are secretly married in church). The regime has complained that even Komsomol and Party members marry in church, baptize their children, and bury their dead religiously.

On the other hand, it would be illusory to underrate the Soviet war against the Church and think that it is ineffective. The intensive atheistic education will turn some into militant atheists, cause others to become indifferent to religion, and force an even greater number to conceal their convictions. It would seem that the majority, however, will remain loyal to the religion of their fathers. The point of view of that majority has been well stated in a young girl's letter, signed "a Lithuanian Catholic," which the Communist Party paper *Tiesa* printed in 1960 so that the former priest J. Ragauskas might have the opportunity to rebuke her. She wrote:

> I am a Catholic. From my very infancy my life has been tied to religion, to the Church. No arguments that God does not exist will destroy my faith, and if necessary, I will choose death rather than lose my faith. I, as a Catholic, conscientiously attend church; I see many priests, but I have never met the sort the papers write about. They exaggerate and shout to the four winds every mistake made by a priest.
>
> I am only twenty years old and my whole life is before me. . . . I find many good things in present-day life. I work and also study. . . .
>
> Nevertheless, I cannot divide my heart; the whole of it belongs to the Church. Religion is my very heart, and to take away my religion would be to tear out my heart.[16]

11. Soviet Social Engineering in Lithuania: An Appraisal

V. STANLEY VARDYS

Soviet ideologists continue to claim that a nation can be radically transformed by changing its productive system. Its transformation from capitalism to socialism, and eventually to communism, they say, gives rise to different social institutions, and in turn, to a completely different national culture, i.e., to a different national identity, to the "new Soviet man."

The experience of Soviet rule in Lithuania, however, does not support this Marxist-Leninist fiction. The sovietization of Lithuanian society did not result from natural changes in productive forces and relations, but was a product of planned social engineering executed by force and manipulation, both applied under laboratorylike conditions of complete social isolation. The purpose of this chapter is to examine this social engineering by the Soviets and to appraise, as much as available evidence allows, how it has affected Lithuania's demographic, sociopolitical, and cultural-ideological personality.

THE SOVIET GOAL IN LITHUANIA

At the beginning of the Soviet occupation in 1940, the Lithuanians were apprehensive about their future, but not even the Lithuanian Communists knew exactly what demands the Soviets would make and how the satisfaction of these demands would affect the Lithuanian society. The gravest doubts centered around the questions of Lithuanian nationalism—political, economic, cultural.[1]

Generally, the Soviets promoted the view that their attitudes on nationalism radically differed from the Czarist policies. The

Leninist-Stalinist formula, "national in form, Socialist in content," was proposed as offering a genuine promise of national autonomy in cultural affairs. It therefore took time for the populace to realize that Moscow had more than merely political and ideological claims on Lithuanian society. Mounting evidence pointed to the disturbing conclusion that under the Leninist-Stalinist nationality policy, Moscow sought culturally to assimilate and Russianize the newly occupied land. Indeed, by the time Lithuania was annexed, the policy formula no longer applied in the Soviet Union itself. It simply shielded Russian nationalism, which Stalin had revived in the mid-thirties.

This situation did not change after Stalin's death. Although the slogan "national in form, Socialist in content" was left unaltered, its meaning was so broadened that the Party's 1961 program, using euphemistic Marxist-Leninist slogans, legitimized the policy of Russification. The Soviet Union, according to the program, had advanced to a stage of economic and social unity at which not only identity of cultural contents, but also assimilation of national forms of Soviet nationalities was indispensable. This assimilation should occur through the medium of the Russian language. In 1963, courageous students of the Vilnius Pedagogical Institute publicly denounced this new program as the Communist Party's plan to de-Lithuanianize the country.[2] There is little doubt that these students were right. Experience of the last quarter of the century, and especially after Khrushchev's ascendancy in 1957, fully supports the charge. Decisions of a conference at Frunze of October 9–12, 1963, dedicated to a systematic study of *rapprochement* and fusion of Soviet Socialist nations also support the view that Moscow pursues a policy of intensified Russianization.[3]

What then is the ultimate Soviet objective in Lithuania, as crystallized and articulated by Soviet policy-makers and propagandists? It is the ideal of a "new Communist man," which means a collectivist, atheistic Russophile, unreservedly loyal to the Party and to the Moscow directed state.[4] This new Lithuanian is supposed to be an "internationalist," that is, in favor of an eternal union with the Russians, whom he must regard as "elder brothers." In the future, he will be completely bilingual, fluent not only in his native tongue, but also in Russian. His loyalties to the ethnic Lithuanian community are to be superficial, extending only to national costumes, dishes, etc. He must love his native land no more than he would "a lovely, dear corner in a large apartment."[5] It is the apartment however, that is his home. This new man will subscribe to the principle of "friendship among peoples," which the Soviets explain by the example of "friendship and fraternity" in the Red Army.[6] This analogy underscores the ideal of Soviet nationalities disciplined in a common organization under a common language to serve their Russian superiors and leaders.

The creation of such a man was emphasized at the Twenty-second Party Congress and afterward. However, it is not an exaggeration to say that the Soviets have been working toward this goal ever since the beginning of the occupation of Lithuania. I do not mean to suggest that Moscow's policy-makers had a detailed model on which they wanted to pattern all their moves. Exigencies of power, domestic as well as international, the war, resistance in the occupied area, economic needs, and human factors of administration did not allow a continuous concentration on the long-range objective. Until the early 1960's, the model was not even clearly described, possibly because of the fear of what its effects might be on the yet not fully subdued population groups in Lithuania. The model was completely unfolded, so to speak, after Khrushchev took over unchallenged direction of the Soviet Union.

THE DESIGN OF SOVIET SOCIAL ENGINEERING, STAGE ONE:
THE DESTRUCTION OF THE OLD AND SETTING UP OF THE
NEW SOCIAL ORGANIZATION

In Lithuania, as in many other countries, the Marxist-Leninist design provided for two stages of social engineering: first, for economic and political action; second, for ideological warfare. The first stage called for the destruction of the old system and of the classes that were considered its mainstays; the ideologies allegedly supported by these classes were believed to die out automatically. This destructive action was to be combined—either immediately or subsequently—with the construction of a new economic and political order and of new classes supporting it. The second stage of this social engineering provided for the "mopping up" of the "remnants" of hostile ideas and for a positive ideological molding of the already conditioned populace.

The first stage of the design was begun immediately after the annexation of Lithuania in 1940 and was completed, the Soviets claimed, in 1951. Industry, commerce, and finances, nationalized

during the summer months of the 1940 occupation, had not been
returned to private ownership by the Germans, and the Soviets
therefore could immediately take over their management. Further
industrialization was decreed in 1946, with Lithuania's inclusion
in Moscow's Five-Year Plan. Thus the creation of a working
class, hitherto small, was begun; the regime hoped it would become one of the main pillars of their "socialist" society. The wip-
ing out of private farming, begun in August, 1940, was continued
with the land reform of August, 1944. Collectivization did not
begin immediately after World War II, but in four years' time it
was going at full speed, although not all local Communists were
yet ready for it. Thus, the independent farmer was replaced by
the kolkhoznik, intended to stand as the other pillar of the Soviet
social order. This synthetic revolution was duly accepted by a
constitutional reform[7] which eliminated concessions made to private enterprise in 1940. This move brought the republic's constitution into line with the Stalinist constitution of 1936, which
claimed to have established a socialist system in the Soviet Union.
Lithuania, the regime announced in 1951, also had become a
"socialist nation." This of course merely meant that sovietization
had been completed and the pattern of the Party-oriented Soviet
society fully imposed. Achieving this Party-oriented society (instead of the ideologically postulated classless one) was costly in
human suffering and materially wasteful. It not only disrupted
Lithuanian society, but also greatly affected Lithuania's demographic personality and political leadership.

Lithuania's demographic personality. Lithuania's population was
affected in several ways. First, the "achievement of socialism"
(1940–41 and 1944–51) cost an estimated 500,000 people—liquidated, confined to camps, dispersed, deported (there were several
mass deportations, in 1941 and 1946–50).[8] Because of this mass
destruction, Lithuania was unable to make up for the demographic losses inflicted by the Nazis (these amounted to 250,000–
300,000 persons) and those caused by the migration of the German
and Polish populations (about 250,000). Thus, between 1944 and
1950, while the other European countries were recouping their
wartime population losses, Lithuania, a country with a high birth
rate, was still suffering a population decrease. According to Soviet
statistics, Lithuania's population in 1959 was 5.8 per cent smaller
than in 1939.[9] At the beginning of 1962, it reached 2,852,200,
which, however, was still 27,000 below the 1939 level.[10] Also, the

population density was somewhat smaller because Lithuania in 1959 covered a territory 2,209 sq. mi. larger than that of October, 1939. (In 1959, Lithuania covered an area of 25,167 sq. mi.)

Second, the Soviets obviously aimed not only at the destruction of unreliable elements but also at the dispersal of others. According to a Soviet census of 1939, about 32,000 Lithuanians lived in the Soviet Union outside Lithuania. In 1959, this figure was close to 200,000,[11] almost 10 per cent of the total number of ethnic Lithuanians within the confines of the Soviet empire. The new figure included deportees who were not allowed or unable to return, "volunteers" working on the virgin lands, graduate specialists assigned to work outside Lithuania in payment for scholarships, some demobilized members of the armed forces. This dispersal is continuously promoted by ideological campaigns for volunteers to "build Communism" outside the Lithuanian borders, yet there is a chronic labor shortage in Lithuania itself.

The third result of "socialist construction" was the strengthening of the Russian minority in Lithuania. The number of Russians almost quadrupled. It is today the largest non-Lithuanian minority in the country, having increased from 2.3 per cent in 1939 to 8.5 per cent in 1959 (or 10.3 per cent if the Ukrainians and Belorussians are added). The Russian group increased not only in numbers but also in influence. Although a substantial number of Russians work in urban centers as simple laborers, an unusually high proportion manage Party, government, and industrial offices and enterprises. Only a negligible number works in villages and kolkhozes. They belong to the class of higher income, prestige, and power. They are treated as a privileged group by the courts and by administrative agencies. The Russians, however, do not isolate themselves in Lithuania as they do in Central Asia, or as the French did in Algeria. Moscow's policy has been one of mingling with the local population at all social levels. Intermarriage with native Lithuanians also has been encouraged.

The position of other minorities in Lithuania also changed. This happened not so much as a result of Soviet as of Nazi policies. Thus, the largest prewar minority, the Jews, were almost completely wiped out by the Nazis (of the 250,000–300,000 people liquidated or deported by the Nazis, an estimated 190,000 were Jewish). In 1959, Jews constituted only 0.9 per cent of the population, as compared to 8 per cent in 1939. The Germans, too, diminished as a consequence of their voluntary repatriation in 1941—from the prewar 4 per cent to 0.4 per cent. The number of Poles, on the other hand, increased considerably (from 3.04 per cent in 1939 to 8.5 per cent in 1959), although a considerable number of Poles voluntarily returned to Poland after the war. Polish-language schools still exist; the regime also allows the publication of a Polish weekly paper. Most of the Poles are found in the Vilnius area restored to Lithuania in October, 1939.

The percentage of ethnic Lithuanians, the majority of the republic's population, has remained stable. The natural increment of the twenty postwar years has almost made up for the losses; in 1959, the Soviets reported that Lithuanians constituted 79.32 per cent of the total population. Before the war they accounted for 80.9 per cent.

Finally, a more usual demographic change because related to economic reorganization has been the rather rapid urbanization. In 1962, approximately 41 per cent of the total population lived in cities and towns. This represents an estimated 18 per cent increase in 20 years. The rate of urbanization, therefore, appears to be twice as rapid as before the war, when in the course of twenty years an estimated 9 per cent of the population moved to the cities. This growth of cities and the expansion of new ones is, of course, a direct product of industrialization. It has also been helped by the low standard of living in rural areas, which has brought on a steady exodus from villages to towns. Moreover, the cities have absorbed most immigrant Russians assigned to administrative jobs in the republic or those who set out on their own in search of greener pastures. Whether by design or not, urbanization has helped to Russify several population centers. For example, the capital, Vilnius, and the port of Klaipėda are reported to be at least 50 per cent Russian.

Political leadership. This Russification of the population centers has been symptomatic of the shift of influence and power, even the power that the limited Soviet federalism allows, to the Russian minority. The preceding studies have amply illustrated that although Lithuania is ruled by the Lithuanian Communist Party, the Party itself is ruled by the Kremlin through Russians sent in from the Party's headquarters in Moscow. In the past, Lithuanian leaders were unsuccessful in defending their ground against Moscow's order on any important issue, such as construction of hydroelectric stations they wanted, the reform of education they advocated, the agricultural policy they supported, or even the restoration of cultural monuments initiated by them. The most recent data further indicate the degree to which the Lithuanian Party itself is dominated by the Russians.

According to statistics provided by the Mandate Commission of the Fourteenth Conference of the Lithuanian Communist Party (January 9–11, 1964),[12] the Party in 1964 had 69,522 full members and 7,968 candidates. At the conference, this membership was represented by 864 delegates. Of these, 580 were Lithuanians, 180 Russians, 31 Ukrainians, 25 Belorussians, and 48 others. This delegate distribution, the Mandate Committee Chairman, A. Britov (a Russian), said, "testified to the immutable sacred friendship among nations of the Soviet Union and the adherence of the republic's Party organization to the spirit of internationalism." It also revealed that 32 per cent of the conference delegates, and thus approximately the same percentage, or about 23,000 Party members, were not Lithuanians; furthermore, it revealed that some 18,000 members, or about 20 per cent of the total Party membership, were Russians although the Russian percentage in the population, according to official statistics, was less than 9 per cent. Similarly overrepresented were the Ukrainians and Belorussians, who for practical purposes must be classified with the Russians because most of them generally stay with the Russian community while residing in the non-Russian republics of the Soviet Union. The composition of the new Central Committee is also very similar, though in the Presidium and the Secretariat only one member, B. Popov, is a Russian sent from Moscow. This preserves appearances; actually, the First Secretary, Antanas Sniečkus, hardly acts without approval from the Second Secretary, Popov.

THE DESIGN OF SOCIAL ENGINEERING, STAGE TWO: POLITICO-IDEOLOGICAL STRUGGLE

Political and economic measures taken to destroy the old and to create a new society were accompanied by the struggle against "bourgeois" ideology, especially nationalism, and in 1951 the regime claimed to have destroyed it because it had demolished those social classes which allegedly supported this ideology. Therefore, only "remnants" of the "bourgeois" ideology remained. The record shows, however, that it was much easier for the Soviets to impose their economic and political institutions than to liquidate these "remnants," which appeared to be more than simply survivals of another age. Furthermore, they were sustained by much larger forces than the liquidated classes or their economic organization.

These "remnants" of "bourgeois ideology" may be divided into three groups: (1) attitudes on property and social ethics that are contrary to the officially postulated collectivism and Communist morality; (2) religious "superstitions"; and (3) manifestations of "bourgeois" and also nonbourgeois nationalism. An examination of these factors throws some light on the effectiveness of Soviet ideological indoctrination.

The Collectivist Mode of Life. Although an appraisal of attitudes toward Soviet collectivism of necessity is impressionistic, Soviet newspaper data and information from recent Lithuanian repatriates allow an interesting generalization, namely, that the more Soviet a collectivist institution, the less it is accepted by the population. This is demonstrated by a review of Lithuanian responses to three such institutions: social security and medical care, state ownership of industry and its centrally planned management, and collectivized agriculture.

The first institution, providing pensions, medical service, paid vacations, privileges at work while attending school, etc., seems to enjoy universal approval. Independent Lithuania, to be sure, had a reasonably well-developed pension and medical plan, but the present program provides a much broader and almost universal coverage. The quality of services rendered varies locally and frequently is inadequate, but city workers with an average income of between 50 and 80 rubles a month and collective-farm peasants with hardly any cash income at all could not afford any services unless provided by the state. Thus, although there are many complaints voiced in the official press about the lack of medicines, medical supplies (a hospital, for example, might have an X-ray machine but no film), shortages of hospital beds, the necessity of bribing doctors to receive decent care, etc., these services constitute an integral and seemingly permanent part of Lithuanian social services. Of course, there is nothing specifically Soviet about this institution; the Bolsheviks were not the first to introduce this either in Europe or in Lithuania.

Similarly, the Lithuanians were acquainted with state ownership of manufacturing and commercial enterprises and with cooperatives, and the latter enjoyed almost a monopoly position in important segments of the rural economy and foreign trade in independent Lithuania. Ownership of these institutions by the

Soviet state, therefore, at least to the middle-aged generations, is neither strange nor revolutionary. The populace, however, refuses to accept the total prohibition of any private enterprise and the centrally planned management of the economy. This is seen in the never-ending efforts to "beat the system." Thus, there still are people, even entire families, who manage to avoid working in factories or on collective farms and yet they earn a better living than those working for the state. For example, individuals and teams rent themselves and their horses out for construction jobs. Illegal taverns also abound. Other self-employed persons make cemetery monuments, keep small tailoring shops, photo studios, etc. Since heavy taxes on such private "businesses" make "privateering" unprofitable, its practitioners secure labor cards (every person in Lithuania must have one) by bribing factory, collective-farm, or other officials and thus do not register as "privateers" at all. In 1961, the regime passed legislation against such "idlers and parasites," leveling stiff penalties against violators. However, this law has not been rigidly enforced, if at all. There are no penalties for "part-time privateers" who work for others on weekends. Another decree, passed on August 30, 1962, also has not been widely enforced. This one provides for the expropriation of privately built homes if the owners cannot prove the legality of either financing, materials, or labor. The law not only acknowledged the existence of widespread private construction activity, but even more, of considerable black marketeering, stealing, and *blat,* that is, the granting of favors in return for favors granted, without regard to official regulations. Antanas Snieckus had good reason for his warning in 1962 that "the psychology of private ownership is very much alive" and that some Party organizations are not aware of how dangerous that psychology and "the trend toward private ownership was."[13]

It seems that a certain amount of "privateering" and especially institutional *blat* is tolerated officially because it helps to satisfy individual needs as well as those of the state. Without such free enterprise many legitimate demands would not be met and many plans would remain unfulfilled. The impression is gained that the collectivist Soviet system itself survives only because the regime unofficially allows it to be broken and fed from the boundless resourcefulness and energy of the individualistic human nature. Incidentally, Khrushchev's reforms in the economic field are actually attempts to incorporate this "privateering" into the official collectivist system. The treatment of the professional *blat* practitioner ("the fixer") in Lithuania demonstrates how much the regime needs flexible private initiative under the inflexible central system of management. The fixer is a hybrid between a sales and procurement officer, public relations specialist, and expert in black marketeering. He helps to get unavailable supplies, to cut red tape, thus aiding the fulfillment of the very plans that do not provide for his existence. The man's importance in the Lithuanian economy was very picturesquely explained by a satirist in *Šluota* (*The Broom,* the Lithuanian counterpart of the Russian *Krokodil*) in a poem describing how conscience-stricken authorities decided to bury Comrade *blat*. They put him in a coffin and lowered it into the grave, but all of a sudden realized that the coffin had not been nailed. They sent an attendant for some nails, but he could not find any far and wide. Hearing the commotion outside, Comrade *blat* inquired about the difficulty and promised to help if the authorities in turn would help him out of the coffin. They did and he reciprocated. "And thus," the writer ended, "*blat* retained the most honorable position in the entire enterprise."[14]

The other important Soviet institution, that of collectivized agriculture, is thoroughly disliked. Manifestations of this dislike are very numerous. Kolkhoz buildings are left in disrepair, farm machinery rusts in the fields through the winter, communal produce is used for private purposes, work discipline is very poor, and production figures are often lower than before the war. Young people trained for skilled jobs in rural areas do their utmost to be assigned to work in cities, even if this involves change of profession. Teachers appointed to rural schools desert by the thousands. Alcoholism, widespread in the cities but rampant on farms (it is very helpful for *blat*), is still another sign of disaffection in the village. As in industry, here, too, the collectivist system feeds on concessions to individualism. Thus, kolkhoz members are given private plots that not only provide for them, but also produce a large percentage of the total agricultural production (for example, almost a half of all dairy and meat products) although their acreage is but a fraction of that of collective farms. Furthermore, the Lithuanian collective farmer is still allowed to live on his old farmstead, which has preserved a degree of privacy. This apparently is tolerated because the regime neither financially nor politically can afford a massive transferral into village housing.

It must be added that the kolkhoz system is detested not only because of its foreign nature and radicalism that destroyed the traditional "peasant way" of life, but also because the Soviets, by collectivizing agriculture, imposed semifeudal restraints on the farmer and substantially reduced the rural standard of living. The kolkhoznik's dissatisfaction with conditions has forced the regime to keep him bound to the kolkhoz by law, thus making it almost impossible to quit the kolkhoz for a job in the city where there is more opportunity and a guaranteed wage, however small. The kolkhozniks are tied down to their kolkhozes as in feudal times and only the younger generation can escape, mainly by way of education. Moreover, economically the collective-farm members are much worse off than average farmers in independent Lithuania or than the present urban population. Despite increased farm mechanization and the introduction of certain amenities like electricity, the life of a *kolūkietis* (the Lithuanian word for kolkhoznik) is very hard. It can be visualized from this recent description by a Soviet Lithuanian writer:

> Our villages, generally, lag behind our towns in standards of living and of culture. The most important reason for this is the poor pay, which forces the kolkhoznik to rely for his livelihood mainly on his private plot (vegetable garden, cow, pigs). Work on this plot of land consumes most of his free time, and thus does not allow him fully to utilize the means for cultural activity. Instead, it pushes the villager into a crude materialism. It is not surprising therefore that a city dweller who volunteers to work on a collective farm is looked upon either as a crackpot or a hero.[15]

The impact of such a system can be fully understood when it is remembered that almost 59 per cent of the total population lives under these conditions. Collectivized agriculture is the regime's Achilles heel. None of the agricultural reforms promulgated by Moscow so far has achieved success in Lithuania.

The Struggle Against Religion. In 1964, religious persecution continued unabated despite a certain easing of relations between Moscow and the Vatican under Pope John XXIII. The regime has allowed delegations of the Lithuanian Catholic clergy to attend the sessions of the Ecumenical Council and also to attend Pope John's funeral, although none of Lithuania's bishops were granted permission to go to Rome. Contacts with the Vatican, however, did not lead to a reduction of pressure on the Roman Catholic Church and on other religious denominations in Lithuania. In the early 1960's, religious activities were further curtailed by prohibiting priests to administer last rites, even at the request of the dying, by forbidding the annual visits to parishioners' families (*calenda*), and by reducing the number of theology students at the only Roman Catholic seminary from forty to twenty-five. Meanwhile, antireligious activities and propaganda have been intensified. The smaller Christian denominations also have been severely punished, especially the Pentecostals and the Baptists. In 1962, the heads of the Jehovah's Witnesses sect were put on trial for "subversion" and received long prison sentences. The Baptists and others had their children taken away for refusing to send them to state schools and for "indoctrinating" them at home.[16]

The regime has been preoccupied, however, with the affairs of the Catholic Church because it is the largest and because it has been traditionally identified with Lithuanian nationalism. The regime's leaders have continuously emphasized this connection as one of the compelling reasons for atheist propaganda. "In the minds of many regressive people," Antanas Sniečkus repeated in 1963, "the remnants of nationalism are closely related to religious superstitions. This fact especially compels Party organizations actively to further atheist work as an integral part of the struggle against the ideology of bourgeois nationalism."[17] The regime so far has been able to undermine the Church's economic and social strength; it has reduced the Church's influence in cities and has succeeded in producing religious indifference among large segments of youth. However, it has neither won over the clergy (only about a dozen in the entire republic have given up the priesthood) nor separated its organization from Rome. A quarter of a century of relentless suppression, nevertheless, has fostered a desire for accommodation among some of the clergy eager to alleviate the persecution. Delegations sent to Rome under the auspices of the regime apparently were intended not only to demonstrate "freedom" of religion in Lithuania but also to pressure the Vatican into accepting compromises with the Soviets. This, of course, would ensure Vatican approval for Moscow's present policies toward Catholicism in Lithuania. However, thus far these attempts have been unsuccessful. All the more important and interesting, therefore, is the question whether the religious suppression and atheistic propaganda has influenced the Lithuanian nationalist personality; religion so far has been the stanchest ally of nationalism. Admittedly, inroads have been made by the Soviets in undermining this alliance.

THE DESIGN OF SOCIAL ENGINEERING, STAGE TWO: LITHUANIAN NATIONALISM

Nationalism as a Social Force After World War II. The effects that the replacement of the old order with the "Socialist system" had on Lithuanian nationalism are of particular significance, because nationalist attitudes have a more direct bearing on political loyalties and commitments.

Since the end of World War II, Lithuanian nationalism has manifested itself in two ways: first, as an aggressive organized movement, especially during the period of the so-called "construction of Socialism"; later as a cautiously calculated activity, from the mid-1950's until now. In the early postwar years, that is, through the politico-economic action stage of social engineering (1944–51), the Lithuanians fought the regime by force of arms. The eight-year guerrilla war (1944–52) was costlier and more destructive than the Algerian rebellion against the French, which won independence for the Algerians. In addition, the Lithuanians supported a number of clandestine organizations, dedicated to cultural resistance against sovietization, especially of schools. Later, in the 1950's, after organized resistance was crushed, individual groups continued their opposition by sabotage and propaganda. The Communist Party daily, *Tiesa*, reported that in 1957–58, such groups sabotaged factories, robbed offices for money and supplies, etc.[18] The Hungarian Revolution was celebrated in Lithuania by public demonstrations in Vilnius and Kaunas. It is important to note that the demonstrators were primarily young people, not just college students but factory workers as well. The demonstration in Kaunas was analyzed in Vytautas Rimkevičius' novel *Studentai* (*The Students,* 1957), which was quickly withdrawn from the bookstores. Meanwhile, individual guerrilla groups continued to hide out; *Tiesa*, for example, reported the capture of such a group in 1961.[19] The last-known trial of a partisan leader was held in Kėdainiai on May 6–8, 1963.[20]

After 1951, the Soviets claim, only "remnants" of nationalism survived. According to their ideologists, present-day manifestations of Lithuanian nationalism are "subtle" and "masked," "indirect" and "unconscious."[21] However, nationalism is still regarded to be the main obstacle to the "drawing closer of Socialist nations."[22] Despite the destruction of the social classes that allegedly were the sole supporters of nationalism in the past, people "infected with bourgeois nationalist ideology and psychology"[23] still exist. Indeed, according to Genrikas Zimanas, editor of *Tiesa,* manifestations of nationalism are found even among true and loyal "Soviet people."[24] Nationalism, in other words, is admitted to have a broad basis and still is feared as a dangerous social force. It therefore has been on the agenda of every conference of the Lithuanian Communist Party, and a topic of discussion in almost every plenum of its Central Committee.

The list of these "remnants" of nationalism is long. It includes localism, that is preference for the local Lithuanian needs, dislike for the Russians and the Russian language, nationalist interpretation of Lithuanian's cultural heritage, nationalist history writing, emphasis on nationalist peculiarities in cultural and other activities and in the selection of the cadres, a non-Marxist explanation of the origin of nations (they rise as a result of certain economic conditions, Marxist-Leninists say, but they will eventually disappear in the Communist society), a view that not classes but nations are responsible for historical development. The regime also considers that "objectivism" in teaching, research, and creative writing, as well as petty-bourgeois attitudes prevalent especially among middle-income groups, are screens that hide nationalism. These manifestations are found not only among the masses, but also among the intelligentsia, in the government, and even in the Party.

Nationalism in the Party, Government, and in Public Institutions. The Lithuanian Communist Party has not experienced purges of high leadership because of nationalist deviations as has happened in Latvia and some Central Asian and Caucasian republics. However, individual *apparatchiki* and Communists in non-Party positions have been accused of tolerating expressions of anti-Russian sentiment, closing their eyes to the unlawful rehabilitations of "bandits" (nationalist partisans), tolerating nationalist teachers, etc. Among these, the most famous case was that of Professor Juozas Bulavas, who was fired as rector of Vincas Kapsukas University in Vilnius and expelled from the Party for "nationalist deviations in the work with the cadres."[25]

Nationalist tendencies in government are more widespread. During the immediate postwar periods, the regime was forced to . use some surviving "bourgeois" administrators who "distorted the Party's policy, misled and disoriented the masses."[26] These, however, were replaced by Soviet managers as soon as the latter, primarily of Russian nationality, became available. After Stalin's death, many of the Russian replacements were in turn replaced by Lithuanians. These appointments immediately resulted in rising nationalist feelings and demonstrations. In 1959, the Party, this time under Khrushchev's firm control, clamped down again in a variety of ways, especially by revising its cadres policies, which again gave Russians a disproportionate share of jobs and re-emphasized ideological activism as a condition for receiving appointments. Nationalist manifestations, however, did not cease. For example, charges of "ideological mistakes in appraising traditions of Lithuania's past" led to dismissals of the managers of the State Committee for Construction and Architecture and the revamping of its plans to restore about 200 Lithuanian castles and churches. It is interesting to see, though, that the "reform" was made only after Nikita Khrushchev publicly complained about the renovation program at the January, 1961, Plenum of the Central Committee. The Publishing House for Political and Scientific Literature was similarly chastised, particularly for publishing the historical writings of J. Jurginis, a Party member and historian, who simply did not do a sufficiently good job of Russifying Lithuania's history. After his original history of Lithuania was banned, he prepared a book of readings (1964), which, however, also was severely criticized for underplaying Lithuania's alleged historic reliance and dependence on Russia and for failing clearly to apply the Marxist periodization of history.[27]

The republic's schools, however, remained the most nationalistic institutions. Their staffs therefore have been repeatedly purged and warned.[28] For example, the University of Vilnius lost its rector and a number of professors on charges of nationalism. The deputy dean of the city's pedagogical institute and some professors also were fired on similar grounds. Heads and faculty members of other institutions have been reprimanded for publicly defending religion, for "apolitical" teachings, for "objectivist" research. Similar sins have been discovered in schools of general education. Thus, in 1961, a teacher was fired because he said that "the Soviet rule would not survive."[29] In 1963, *Tiesa* complained that teachers as well as students of a provincial school praised independent Lithuania.[30] Many teachers, the complaint goes, preach nationalism, attend church services, baptize their babies. Teachers and scientists are still regarded as sections of the intelligentsia infested with "bourgeois-nationalist ideology." Thus, the members of the Lithuanian S.S.R. Academy of Sciences were specifically asked in their 1963 meeting to struggle against nationalism.[31] Yet at the very time that this was demanded, college faculty members were crying for greater recognition for the Lithuanian language, literature, and creative arts. For example, some instructors at the Vilnius Pedagogical Institute demanded more weekly teaching hours of Lithuanian in secondary schools.[32] Others asked for an additional twelfth year of secondary schooling, or at least the establishment of special classes in humanistic studies that would allow a more intense study of Lithuanian literature.[33] Still others wanted to hear more music by Lithuanian composers.

Nationalism in Daily Life. This nationalism of the teachers not only conveys attitudes of a particular social group, but also mirrors the feelings of the Lithuanian intelligentsia and, generally, of broad segments of the Lithuanian population. To begin with, the populace today does not seem to accept the Communists any more than it did a decade ago. Despite the fact that between 1954 and 1964, the Party's membership has doubled (from 34,544, in 1954, to 77,499, in 1964),[34] the percentage of Party members in Lithuania still is much below the Soviet average; only about 2.5 per cent of the population belongs to it. This percentage is even smaller among the ethnic Lithuanians (less than 2 per cent). The ideological commitment of many of those Party members also seems to be doubtful. Many people, the Soviets publicly complain, join the Party for opportunistic reasons. The fervor of older Party members has declined. Their commitment to Communist social ethics also is questionable. In 1961, for example, two members of the Central Committee of the Party were expelled and sentenced to prison terms for *blat* activities.[35] In 1963, another Central Committee member was purged.[36] Although reasons for his dismissal were not given, there is no indication that it was caused by an intra-Party feud.

Furthermore, examples given by the Soviet press suggest that a large number of parents and families have not yet dropped their opposition to various Communist activities and further indoctrination. Thus, there still are parents who have the courage to forbid children to join the Komsomol.[37] Pioneers are frequently sneered at.[38] *Komjaunimo Tiesa* once described a family that refused to praise their daughter who had run away from home to join the Komsomol and was liquidated by the nationalist guerrillas.[39]

Russian influence and even identification with Soviet citizenship are shunned and even detested. Thus, people sometimes refuse to speak Russian in public;[40] parents forbid young adults to marry Russians.[41] A very revealing story in *Tiesa* tells of Lithuanian tourists in satellite countries keeping away from the Soviet group with which they traveled, demonstratively refusing to speak Russian, and even attempting to pass for Western visitors.[42] On another occasion, the Communists were appalled by a refusal of a workers' collective to condemn youths for trying to flee the Soviet Union.[43]

It is a small wonder, therefore, that in such an atmosphere functionaries of the regime feel that at least occasionally they have to come out in defense of Lithuanian national culture and cultural aspirations. This helps to explain, for example, the letter by Mečys Gedvilas, the Minister of Education, which he published in *Izvestiia* on March 22, 1964. In it, this old-guard Communist and former important government leader, demanded the safeguarding of the Lithuanian language in the newly planned educational reform of the Soviet Union. The plan provided for the return to *desitiletka* (ten-year secondary education). Gedvilas argued that national republics should be allowed to keep the eleventh year of education because, he said, students there have to spend one full year learning Russian and thus are deprived of adequate time to study their native languages. However, Moscow disregarded this plea, and in September, 1964, secondary schooling was reduced to ten years.

The Struggle for the Youth. The letter by Gedvilas is symptomatic of competition for the loyalties of the republic's younger generation. The youth has been the regime's special target, particularly since 1958. In that year, the Soviets started a post-Stalinist offensive against nationalism and religion and pressed for more tangible ideological gains among the youth.[44] "The new Soviet man," of course, was the ideal to be achieved. First, however, the youths were to be alienated, divorced from their native history, traditions, and social institutions. In December, 1957, the Central Committee's Plenum in Moscow initiated certain policies designed to intensify this alienation process (as well as a greater integration into the general Soviet framework). In Lithuania, the regime mobilized everything, including films, TV, and show trials, to rewrite Lithuania's history, to intensify atheist propaganda, and by various fabrications to destroy the moral authority of Lith-

uanian nationalist leaders, guerrillas, and other alleged supporters
of nationalism, especially the United States, the Vatican, and
Lithuanian refugees from Soviet rule. One of the obvious purposes of this activity was to demonstrate that Lithuania's "des-
tiny" was to stand together with the Russians. Another objective
was to alienate the youth from the strongest native institution,
Roman Catholicism. At the same time, Party ideologists uninhib-
itedly promoted the image of the pro-Russian, atheistic Soviet
patriot and greatly expanded efforts to promote the Russian
language as the medium of the new man and his new culture.

In this new campaign, the regime no longer relied on the direct
use of force as in Stalinist times, but rather on social pressure,
individual persuasion, and material inducements. Only rarely is
police power used directly; however, it lurks in the background
and creates a proper atmosphere for a favorable compliance with
these Soviet pressures and blandishments.

Such concentrated onslought, to which there is no parallel in
Lithuania's experience under the Soviets, undoubtedly must have
made some progress. For example, after the wholesale dismissal of
the Lithuanian Komsomol leadership (all of the secretaries, and
76 of the 81 members of the Central Committee), the Komsomol
membership very rapidly rose to 209,000 (January, 1964), about
double that of 1957.[45] This constitutes an estimated 40 per cent
of the total Komsomol-age population of the republic. Similarly,
numerous teenagers have been scared or lured away from attending church.

Interestingly enough, however, these statistical successes are
much more impressive than the actual ideological penetration.
The superficiality of ideological gains can be reasonably well ascertained, at least in certain aspects of propaganda work on nationalism and atheism. It is quite apparent that the youth do not
accept Soviet propaganda uncritically. Thus, students still refuse
to believe that Lithuania's material advances (for example, the
rapid industrialization and the impressive development of post-
primary education) were made possible only by the Soviet system.[46]
The regime's agitators are angered and frustrated by assertions
that independent Lithuania would have achieved these material
gains on its own, even without paying such a high price in suffering, misery, and waste. Similarly, even Soviet-born and -educated
students publicly question the motives of the Soviet nationality
policy and have denounced the 1961 Party's program as a plan for
Lithuania's Russianization.[47] They also refuse to accept Soviet

claims of the good life in the Soviet Union and the bad life in the West. In the fall of 1963, *Tarybinis Studentas,* a newspaper of the University of Vilnius, denounced the Russians, criticized Soviet standards, and praised the West.[48]

The young generation also has refused to identify itself with Russia or the Russian traditions. Almost all the demonstrators sympathizing with the Hungarian Revolution of 1956 and celebrating Lithuania's Independence Day on February 16, 1957, were young people. They are unmistakably proud of Lithuania's old traditions of statehood when, as a young writer recently put it, "both the East and the West trembled before its [Lithuania's] power."[49] Some of them are outrightly disloyal, as exemplified by two young Lithuanians who attempted to escape into Turkey.[50] One of these young men, a teenager, was the son of a pro-Soviet educator and writer. This points to another problem that the regime has to face, namely, nonbourgeois, pro-Communist nationalism. Such tendencies were detected especially in the Kaunas Party organization and Komsomol after the Hungarian Revolution. This nonbourgeois nationalism, however, seems to be a broader phenomenon. At the most recent Komsomol convention, its leader, A. Česnavičius (a former altar boy), warned the youth not only against the bourgeois but also "any other" nationalism.[51]

Soviet achievements in atheist indoctrination seem to be similarly modest. Very many Komsomols still attend church, read religious books, sometimes hold religious reading sessions in the official "houses of culture," and occasionally even create havoc by applying for admission to the country's only theological seminary. Furthermore, very few young people become active atheists. It is interesting to see that the Soviets merely succeed in producing philosophical agnostics. The view fashionable among the youth is that religion, like *Weltanschauung,* is a private affair. The hatred for religion has failed to materialize. It also seems that the propaganda saturation campaign has backfired, creating an aversion to all ideology. A large segment of the youth has been scared away from thinking on their own; they concentrate on good times, the good life, and generally display a restlessness and nihilism that now seems to be sweeping the youth of the Soviet Union and the satellite countries. Still others simply brush aside Communist propaganda and eagerly imitate Western fashions, music, art, etc.

Intelligentsia: Which Way? Similar observations can be made about the ideological development of the Soviet-educated intelligentsia, which plays an influential part in present-day Lithuania. Although converts have been made and this intelligentsia has learned to observe the limits of the regime's tolerance, the Soviets have failed to produce Communist militants who frown upon nationalistic Lithuanian identification. Questions about Lithuanian culture and national survival seem to concern all, not just the more courageous, who show this interest by public utterances or deviationism. This is the more remarkable because the regime has made intense efforts to integrate this intelligentsia, especially its creative talent, into the Soviet system by awarding it the Lenin Prize and other medals, offering professional opportunities in Moscow and in Russian establishments, lending an all-Soviet professional aura to certain cultural achievements and celebrations.* However, thus far the faceless pro-Russian "internationalism" has destroyed neither the "national particularities" nor the desire to be different from the Russians. Similarly, atheism has not yet won out over religion. The students and the intelligentsia do not subscribe to atheism or doctrinaire Marxism-Leninism, but rather to agnosticism, ideas of tolerance, humanism, Western modernism, or simply to cynical nihilism. Secret religious communicants, too, are numerous in these circles.

The intelligentsia, generally, seems to be tired of the hatred and fault-finding with political opponents that the Communists continue to promote. Also, they are weary of the Party's manipulations to prevent social peace among all elements of society and between the past and the present. Teachers, doctors, scientists, and other professionals demonstrate this by deliberate restraint in Communist propaganda activities, especially atheist campaigns in which they are forced to participate. A surprisingly large part of the intelligentsia finds ideological warfare either distasteful or inconsequential. Ideological militancy seems to be regarded as unbecoming to educated people.[52]

---

* For example, in 1962, Eduardas Mieželaitis won a Lenin Prize for his book of poems, *Žmogus (Man)*, which was published in Russian before it was published in Lithuanian. In 1963, the sculptor Gediminas Jokubonis was awarded a Lenin Prize for a monument to the victims of the Lithuanian village Pirčiupis, whose entire population was burned alive by the Nazis during the war. The sculptor's work was directed by a supervisory committee. A number of Lithuanian artists, among them an old nationalist, A. Žmuidzinavičius, and a younger Communist, Vytautas Jurkūnas, have been made People's Artists of the Soviet Union. One of the conductors of the *Bolshoi* theater in Moscow is a young Lithuanian, Žiūraitis. In 1964, the 250th anniversary of the birth of Kristijonas Donelaitis, a classical Lithuanian poet, was celebrated in Moscow.

This desire for social peace and ideological tolerance is also reflected in the most recent literary production. For example, A. Pocius, a young writer, in a short story on resistance to the Soviet regime, heretically puts a pro-Communist official seeking refuge from nationalist guerrillas and the official's non-Communist friend running away from the Soviet police in the same hiding place.[53] The Chairman of the Lithuanian Writers Association, A. Sluckis, the critic Sluckaitė, and even the Lenin Prize winner Eduardas Mieželaitis have been criticized for tendencies of "general humanism."[54] The critics especially objected to Mieželaitis' advice to forget about mutual recriminations and the beating of dead horses.[55] Despite the official Communist attempts to whip up campaigns of hatred against "bourgeois nationalists and their supporters,"[56] the opinions among the very youngest writers suggest "forgiveness and forgetfulness" even toward persecuted families of alleged "Hitlerites."[57]

The Lithuanian intelligentsia is politically realistic. Mindful of the international situation, it no longer expects the immediate overthrow of the regime its seniors hoped for in the aftermath of World War II. It also differs from the elder generation in that it is not divided along prewar partisan lines. According to recent *emigrés*,[58] however, the intelligentsia reflects a variety of attitudes on the country's present political situation and possibilities. There is, for example, a pro-Soviet view advocated largely by those who somehow benefit from the regime and who justify the Soviet rule by economic advantages they believe accrue from being part of the Soviet Union. The second view, expounded by "national Communists," demands a greater national autonomy than now granted by Moscow. Another opinion, especially popular since Stalin's death, advocates a satellite status for Lithuania as the first realistic step toward full independence. In addition to these, there are still those among the intelligentsia who expect another world war and hope that this war will bring freedom to their land.

SOME CONCLUSIONS

With the superior power at their command, the Soviets could quickly destroy the old and impose the new order; this imposition, however, so far has failed radically to change the ideological views of the new social classes and of the younger generation. Gains, admittedly, have been registered; different norms of behavior and different customs have made some headway, attitudes toward industrial property and state services are generally socialistic, but these have not transformed the Lithuanian community's basic loyalty to itself into loyalty to the foreign occupant. The concept of Lithuania as "a lovely dear corner in a very large Soviet apartment" has not yet sunk into the consciousness of even the Lithuanian born under Soviet rule. For him, as the young writer Romualdas Lankauskas wrote in a much-denounced novel, Lithuania still is "the green country, covered with the bones of his forefathers who for centuries fought for their freedom. He felt how priceless this holy land was for him."[59]

The majority of Lithuanians, especially the dominant middle-aged and younger intelligentsia, simply know that under circumstances they have no other choice but to put up with the regime while constantly probing the limits of its tolerance for efforts to preserve Lithuanian nationalist identity and culture. The youngest generation, born and educated under the regime, seems to be fully aware of its ethnic and cultural particularities. Nationalism may not even substantially suffer from the damage inflicted on the alliance between nationalism and Catholicism. The tradition of Lithuanian secular and anti-clerical nationalism reaches back into the second half of the last century, and the divorce of the two at present may not hurt either. Nationalism can and does exist without this alliance even now.

This limited ideological success disproves the Marxist-Leninist thesis that the change in productive relations and social classes automatically transforms people into supporters of the Soviet regime, into "Soviet men." Conversely, it may be argued that if nationalism is not overcome by the change in socio-economic institutions, it possibly is not a product of solely these institutions, as Marxists-Leninists teach. The institutional framework apparently functions as a qualifying, not the determining factor. It is obvious in the Lithuanian case that the attitudinal changes, just as the Soviet system itself, have been enforced from above.

However, the fact that the regime's ideological penetration has been superimposed and neither very deep nor broad, does not mean that the process of cultural alienation, by producing ideologically superficial or even nihilistic people, is not making it easier for the regime to obtain political loyalties. Although such limited achievement does not seem to satisfy the Party, the regime doubtlessly has profited from its own inability to indoctrinate be-

cause it is not very difficult to buy obedience from people dis-
abused of independent thinking.

Yet neither this brainwashing nor collectivization of economy
present the main danger to Lithuania's nationalist identity. The
experience of the last quarter of our century suggests that Lithuania's nationalist future is rather threatened by the economic,
demographic and similar policies of Moscow that eventually may
destroy conditions under which it is still possible to resist indoctrination and Russification. This could happen if Lithuanians
were reduced to a minority in their own country. Such prospect
is within the realm of possibility. Since 1961, Soviet leaders have
been integrating economic, administrative, and Party management and again concentrating control in Moscow. Lithuania
today is a part of the Western economic region; large segments of
its economy are directed from centers outside Lithuania. Meanwhile, certain aspects of the Kaliningrad economy have been
integrated with that of Lithuania. It is probable that the new
Soviet constitution, in preparation since 1961, will politically
"recognize" this "new stage of economic development" by integrating Lithuania into some larger unit, say, a Baltic federation,
to which even Kaliningrad might be added. This would radically
change the demographic balance in favor of the Russians. This
fact, aided by the present policy of industrialization and privileges
given to Russians, and combined with measures that narrow
freedom and opportunities for the Lithuanian-speaking youth,
may indeed threaten the very survival of Lithuanian identity. In
the past twenty-five years, however, the Soviets succeeded merely
in swallowing Lithuania, not in digesting the Lithuanian people.

Notes

1. LITHUANIA FROM MEDIEVAL TO MODERN TIMES: A HISTORICAL OUTLINE
(pp. 3–19)

1. Vaižgantas (Juozas Tumas), *Tiesiant Kelią į Lietuvos Nepriklausomybę 1916–1917* (Vilnius, 1919), p. 35.
2. *Ibid.*, p. 36.
3. Juozas Žiugžda (ed.), *Lietuvos TSR Istorijos Šaltiniai* (Vilnius, 1958), III, 27.
4. *Keleivis* (Boston), April 17, 1918, citing *Lietuvių Balsas* (Voronezh, Russia), No. 86 (1917).
5. Petras Klimas, "Lietuvos Valstybės Kūrimasis 1915–1918," in *Pirmasis Nepriklausomos Lietuvos Dešimtmetis* (2d ed.; London, 1955), pp. 15–16.
6. Alfred E. Senn, *The Emergence of Modern Lithuania* (New York, 1959), pp. 30–32.
7. Adolfas Šapoka (ed.), *Lietuvos Istorija* (2d print.; Felbach-Württemberg, Germany, 1950), p. 544.
8. Department of State, *Papers Relating to the Foreign Relations of the United States*, II: *Paris Peace Conference* (Washington, D.C., 1942), pp. 24–25.
9. Vincas Mickevičius (Kapsukas), "Borba za sovetskuiu vlast' v Litve i zapadnoi Belorussii, 1918–1919," in *Proletarskaia Revolutsiia*, No. 108 (1931), p. 65.
10. Adam Zoltowski, *Border of Europe* (London, 1950), p. 194.

2. INDEPENDENT LITHUANIA: A PROFILE
(pp. 21–46)

1. Area and population figures from Anicetas Simutis, *The Economic Reconstruction of Lithuania After 1918* (New York, 1942), pp. 13 ff. For a bibliography on various aspects of Lithuanian life, see Jonas Balys, *Lithuania and Lithuanians: A Selected Bibliography* (New York, 1961).
2. Simutis, *op. cit.*, p. 67.
3. Among many other sources, see the account by Malbone W. Graham, Jr., *New Governments of Eastern Europe* (New York, 1927), esp. pp. 383–85.
4. *Ibid.*, p. 383.
5. A. Bilmanis, *The Baltic States in Post-war Europe* (Washington, D.C., 1944), p. 32.
6. Simutis, *op. cit.*, p. 27.
7. *Lietuvos Žemės Ūkis ir Statistika* (Dillingen, Germany, 1948), II, pp. 20–21.
8. Data on agriculture from Simutis, *op. cit.*, pp. 19–55; also from J. Krik-

ščiūnas, *Agriculture in Lithuania* (Kaunas, 1938), esp. pp. 67–87. In cases of conflicting data, reliance was placed on the work of Krikščiūnas, a specialist on Lithuanian agriculture. Data on industry from Simutis, *op. cit.; Ten Years of Lithuanian Economy,* Report of the Chamber of Commerce, Industry and Crafts (Kaunas, 1938); and *Lietuvos Žemė Ūkis ir Statistika.*

9. K. Meškauskas, in *Komunistas* (Vilnius), No. 7 (July, 1963), p. 40.

10. Simutis, *op. cit.,* p. 71.

11. Bilmanis, *op. cit.,* p. 38.

12. J. Purickis, "Seimų laikai," in *Pirmasis Nepriklausomos Lietuvos Dešimtmetis, 1918–1928* (2d ed.; London, 1955), p. 141.

13. Simas Sužiedelis, "Steigiamasis seimas," *Į Laisvę* (New York), No. 6 (June, 1955), p. 23.

14. The texts of all three Lithuanian constitutions are available in *Lietuvos Valstybės Konstitucijos* (Toronto, 1952).

15. For a brief discussion of elections to the Constituent Assembly and the three regular legislatures, see M. Mackevičius, "Seimas," in *Lietuvių Enciklopedija* (Boston, 1960), XXVII, 163–67; for a chart on partisan composition of all the *Seimas,* see Graham, *op. cit.,* insert between pp. 398 and 399.

16. Cf. Colonel K. Škirpa, chief of staff of Lithuania's armed forces at the time, in A. Rūkas (ed.), *Mykolas Šleževičius* (Chicago, 1954), pp. 249 ff.; K. Žukas, *Žvilgsnis į Praeitį* (Chicago, 1959), pp. 455 ff.

17. See *Lietuvių Enciklopedija,* XXII, 339–40.

18. *Ibid.,* XXII, 340. For a highly critical evaluation of the coup written by members and supporters of the overthrown government, see Rūkas, *op. cit.,* pp. 147–64, 247–300.

19. Aleksandras Merkelis, in *Lietuvių Enciklopedija,* XXVIII, 177.

20. Kazys Pakštas, *Lithuania and World War II* (Chicago, 1947), p. 22.

21. Pilsudski himself admitted the authorship of this coup. Quoted in John Gunther, *Inside Europe* (New York, 1938), p. 423. For recognition of Lithuania's claims, see Josef Pilsudski, *Erinnerungen und Dokumente* (Essen, 1936), IV, 84.

22. Purickis, *op. cit.,* p. 132.

23. The fullest documentation of the conflict, giving both the Lithuanian and the Polish documents, is *Documents Diplomatiques, Conflict Polono-Lithuanien, Question de Vilna, 1918–24,* published by the Lithuanian Foreign Ministry (Kaunas, 1924). The Polish version is found in *Documents diplomatiques concernant les relations Polono-Lithuaniens* (Warsaw, 1920–21), I: *décembre, 1918–septembre, 1920;* II: *avril–juin, 1921.* On the decision of the Conference of Ambassadors, see *The Vilna Question: Consultations of MM. A. D. Lapradelle, Louis le Fur, and A. N. Mandelstam Concerning the Binding Force of the Decision of the Conference of Ambassadors of March 15, 1923* (London, 1929). A dispassionate British account of the conflict was given by Professor A. J. Toynbee in *Survey of International Affairs, 1920–1923* (London and New York, 1924), pp. 248–56. A legalistically oriented American study of the conflict is found in F. Keller and A. Hatvany, *Security Against War* (New York, 1924), I. A competently narrated account of the conflict from the Lithuanian point of view is in Adolfas Šapoka, *Vilnius in the Life of Lithuania* (Toronto, 1962); the Lithuanian-Polish confrontation in the late 1920's is well analyzed by Alfred E. Senn, "Polish-Lithuanian War Scare," *Journal of Central European Affairs,* October, 1961, pp. 267–89.

24. See the interesting memoirs on the ultimatum written by a former high

officer of the Lithuanian Foreign Ministry, Dr. Petras Mačiulis, *Trys Ultimatumai* (Brooklyn, N.Y., 1962), esp. pp. 9–50.

25. O. Rutter, *The New Baltic States* (London, 1925), p. 77, quotes Georges Clemenceau's note of June 16, 1919: "The district in question has always been Lithuanian, the majority of population is Lithuanian in origin and speech, and the fact that the city of Memel itself is in large part German is no justification for maintaining the district under German sovereignty, particularly in view of the fact that the port of Memel is the only sea outlet for Lithuania."

26. For an authentic story of the revolt, see the article by its leader, Jonas Budrys, in *Lietuvių Enciklopedija*, XII, 39–43.

27. See Jonas Budrys, "Lietuvos teisės į Klaipėdos kraštą," *Į Laisvę* (Chicago), No. 20 (March, 1960), pp. 25–28.

28. A Lithuanian monograph analyzing the entire spectrum of Klaipėda's problems is not available. An intensely nationalistic German account is found in Ernst-Albrecht Plieg, *Das Memelland, 1920–39* (Würzburg, 1962). The Lithuanian Foreign Ministry has published *Documents diplomatiques. Question de Memel* (2 vols.; Kaunas, 1923–24).

29. William L. Shirer, *The Rise and Fall of the Third Reich* (New York, 1960), p. 462. In his book *Die Sowjetunion, die Baltischen Staaten, und das Völkerrecht* (Cologne, 1956), p. 22, Professor Boris Meissner maintains that the German demand to cede the Klaipėda region and the cession itself did not violate international law and that the Lithuanians gave in not so much because of German pressure as because of their understanding of the necessity for a final purification of German-Lithuanian relations.

30. For a somewhat different explanation of the background of the pact, see Leonas Sabaliūnas, "The Politics of the Lithuanian-Soviet Non-Aggression Treaty of 1926," *Lituanus*, VII, No. 4, 97–102.

31. Cf. Pakštas, *op. cit.*, p. 22.

32. Adolfas Šapoka (ed.), *Lietuvos Istorija* (3d ed.; Fellbach-Württemberg, 1950), p. 588.

3. AGGRESSION, SOVIET STYLE, 1939–40
(pp. 47–58)

1. For the text and for other related documents, see Department of State, *Nazi-Soviet Relations, 1939–41: Documents from the Archives of the German Foreign Office* (Washington, D.C., 1948), esp. pp. 76–78, 107, 112–19, 176, 267–68.

2. See the report of the American Minister in Latvia to the Secretary of State, in *Foreign Relations of the United States, Diplomatic Papers: The Soviet Union, 1933–1939* (Washington, D.C., 1952), p. 938; statement of policy by the Lithuanian Foreign Minister Juozas Urbšys in U.S. House of Representatives, 83d Cong., 2d sess., *Third Interim Report of the Select Committee on Communist Aggression* (Washington, D.C., 1954), p. 444 (hereinafter cited as *Third Interim Report*); a discussion of this story in Albert N. Tarulis, *Soviet Policy Toward the Baltic States* (Notre Dame, Ind., 1959), pp. 129–36. The Soviets popularize a cleverly fabricated claim that Lithuania itself sought a German alliance and protectorate. See, for example, *Tėvynės Balsas* (Vilnius), No. 81 (1963), p. 3; *Komunistas* (Vilnius), No. 6 (June, 1960), pp. 35 ff.

3. See a photostatic copy of this map in *Memorandum on the Restoration*

of Lithuania's Independence, published by the Supreme Lithuanian Committee of Liberation (Reutlingen, Germany, 1950), insert between pp. 36 and 37.

4. Text in Jane Degras (ed.), *Soviet Documents on Foreign Policy, 1917–1941* (London and New York, 1951–53), III, 380–82.

5. *Izvestiia,* November 1, 1939.

6. *Third Interim Report,* p. 318.

7. Text in *ibid.,* pp. 320–21.

8. Dr. Petras Mačiulis, *Trys Ultimatumai* (Brooklyn, N.Y., 1962), pp. 94–95. An account by a former chief of the Soviet division in the Lithuanian Foreign Office.

9. See reports by the Lithuanian envoy to Moscow, Ladas Natkevičius, to the Lithuanian Foreign Office, *Third Interim Report,* pp. 322–32.

10. Text in *ibid.,* pp. 332–33.

11. Cf. Stasys Raštikis, *Kovose dėl Lietuvos* (Los Angeles, 1957), II, 23–25.

12. See some of the pertinent documents in Lietuvos TSR Mokslų Akademija, Istorijos Institutas, *Lietuvos TSR Istorijos Šaltiniai* (Vilnius, 1961), IV, 772–73.

13. *Third Interim Report,* p. 339.

14. Tarulis, *op. cit.,* p. 210.

15. For the full text, see *Third Interim Report,* pp. 341–44.

16. See *ibid.,* p. 340.

17. Tarulis, *op. cit.,* p. 217.

18. Text in *Third Interim Report,* pp. 445–48.

19. Report of the Supreme Electoral Commission, *Third Interim Report,* pp. 355–57.

20. English translation in *Third Interim Report,* pp. 360–61; Russian text in Akademiia Nauk SSSR, Institut prava im. A. Ya. Vishinskogo, *Istoriia Sovetskoi Konstitutsii,* Sbornik dokumentov (Moscow, 1957), pp. 389–91.

21. Department of State *Bulletin,* III, No. 57 (1940), 48.

4. LITHUANIA DURING THE WAR: RESISTANCE
AGAINST THE SOVIET AND THE NAZI OCCUPANTS
(pp. 61–84)

1. Department of State *Bulletin,* III, No. 57 (1940), 48.

2. *Lithuanian Bulletin* (New York), IV, No. 3 (1946), 32.

3. Stasys Raštikis, "Lietuvos kariuomenės tragedija," *Lietuvių Archyvas: Bolševizmo Metai* (Brooklyn, N.Y., 1952), pp. 284–365; Lt. Trečiokas, "Atsiminimai iš 9 pėstininkų D.L.K. Vytenio pulko gyvenimo," *ibid.,* pp. 366–84.

4. Julius Vidzgiris, "Lietuvių pasipriešinimas Okupantams," *Į Laisvę* (Chicago), No. 22 (1960), p. 2.

5. Kazys Škirpa, "Apie tris birželio įvykius," *Lietuvių Dienos* (Los Angeles), No. 6 (1959), pp. 4–5, 16; "Gairės į tautos sukilimą," *Į Laisvę* (Chicago), No. 27 (1961), pp. 1–13; "Tautos sukilimo idėja," *Sėja* (Chicago), No. 4–5 (1961), pp. 4–14.

6. Among the so-called scholarly Soviet works are: A. Gaigalaitė, *Buržuaziniai Nacionalistai Hitlerinės Vokietijos Tarnyboje 1939–41,* published by the Lithuanian S.S.R. Academy of Sciences, series A, 2 (9), 1960, pp. 133–51; J. Dobrovolskis, *Lietuviškųjų Buržuazinių Nacionalistų Antiliaudinis Veikimas Okupaciniame Hitlerininkų Valdžios Aparate 1941–44,* series A, 2(13), 1962, pp. 155–74. Popularized descriptions are found in B. Baranauskas,

"Penktoji Kolona Lietuvoje 1940–41," *Mokslas ir Gyvenimas*, No. 4 (1960), pp. 33–35; A. Endzinas, "Lietuviškieji 'aktyvistai' hitlerininkų tarnyboje," *Kauno Tiesa*, No. 123 (May 26, 1961). In 1960–62, the Academy of Sciences of the Lithuanian S.S.R., in the series "Facts Accuse," published five booklets called "Archive Documents." The LAF is treated in the fourth collection, prepared by B. Baranauskas, *Hitlerininkų Penktoji Kolona Lietuvoje* (Vilnius, 1961), pp. 5–227. Among other materials, the work prints testimony doubtlessly obtained by torture of some of the organizers (Kl. Brunius, Ant. Valiukėnas) of the LAF in Berlin. Testimony of a courier, Mykolas Naujokaitis, is also found (pp. 107–19). Because the revolt of June 23, 1941, revealed the real Lithuanian attitude toward the Communist order, Bolshevik propaganda, especially since 1959, has been falsely charging that the LAF served only Nazi interests. See the works of A. Gaigalaitė and J. Dobrovolskis. These authors used source material from the main state archives in Vilnius, the manuscript section of the Academy of the Sciences main library in Vilnius (where most of the material on the LAF is to be found), and the Party Archive of the Central Committee of the Lithuanian Communist Party.

7. A large proportion of these proclamations have been collected by the Communists in the library of the Academy of the Sciences. See A. Gaigalaitė, *op. cit.*, p. 142.

8. Škirpa, in *Į Laisvę*, No. 27 (1961), p. 7.

9. *Ibid.*, pp. 7–8. Cf. testimony of M. Naujokaitis in Baranauskas, *op. cit.*, pp. 112–16.

10. Škirpa, in *Sėja*, No. 4–5 (1961), p. 12; also in *Į Laisvę*, No. 27 (1961), p. 7.

11. Antanas Pocius, "Kap. Pranas Gužaitis ir pogrindis," *Į Laisvę* (Chicago), No. 8 (1955), p. 27.

12. Škirpa, in *Lietuvių Dienos*, No. 6 (1959), p. 5.

13. Leonas Prapuolenis, "Tautos Istorinio Laimėjimo Sukaktis," *Į Laisvę* (Chicago), No. 25 (1961), p. 8.

14. Stasys Raštikis, *Kovose dėl Lietuvos*, II, 163–64. Hereinafter cited as *Kovose*.

15. *Ibid.*, p. 173.

16. *Į Laisvę*, No. 21 (October 30, 1943), p. 1. (All future references to *Į Laisvę*, unless otherwise indicated, are to the underground newspaper published in Lithuania during World War II.) Ten years later, Kleist passed over this mission almost in silence and criticized only the mistakes of the Zivilverwaltung. See P. Kleist, *Zwischen Hitler und Stalin, 1939–1945: Aufzeichnungen* (Bonn, 1950), pp. 152–61.

17. Cf. Raštikis, *Kovose*, II, 305–7; *Lietuvių Enciklopedija*, XXIX, 178.

18. This question is treated in more detail by Alexander Dallin, *German Rule in Russia, 1941–1945: A Study of Occupation Policies* (London and New York, 1957), pp. 183–86; cf. also Dobrovolskis, *op. cit.*, pp. 159–60. For an account of the pamphlets and articles on colonizing and Germanizing the Baltic that appeared during World War I, see M. Urbšienė, *Vokiečių Karo Meto Spauda ir Lietuva* (Kaunas, 1939), pp. 59–82. Hitler's plans were incomparably more stringent.

19. Raštikis, *Kovose*, II, 316.

20. Dallin, *op. cit.*, pp. 50–53, 182–86.

21. Antas Mikonis, *Bala* (Leipzig and Berlin, 1943), p. 362.

22. See Bronius Kviklys, *Lietuvių Kova su Naciais 1941–1944* (Memmingen,

1946). His information was taken from the commerce section of the *Neue Zürcher Zeitung*, September 2, 1943, pp. 13–14.

23. See Dobrovolskis, *op. cit.*, p. 162.

24. Dallin, *op. cit.*, p. 193.

25. *Ibid.*, p. 188.

26. *Ūkininko Patarėjas* (Kaunas), No. 24 (June 19, 1942).

27. *Į Laisvę*, No. 22 (1943).

28. *Nepriklausoma Lietuva*, No. 11–12 (1943).

29. *Į Laisvę*, No. 23 (December, 1943).

30. Dissension among various German officials is documented by Dallin, *op. cit.*, pp. 182–98. See also Kleist, *op. cit.*, pp. 141–69.

31. Adolfs Blodnieks, *The Undefeated Nation* (New York, 1960), p. 260. German statistics are found in *Ostland in Zahlen* (Riga, 1942).

32. *Ateitis* (German-licensed daily in Kaunas), No. 54 (March 6, 1943).

33. Juozas Žiugžda (ed.), *Lietuvos TSR Istorija* (Vilnius, 1958), p. 417; Cf. a collection of articles, *Hitlerinė Okupacija Lietuvoje* (Vilnius, 1961), p. 173.

34. Cf. Raštikis, *Kovose*, II, 326.

35. Raštikis, *Kovose*, II, 326–27.

36. *Laisvės Kovotojas*, (underground newspaper in Lithuania), No. 13 (1943).

37. *Ateitis*, No. 81 (April 7, 1943). Von Renteln's announcement warned: "It is a fact that some of the men who had to register failed to do so because of the warnings of a politicking intelligentsia and thus invited punishment upon themselves."

38. *Į Laisvę*, No. 4 (27) (1944).

39. The underground press collected and extensively published facts about the tragedy of the Territorial Defense Force. For the list of names of executed soldiers see *Į Laisvę*, No. 10 (33) (June 1, 1944). The arrests of the commanders of the Force were immediately reported in *Į Laisvę*, No. 9 (32) (May 17, 1944), and other papers. Bolshevik assertions (see Žiugžda, *op. cit.*, p. 417; *Hitlerinė Okupacija Lietuvoje*, p. 178) that the Force fell apart by itself are completely false. J. Dobrovolskis resorts to complete falsification (*op. cit.*, p. 169) when he asserts that "when the soldiers of the Force discovered that the Hitlerites planned to throw them into the front against the Soviet Army, mass defections from the Force began [May, 1944]. . . . Thus, the Lithuanian people . . . refused to oppose the liberating Soviet Army."

5. THE PARTISAN MOVEMENT IN POSTWAR LITHUANIA
(pp. 85–108)

1. There seems to be general agreement on these dates. Colonel Burlitski, a former NKVD officer who participated in action against Lithuanian partisans, testified that the partisan movement existed "up to 1953." See U.S. House of Representatives, 83d Cong., 2d sess., *Fourth Interim Report of the Select Committee on Communist Aggression* (Washington, D.C., 1954), p. 1372 (hereinafter cited as *Fourth Interim Report*). Similarly, Romas Šarmaitis, director of the Lithuanian Communist Party's history institute at Vilnius, related in an interview to George Weller, an American correspondent, that the partisan war lasted eight years, which must mean the period 1944–52, since the Soviet re-occupation did not begin until 1944. See *Chicago Daily News*, August 17, 1961. See also *émigré* sources: Professor J. Brazaitis' article, "Partizanai," in *Lietuvių Enciklopedija*, XXII, 44–52; V. K. Tauras, *Guerrilla Warfare on the*

Amber Coast (New York, 1962), p. 96; and Professor Stasys Žymantas, "Twenty Years Resistance," *Lituanus*, VI, No. 2 (September, 1960), 44. G. Zimanas, editor of *Tiesa* (the *Pravda* of the Lithuanian Communist Party), writing in *Pergalė* (Vilnius), No. 9 (September, 1960), p. 103, held a slightly different opinion: "It is possible to affirm that banditism was essentially liquidated by 1950."

2. J. Daumantas (pseudonym of Juozas Lukša), *Partizanai Už Geležinės Uždangos* (Chicago, 1950), p. 81. This book is a firsthand account of partisan activities in 1944–47 written by a prominent partisan leader during his sojourn in the West. The author's identity was revealed by the Communists in a series of articles in *Tiesa* in the summer of 1959. In 1960, these were published in book form. See M. Chienas, K. Šmigelskis, and E. Uldukis, *Vanagai iš Anapus*. (Hereinafter cited as *Vanagai*.) Specific Communist references to Daumantas' book are found on p. 121. New Soviet sources, not available at the time this essay was originally written, point to the need for a closer study of *Lietuvos Laisvės Armija* (*Lithuania's Freedom Army*) and its influence on the organization of the partisan movement and the conduct of guerrilla war.

3. K. Volčkova, "Komunistų partijos kova už Lietuvos liaudies ūkio atstatymą ir išvystymą pokario laikotarpiu (1945–1953)," *Komunistas* (Vilnius), No. 5 (May, 1960), p. 37.

4. A. Vabalas (ed.), *Kraują Sugėrė Dzūkijos Smėlis* (Vilnius, 1960), p. 67. The author discusses a meeting of the leaders of the movement in February of 1959.

5. *Ibid.*

6. Quoted by George Weller, *Chicago Daily News*, August 17, 1961.

7. S. Žymantas, "Aktyviosios Rezistencijos Tragedija," *Santarvė* (London), No. 4 (1953), p. 16.

8. Daumantas, *op. cit.*, p. 106.

9. S. Žymantas, "Laisvės Rytojus Jau Švinta," *Santarvė*, No. 4–5 (1955), p. 177.

10. K. Pakštas, *Lithuania and World War II*, pp. 31–32; K. Pelėkis, *Genocide* (Germany, 1949), pp. 68–84; E. J. Harrison, former British Vice-Consul in Lithuania, *Lithuania's Fight for Freedom* (New York, 1952), pp. 30–31; Albert Kalme, *Total Terror* (New York, 1948), pp. 40–47. On the introduction of Soviet rule in 1941, see Albert N. Tarulis, *Soviet Policy Toward the Baltic States*. See also *Third Interim Report of the Select Committee on Communist Aggression;* this study of the Baltic states between 1918 and 1940 was prepared by the Library of Congress.

11. For the story of the revolt, see *The New York Times*, June 24, 25, 29, and July 2, 1941; also Pakštas, *op. cit.*, p. 35; Pelėkis, *op. cit.*, pp. 93–99; Harrison, *op. cit.*, p. 31; Professor Z. Ivinskis, "Kaip laikinoji vyriausybė išsilaikė šešias savaites," *Į Laisvę* (New York), No. 6 (June, 1955), pp. 31–40; the article by the Prime Minister-designate of the provisional government, K. Škirpa, "Gairės į tautos sukilimą," *Į Laisvę* (Chicago), No. 27 (December, 1961), pp. 1–13; S. Raštikis, *Kovose Dėl Laisvės*, II, 293–317; a series of articles by S. Žymantas in *Nepriklausoma Lietuva* (Montreal), May 17, 24, 31, June 7, 14, 21, 28, and July 12, 1961.

12. E.g., P. Rimkus, *Tai Buvo Leipalingyje* (Vilnius, 1961), p. 44. The wide acceptance of this view deeply disturbed the Communists. See, for example, J. Žiugžda (ed.), *Lietuvos TSR Istorija*, p. 491.

13. Daumantas, *op. cit.*, p. 81; B. Baranauskas and G. Erslavaitė (eds.),

Žudikai Bažnyčios Prieglobsty (Vilnius, 1960), pp. 50 ff. (hereinafter cited as *Žudikai*).

14. J. Ragauskas, *Ite Missa Est* (Vilnius, 1960), p. 448; *Lietuvos Pionierius*, January 31, 1962, p. 2.

15. *Žudikai*, pp. 28, 33, 85, 119–20.

16. A statement by Bishop P. Ramanauskas to his Communist interrogators. See *ibid.*, p. 122.

17. Soviet writers claim that this Western orientation turned Lithuania into a "backwater of Europe." See G. Metelsky, *Lithuania: Land of the Niemen* (Moscow, 1959), p. 150.

18. Cf. Zimanas, *Pergalė*, No. 9 (1960), pp. 104–5; V. Radaitis, *Pergalė*, No. 2 (February, 1961), p. 122.

19. Pelėkis, *op. cit.*, p. 179; *Į Laisvę*, December 8, 1943; *Laisvės Kovotojas*, February 16, 1944.

20. Views attributed by the Soviets to Bishop V. Borisevičius. *Žudikai*, pp. 33, 49.

21. Editorial in *Laisvės šauklys*, a partisan paper, on March 20, 1947, quoted in S. Žymantas' article on the partisan press, *Santarvė*, No. 4–5 (June–July, 1955), p. 173.

22. Editorial in *Aukštaičių Kova*, another partisan paper, dated April 16, 1947, quoted by Žymantas, *op. cit.*, p. 175.

23. Daumantas, *op. cit.*, pp. 238–41; for a brief account of anti-Nazi resistance, see Pelėkis, *op. cit.*, pp. 103–74.

24. For documentation, see Daumantas, *op. cit.*, pp. 30–37, 47–48, 75, 79, 81, 84, 103.

25. R. Žiugžda, A. Smirnov, *Litovskaia SSR* (Moscow, 1957), pp. 105 ff.; "Litovskaia SSR," in *Bolshaia Sovetskaia Entsiklopediia*, (2d ed.), XXV (1954), 260. The Soviets found many such farmer "collaborators," because a full delivery of the quota of agricultural products as requisitioned by the Germans was regarded to be an act of collaboration. To make matters worse, special Soviet commissions decided whether this delivery was "full" or only "partial." The status of the "kulak" also was defined very arbitrarily and did not depend on the amount of land owned. See Daumantas, *op. cit.*, pp. 105–6; also "Memorandum to the United Nations and the Four Power Foreign Ministers Council by the United Democratic Resistance Movement (B.D.P.S.) of Lithuania," *Lithuanian Bulletin* (New York), VI, Nos. 11–12 (November–December, 1948), 11 (hereinafter cited as "Memorandum").

26. See "Order of the People's Commissar for the Interior of Lithuanian SSR of Year 1940," reprinted in translation in the *Third Interim Report*, p. 471; also "Instructions Regarding the Manner of Conducting the Deportation of the Anti-Soviet elements from Lithuania, Latvia, and Estonia," signed by Ivan Serov, Deputy People's Commissar for State Security of the USSR, *ibid.*, pp. 464–68. Other translated documents, *ibid.*, pp. 464–529; reprints of photostatic copies of originals in Russian and Lithuanian are found in the *Lithuanian Bulletin*, III–IX (1945–51). The Soviets apparently realized that these deportations were at least partly responsible for the violently anti-Soviet attitude of the Baltic peoples during and after the war. Some twenty years later these deportations were regretted as "exceedingly strong measures" and blamed on Stalin and his collaborators. See a public letter by Vilhelms Munters, the former Minister of Foreign Affairs of independent Latvia, in *Izvestiia*, April 8, 1962, p. 5.

27. "Memorandum," p. 11.

28. See "Order of the People's Commissar for Internal Affairs of the Lithuanian SSR," issued by the Commissar, Major General Bartašiūnas. This order, dated February 15, 1946, promised amnesty to surrendering "bandits"; 150,000 copies of the proclamation were distributed throughout the country. Photostatic copy in *Lithuanian Bulletin*, IV, No. 4 (November, 1946), 14; also in Pelėkis, *op. cit.*, p. 222.

29. *Žudikai*, p. 10.

30. *Pravda*, October 24, 1961, p. 4.

31. *Ibid.*

32. *Tiesa*, February 8, 1962, p. 3.

33. *Pravda*, October 24, 1961, p. 4.

34. For criticisms of collectivization procedure see M. Gregorauskas, *Tarybų Lietuvos Žemės Ūkis* (Vilnius, 1961); also *Tiesa*, February 8, 1962, p. 3.

35. *Tiesa*, December 20, 1961, p. 2.

36. Discussion of partisan membership is based primarily on Daumantas' work, on *Žudikai*, and on other items from the Soviet Lithuanian press.

37. See *Už Tėvų Žemę*, April 4, 1946. Quoted at length in *Lithuanian Bulletin*, IV, No. 4 (November, 1946), 8–9; also cf. Daumantas, *op. cit.*, p. 236.

38. Daumantas, *op. cit.*, pp. 79–82.

39. *Žudikai*, p. 67; Daumantas, *op. cit.*, pp. 258, 271.

40. See Colonel Burlitski's testimony in *Fourth Interim Report*, p. 1369.

41. Brazaitis, *op. cit.*, p. 44.

42. See Daumantas, *op. cit.*, p. 238; *Žudikai*, p. 64; Vabalas, *op. cit.*, p. 66.

43. See *Žudikai*, pp. 47, 53, 55; Vabalas, *op. cit.*, p. 60.

44. See *Vanagai*, pp. 206, 241; *Žudikai*, p. 63; Daumantas, *op. cit.*, pp. 85, 224, 278.

45. Daumantas, *op. cit.*; Vabalas, *op. cit.*, p. 66.

46. See Daumantas, *op. cit.*, p. 391; *Žudikai*, p. 111.

47. See the 1953 declaration of the Supreme Committee for the Liberation of Lithuania, photostatic copy in Pelėkis, *op. cit.*, p. 179.

48. Vabalas, *op. cit.*, pp. 64–68.

49. Daumantas, *op. cit.*, p. 194.

50. Private document.

51. See, for example, Žiugžda, Smirnov, *op. cit.*, pp. 107 ff.; *Tiesa*, January 31, 1962, p. 3; Daumantas, *op. cit.*, pp. 105–6.

52. See, for example, Daumantas, *op. cit.*, p. 363; *Tiesa*, December 27, 1961; *Tiesa*, December 11, 1960, p. 2; *Sovetskaia Litva*, December 22, 1960, p. 2.

53. *Švyturys* (Vilnius), August, 1961, pp. 6–7.

54. *Tiesa*, February 22, 1962, p. 2; Vabalas, *op. cit.*, pp. 58–59.

55. Testimony of Colonel Burlitski, in *Fourth Interim Report*, p. 1369.

56. *Žudikai*, pp. 23, 80.

57. See for example, *Komunistas*, No. 12 (1960), pp. 51–54; a partial list of liquidated officials in *Žudikai*, pp. 131–43; *Tiesa*, June 1, 1960, p. 3, and October 7, 1960, p. 2; biographies of liquidated teachers in A. Bieliauskas and G. Iešmantas, *Kad Žemėje Žydėtų Gėlės* (Vilnius, 1960).

58. *Lietuvos TSR Istorija*, p. 491.

59. Daumantas, *op. cit.*, pp. 93, 195, 242.

60. *Ibid.*, pp. 187–89.

61. A Communist version of aspects of partisan relations with the West is available in the May and June, 1962, issues of *Švyturys* (Vilnius), No. 9, pp.

10–11; No. 10, pp. 10–12; No. 11, pp. 16–17; No. 12, pp. 10–11. The series, entitled "Iliuzijų Sudužimas," was published under the name of Jonas Deksnys, a liaison man between the Lithuanian émigrés in the West and groups in Lithuania, who was captured by the Soviets sometime in the 1950's.

62. Vabalas, *op. cit.*, p. 67.

63. *Vanagai*, pp. 107 ff.

64. Speech to the Supreme Soviet of the Lithuanian SSR, *Tiesa*, June 8, 1960, p. 2. See also P. Rimkus, *op. cit.*, p. 51. The fact of Lukša and his group's return to Lithuania in 1950–51 is confirmed by Lithuanian nationalist sources. See *Į Laisvę* (Chicago), No. 19 (December, 1959), p. 11.

65. Vabalas, *op. cit.*, p. 70.

66. See Burlitski's testimony in *Fourth Interim Report*, pp. 1373–74; also *Vanagai*, esp. pp. 149–241.

67. Private document.

68. Daumantas, *op. cit.*, p. 239.

69. *Bolshaia Sovetskaia Entsiklopediia*, XLI (1956), 320.

70. Volčkova, *Komunistas*, No. 5 (1960), p. 37.

71. J. Bulota, *Pergalė*, No. 3 (March, 1961), p. 175.

72. See A. Grabauskas, A. Deriūnas, in *Tiesa*, February 8, 1962, p. 3.

73. Burlitski's testimony in *Fourth Interim Report*, pp. 1368–69.

74. *Biographical Dictionary of the USSR* (New York, 1958), pp. 319–20. For a description of Kruglov's activities, see Burlitski's testimony in *Fourth Interim Report*, pp. 137 ff.

75. Daumantas, *op. cit.*, pp. 103, 108.

76. Information from the partisan paper, *Laisvės Varpas*, No. 122 (October 1, 1947). See Žymantas, *Santarvė*, No. 10 (1954), p. 368.

77. *Žudikai*, pp. 6 ff., 125 ff.

78. See Brazaitis, *op. cit.*, p. 47.

79. Daumantas, *op. cit.*, p. 117; also Burlitski in *Fourth Interim Report*, p. 1372.

80. Daumantas, *op. cit.*, pp. 117–20.

81. Žiugžda, Smirnov, *op. cit.*, p. 106.

82. See B. Armonas and A. Nasvytis, *Leave Your Tears in Moscow* (New York, 1961), esp. pp. 37–48.

83. Daumantas, *op. cit.*, pp. 189–90.

84. *Ibid.*, pp. 305–6.

85. Žiugžda, Smirnov, *op. cit.*, pp. 106–10.

86. Vabalas, *op. cit.*, pp. 64–66.

87. Žiugžda, Smirnov, *op. cit.*, p. 109.

88. E.G., see *Tiesa*, May 27, 1960, p. 2; October 30, 1960, p. 2; December 11, 1960, p. 2; *Lietuvos Pionierius*, January 27, 1962, p. 3; *Vanagai*, pp. 48–49.

89. See *Komunistas*, No. 3 (1961), pp. 45–46.

90. Account in *Vanagai*.

6. THE ADMINISTRATION OF POWER: THE COMMUNIST PARTY AND THE SOVIET GOVERNMENT
(pp. 111–40)

1. This account of CPL history is based on an unpublished study by the author, *Communist Party of Lithuania: A Historical and Political Study*, a Ph.D. thesis in Political Science, University of Illinois, 1963. An official history of the CPL has not yet been published by the CPL Institute of Party History.

Contemporary Communist historians, however, have produced several preliminary studies of various aspects of the CPL history which provide useful factual data. Some of the more significant works on the CPL history by Communist historians are: Vincas Kapsukas, *Pirmoji Lietuvos Proletarinė Revoliucija ir Tarybų Valdžia* (2d ed.; Vilnius, 1958); Partijos Istorijos Institutas prie LKP CK, *Revoliucinis Judėjimas Lietuvoje*, a collection of articles edited by R. Šarmaitis (Vilnius, 1957); Vilniaus Valstybinis Universitetas, *Darbai, XXIX: LKP Istorijos Klausimai* (Vilnius, 1959); R. Šarmaitis, *Lietuvos Komunistų Partijos Pirmojo Suvažiavimo Sušaukimo Istorijos Klausimu* (Vilnius, 1959); S. Atamukas, *LKP Kova Prieš Fašizmą už Tarybų Valdžią Lietuvoje 1939–1940 Metais* (Vilnius, 1958). Of great value is the collection of historical documents of the Lithuanian SSR Academy of Sciences, Institute of History, edited by J. Žiugžda, *Lietuvos TSR Istorijos Šaltiniai (The Sources of Lithuanian SSR History)* (Vilnius, 1958, 1960), III and IV.

2. See Kapsukas-Mickevičius report to the Sixth RSDLP(b) Congress; Lithuanian text of the report in *Lietuvos TSR Istorijos Saltiniai*, III, 16–17.

3. Šarmaitis, *op. cit.*

4. According to V. Kapsukas, *op. cit.*, p. 101, Stalin wrote a letter to the Central Committee, CPL&B, instructing it to form a Soviet Government. The text of the letter has never been published.

5. See the resolution of the Eighth Congress of the RCP(b); Lithuanian text in *Lietuvos TSR Istorijos Šaltiniai*, III, 191.

6. For some of the motives and circumstances of the formation of *Litbel,* see the following Soviet studies: A. M. Andreev, *Bor'ba Litovskogo naroda za sovetskuiu vlast', 1918–1919 g.g.* (Moscow, 1954); S. P. Margunskii, *Sozdanie i Uprochenie Belorusskoi gosudarstvennosti, 1917–1922* (Minsk, 1958); also Richard Pipes, *The Formation of the Soviet Union: Communism and Nationalism* (Cambridge, Mass., 1954).

7. See Atamukas, *op. cit., passim.* Atamukas' figures are taken from Party sources and do not appear to be distorted.

8. *Lietuvos TSR Istorijos Šaltiniai*, IV, 631.

9. Party publications, mainly *Komunistas, Balsas, Partijos Darbas,* which were available to the author for the years 1918–33, provided the outlines for the discussion of CPL relations with the Comintern.

10. See A. Butkutė-Ramelienė, *Lietuvos KP Kova už Tarybų Valdžios Įtvirtinimą Respublikoje (1940–41)* (Vilnius, 1958), p. 150.

11. *Ibid.*, p. 167.

12. *Ibid.*, p. 166.

13. For CPL activities during the war, see P. Ataras, in *Hitlerinė Okupacija Lietuvoje* (Vilnius, 1961); the memoirs of J. Macijauskas, *Už Liaudies Laimę* (Vilnius, 1957).

14. *Sovetskaia Litva*, February 18, 1949.

15. The Org Bureau for Lithuania is practically unmentioned in the Soviet press. One Soviet reference to it will be found in the Vilnius State University Faculty of Law publication, *Tarybų Lietuvos Valstybės ir Teisės Dvidešimtmetis* (Vilnius, 1960), p. 161. A detailed description of the Org Bureau, its functions and powers, will be found in testimony of the former MVD border guard Colonel Burlitski, who participated in the sovietization of Lithuania and defected to the West in 1953. His testimony is found in the *Fourth Interim Report of the Select Committee on Communist Aggression*, pp. 1371–72.

16. *Sovetskaia Litva*, January 18, 1947, p. 2.

17. Walter S. Hanchett, "Some Observations on Membership Figures of the Communist Party of the Soviet Union," *The American Political Science Review*, CCXI, No. 4 (December 1958), 1124; Herbert Ritvo, "Twenty-First Party Congress—Before and After" (Part Two), *Slavic Review*, XX, No. 3 (October, 1961), 453. See their notes on the sources and derivations of membership figures for the CPSU.

18. *LKP Istorijos Klausimai*, p. 184.

19. *Tiesa*, November 24, 1955, p. 2.

20. *Ibid.*

21. *Ibid.*, March 5, 1960, p. 1.

22. *Sovetskaia Litva*, February 20, 1949, p. 2; *Tiesa*, March 3, 1960, p. 3.

23. See the quite revealing statistical portrait of the CPSU in *Partiinaia Zhizn'*, No. 1 (January, 1962).

24. *Ibid.*

25. *Tiesa*, January 17, 1959, p. 1.

26. *Ibid.*, February 15, 1959, p. 3.

27. Based on a biographical file compiled by the author.

28. See, for example, his report to the Twelfth CPL Congress in 1959; *Tiesa*, January 15, 1959, p. 5.

29. One of the best political characterizations of Antanas Sniečkus is that by V. Rastenis, "A Diehard Kremlinist," *The Baltic Review*, No. 9 (December, 1956), p. 57.

30. This explanation of political survival has been suggested by Robert Conquest, "The Struggle Goes On," *Problems of Communism*, July–August, 1960, p. 9.

31. *Tarybų Lietuvos Valstybės ir Teisės Dvidešimtmetis*, p. 299.

32. *Sovetskaia Litva*, February 18, 1949, p. 3.

33. For the inclusive collection of laws, decrees, decisions, and rules passed by the Lithuanian Soviet regime, see the following source, in both Lithuanian and Russian: Lietuvos TSR Teisingumo Ministerija, *Lietuvos TSR Istatymų, Aukščiausios Tarybos Prezidiumo Įsakų ir Vyriausybės Nutarimų Chronologinis Rinkinys* (Vilnius, 1957–59), I–VI, covering the period 1940–57.

34. See, for example, the memoirs of the Bolshevik partisan P. Kutka, *Girioj Aidi Šūviai* (Vilnius, 1958).

35. E. Bilevičius, *Nemunas Grįžta į Savo Vagą* (Vilnius, 1961), p. 146.

36. *Fourth Interim Report*, p. 1372.

37. *Tiesa*, August 20, 1946, p. 4.

38. See Sniečkus' admission of extensive violence and "violation of socialist legality" during the postwar years in the report to the Twenty-second Congress of the CPSU, in *Tiesa*, October 24, 1961, p. 3.

39. *Tarybų Lietuvos Valstybės ir Teisės Dvidešimtmetis*, p. 61.

40. *Ibid.*, p. 62.

41. *Ibid.*, p. 65.

42. *Tiesa*, August 15, 1946, p. 1.

43. *Tarybų Lietuvos Valstybės ir Teisės Dvidešimtmetis*, p. 66.

44. *Ibid.*, pp. 62–63.

45. G. O. Zimanas, "Friendship of People of the U.S.S.R. and Overcoming Survivals of Bourgeois Nationalism," *Voprosy Filosofii*, No. 1 (February, 1958), pp. 27–38.

46. See, for example, *Tiesa,* May–August, 1953.
47. *Tiesa,* July 2, 1953, p. 1.
48. See, for example, Zimanas, *op. cit.*
49. For a convincing exposition of reasons for economic decentralization, see Edward Crankshaw, *Khrushchev's Russia* (Baltimore, 1959), pp. 70–79.
50. *Tiesa,* December 3, 1959, pp. 1–3; *Tiesa,* April 5, 1963, pp. 1–3.
51. See the report of the First Secretary in *Tiesa,* September 30, 1961, p. 3.
52. *Ibid.*
53. V. Vaitiekūnas, "Court System of Occupied Lithuania," *Draugas,* July 16, 1960, Part 2, p. 1.
54. *Tiesa,* February 21, 1963.
55. *Ibid.,* December 14, 1962, p. 3.
56. *Ibid.,* January 11, 1963.
57. *Ibid.,* December 9, 1962, p. 1.
58. *Ibid.,* February 8, 1956, p. 1, in an editorial strongly suggesting that agricultural production problems forced the change in command in the Council of Ministers.
59. On the role of the union republics in the foreign affairs of the U.S.S.R., see the excellent study by Vernon Aspaturian, *The Union Republics in Soviet Diplomacy: A Study of Soviet Federalism in the Service of Soviet Foreign Policy* (Geneva, 1960).
60. *Ibid.,* p. 79.
61. *Ibid.*
62. See the interview with the present chairman of the Society, Laurynas Kapočius, in *Tiesa,* November 30, 1962, p. 1.
63. Macijauskas, *op. cit.,* gives the most extensive account of the Lithuanian unit of the Red Army.
64. *Tiesa,* June 8, 1957.
65. *Partiinaia Zhizn',* No. 16 (August 1959) pp. 14–21. For details of the purge of the Latvian Soviet regime in 1959, see Vilis Hazner, "Latvia," in *A Survey of Recent Developments in Nine Captive Countries, October 1959–March 1960* (New York, 1960).
66. *Tiesa,* January 15, 1959, p. 6.
67. *Ibid.,* March 2, 1960, p. 4; *Komunistas,* No. 1 (January, 1959), pp. 9–10.

7. LITHUANIA'S ECONOMY: INTRODUCTION OF THE SOVIET PATTERN
(pp. 141–69)

1. *Lietuvos Statistikos Metraštis 1939* (Vilnius, 1940), pp. 13, 15.
2. *Lietuvos Statistikos Metraštis 1938* (Kaunas, 1939), pp. 104–5.
3. *Lietuvos Statistikos Metraštis 1939,* p. 111.
4. *Ibid.,* p. 125.
5. *Ibid.,* p. 242.
6. *Lietuvos TSR Istatymų, Aukščiausios Tarybos Įsakų Ir Vyriausybės Nutarimų Chronologinis Rinkinys* (Vilnius, 1956), I, 9. (Hereinafter cited as *Lietuvas TSR Istatymų Rinkinys.*)
7. A. Butkutė-Ramelienė, "Tarybinė Agrarinė Reforma Lietuvoje 1940," *Komunistas,* No. 8 (1958), p. 19.
8. M. Gregorauskas, *Tarybų Lietuvos Žemės Ūkis 1940–1960* (Vilnius, 1960), p. 82.

9. *Ibid.*, p. 85.
10. *Ibid.*
11. *Ibid.*, p. 86.
12. Butkutė-Ramelienė, *op. cit.*, p. 22.
13. *Tiesa*, February 6, 1941.
14. Gregorauskas, *op. cit.*, p. 101.
15. *Lietuvos TSR Istatymų Rinkinys*, pp. 88–90.
16. *Ibid.*, p. 88.
17. Gregorauskas, *op. cit.*, p. 134.
18. *Ibid.*, p. 130.
19. *Lietuvos Statistikos Metraštis 1939*, pp. 282–86; Gregorauskas, *op. cit.*, p. 145.
20. Gregorauskas, *op. cit.*, pp. 141, 151.
21. *Ibid.*, p. 137. The discussion on collectivization is also based on this work.
22. *Lietuvos TSR Istatymų Rinkinys*, II, 31.
23. *Tiesa*, March 23, 1957.
24. Gregorauskas, *op. cit.*, p. 163.
25. *20 Metų Tarybų Lietuvos Liaudies Ūkiui* (Vilnius, 1960), p. 152.
26. Gregorauskas, *op. cit.*, p. 206.
27. *Ibid.*, p. 188.
28. *Lietuvos TSR Liaudies Ūkis* (Vilnius, 1957), p. 65.
29. *SSSR v tsifrakh v 1961 godu* (Moscow, 1962), p. 243.
30. Gregorauskas, *op. cit.*, p. 405. For other figures, see the same source.
31. For a detailed discussion of the consequences of collectivization, see P. Zundė, *Die Landwirtschaft Sowjetlitauens* (Marburg, 1962).
32. Pranas Zundė, "Sodybinio Sklypo Reikšmė Kolūkiečiui," *Aidai* (Brooklyn, N.Y.), No. 5 (1962), p. 202.
33. *Narodnoe khoziaistvo SSSR v 1959 godu* (Moscow, 1960), pp. 148 ff.
34. K. Meškauskas, *Tarybų Lietuvos Industrializavimas* (Vilnius, 1960), pp. 129–30.
35. Gregorauskas, *op. cit.*, p. 256.
36. *Tiesa*, December 4, 1960.
37. *Ibid.*, December 31, 1962.
38. *Mokslas ir Gyvenimas* (Vilnius), No. 6 (1962).
39. *Sovetskaia Litva* (Vilnius), April 13, 1962.
40. *Ibid.*, March 10, 1962.
41. *Tarybų Lietuvos Dvidešimtmetis* (Vilnius, 1960), p. 325.
42. *Ibid.*, p. 78.
43. *Ibid.*, pp. 282–83.
44. *Lietuvos TSR Liaudies Ūkis*, pp. 135–36; *Norodnoe khoziaistvo SSSR v 1958 godu* (Moscow, 1959), pp. 502–3.
45. See *Švyturys*, No. 22 (1961).
46. *Czerwony sztandar* (Vilnius), November 2, 1961.
47. *Sovetskaia Litva*, April 4, 1961.

8. SOVIETIZED EDUCATION IN OCCUPIED LITHUANIA
(pp. 171–96)

1. A. Knyva and J. Žiugžda, *Švietimas Tarybų Lietuvoje* (Vilnius, 1950), p. 20.

2. *Tarybinė Mokykla* (Vilnius), No. 7 (July, 1959), p. 8.

3. *Ibid.*, No. 8 (August, 1959), p. 10.

4. *Vyriausybės Žinios* (Kaunas), No. 724 (August 14, 1940). It should be added, however, that the thirteen-year program the Soviets abandoned was not introduced until 1936 and had not yet produced high school graduates with thirteen years of secondary education at the time of the occupation. Primary education was in fact extended to six years.

5. *Pravda*, November 2, 1961, p. 8.

6. *Tarybinė Mokykla*, No. 10 (October, 1961), p. 22.

7. *Ibid.*

8. *Ibid.*, No. 7 (July, 1960), p. 18.

9. *Ibid.*, No. 6 (June, 1959), p. 3.

10. *Ibid.*

11. *Ibid.*, No. 8 (August, 1957), p. 46.

12. *Ibid.*, No. 10 (October, 1961), p. 22; figures for 1962–63 from *Tiesa*, January 22, 1963, p. 3.

13. *Ibid.*, No. 7 (July, 1960), p. 7.

14. *Tiesa*, December 28, 1961.

15. *Sbornik rukovodiashchikh i instruktivnikh materialov po vseobshchemu obucheniiu detei* (Narkompros RSFSR, 1943), p. 13; and *Sobranie postanovlenii i rasporiazhenii pravitelstva SSSR*, No. 10 (1944), p. 195.

16. *Lietuvos TSR Liaudies Ūkis* (Vilnius, 1957), p. 187; and *Tarybinė Mokykla*, No. 7 (July, 1960), p. 18; figures for 1962–63 from *Tiesa*, January 22, 1963, p. 3.

17. *Tarybinė Mokykla*, No. 7 (July, 1960), p. 18; figures for 1962–63 from *Tiesa*, January 22, 1963, p. 3.

18. *Lietuvos Statistikos Metraštis 1939*, p. 72.

19. *Komjaunimo Tiesa* (Vilnius), June 17, 1961.

20. *Ibid.*, July 17, 1961.

21. *Ibid.*, December 5, 1961.

22. *Ibid.*

23. *Tarybinė Mokykla*, No. 7 (July, 1959), pp. 4–10.

24. *Komjaunimo Tiesa*, December 5, 1961.

25. *Tarybinė Mokykla*, No. 7 (July, 1959), pp. 4–10.

26. *Liaudies Švietimas* (Kaunas, 1958), p. 3.

27. *Tarybinė Mokykla*, No. 12 (December, 1960), p. 30.

28. See *Švietimas Tarybų Lietuvoje*, p. 31; *Liaudies Švietimas*, p. 22; *Tarybinė Mokykla*, No. 1 (January, 1958), p. 3; *ibid.*, No. 1 (January, 1959), p. 8; *ibid.*, No. 12 (December, 1960), pp. 26–27.

29. *Lituanus* (Brooklyn, N.Y.), V, No. 1 (March, 1959), 4.

30. *Komunistas* (Vilnius), No. 6 (June, 1960), p. 50.

31. *Tarybinė Mokykla*, No. 1 (January, 1961), pp. 8, 10.

32. *Tarybinis Mokytojas* (Vilnius), February 5, May 25, June 22, 1961.

33. *Ibid.*, January 12, March 19, April 13 and 16, 1961.

34. *Komunistas*, No. 1 (January, 1960), p. 72.

35. Justas Paleckis, *Mintys Apie Vyresny jį Brolį* (Vilnius, 1959).

36. *Švietimas Tarybų Lietuvoje*, p. 44.

37. A. Abrikosovas, *Braižyba* (Kaunas, 1957), Part 1 (for the seventh grade).

38. *Vilniaus Universiteto Žinynas* (Vilnius, 1957), p. 141.

39. *Tarybinė Mokykla*, No. 3 (March, 1960), p. 4.

40. *Komjaunimo Tiesa*, July 14, 1961.

41. *Komjaunimo Tiesa*, May 16, June 17, July 15, 1961; *Tiesa*, June 21, 1961; *Valstiečių Laikraštis* (Vilnius), No. 154 (1961).

42. *Survey of Recent Developments in Nine Captive Countries, July–December, 1961*, published by the Assembly of Captive European Nations (New York, 1962).

43. *Kulturnoe stroitelstvo SSSR* (Moscow, 1956), p. 184.

44. *Lietuvos Statistikos Metraštis 1939*, p. 71.

45. T. Dėjus, *Lietuvių Kalbos Gramatika* (Kaunas, 1957).

46. *Tarybinė Mokykla*, No. 11 (November, 1959), p. 3.

47. *Ibid.*, No. 2 (February, 1958), pp. 6, 8; *ibid*, No. 5 (May, 1959), p. 4.

48. *Ibid.*, No. 5 (May, 1958), p. 12.

49. *Ibid.*, No. 12 (December, 1958), pp. 13–15.

50. *Ibid.*, No. 5 (May, 1961), p. 6; *Tarybinis Mokytojas*, January 7, 1962; *Tiesa*, January 22, 1963, p. 3.

51. *Tarybinis Mokytojas*, January 14, 1962.

52. *Tarybinė Mokykla*, No. 9 (September, 1960), p. 4.

53. *Ibid.*, No. 6 (June, 1960), pp. 4–5.

54. *Ibid.*, No. 8 (August, 1959), pp. 39–41.

55. *Ibid.*, No. 5 (May, 1961), pp. 21, 29, 30.

56. *Ibid.*, No. 1 (January, 1961), p. 18.

57. *The New York Times*, August 1, 1961, p. 19.

58. *Valstiečių Laikraštis*, October 1, 1961.

59. *Tarybinis Mokytojas*, January 4, 1962.

60. *Komunistas*, No. 2 (February, 1963), p. 30.

61. *Ibid.*, No. 9 (September, 1962), p. 58.

62. *Lietuvos TSR Liaudies Ūkis*, pp. 188, 194.

63. *Ibid.*

64. *Tarybinis Mokytojas, September 24*, 1961; *Tiesa*, January 4, 1962.

65. *Tarybinis Mokytojas*, November 12 and 26, 1961.

66. *Tarybinė Mokykla*, No. 6 (June, 1960), p. 15.

67. *Tarybinis Mokytojas*, September 24, 1961, January 7, 1962; *Tarybinė Mokykla*, No. 8 (August, 1961), p. 4.

68. *Tarybinis Mokytojas*, December 28, 1961; January 7, 1962.

69. *Tiesa*, November 24, 1961.

70. *The New York Times*, September 7, 1959, p. 8.

71. *Tarybinė Mokykla*, No. 10 (October, 1961), p. 2.

72. *Tiesa*, November 24, 1961; *Tarybinis Mokytojas*, January 7, 1962.

73. *Komjaunimo Tiesa*, December 9, 1961.

74. *Ibid.*, December 19, 1961.

75. *Į Laisvę* (New York), No. 15 (June, 1958), p. 63.

9. LITERATURE AND THE ARTS IN CAPTIVE LITHUANIA
(pp. 197–213)

1. A. Venclova, speech at the Second Congress of Soviet Writers, published in *Pergalė*, No. 1 (January, 1955), p. 108.

2. K. Korsakas, in *Tiesa*, December 19, 1950.

3. *Literatūra ir Menas*, February 9, 1957.

4. *Ibid.*, February 2, 1957.

5. A. Surikov, in *Pergalė*, No. 1 (January, 1955), p. 96.

6. K. M. Simonov, in *Literatūra ir Menas*, No. 1 (January, 1955).

7. *Tiesa,* August 20, 1950.
8. *Ibid.,* October 9, 1950.
9. *Ibid.,* October 15, 1950.
10. *Literatūra ir Menas,* February 2, 1957.
11. *Ibid.,* March 5, 1950.
12. J. Josadė, in *Pergalė,* No. 1 (January, 1956), p. 119.
13. *Literatūra ir Menas,* No. 3 (January, 1956).
14. A. Gudaitis, in *ibid.,* April 17, 1957.
15. J. Mackonis, in *ibid.,* October 13, 1956.
16. *Ibid.,* July 13, 1957.
17. *Ibid.,* July 27, 1957.
18. *Ibid.,* December 1, 1956.
19. H. Zimanas, in *ibid.,* December 28, 1957.
20. A. Sniečkus, address at the Tenth Congress of the Lithuanian Communist Party published in *ibid.,* February 15, 1958.
21. *Lietuvių Tarybinės Literatūros Istorijos Apžvalga* (Vilnius, 1956), pp. 235–50.
22. *Pergalė,* No. 2 (February, 1958), p. 7.
23. L. Ilychev, in *Literatūra ir Menas,* December 29, 1962.
24. A. Barkauskas, in *ibid.,* January 19, 1963.
25. L. Ilychev, in *ibid.,* December 29, 1962.
26. Quotation from a private letter, in *Draugas* (Chicago), March 23, 1963.

10. SOVIET POLICY TOWARD RELIGION IN LITHUANIA: THE CASE OF ROMAN CATHOLICISM
(pp. 215–35)

1. The pledge, in translation, read as follows: I, ... , the undersigned servant of the cult, residing in . . . . . village, ... district, ... region, with my signature testify that on April . . . , 1941, I was informed of the formal ban against the teaching of religion to school and pre-school children in schools, their parents' homes, my own home or, in other words, anywhere. Equally, I have no right to speak with them on religious questions. It is furthermore known to me that if I violate this law, I will be charged in court.
2. *Lietuvių Archyvas* (Kaunas, 1942), I, 47–49.
3. *Ibid.,* pp. 29–31.
4. Simas Miglinas, *Pavergtoji Lietuva* (Memmingen, 1957), pp. 47–49.
5. *Pravda,* November 11, 1954.
6. *Tiesa,* August 10, 1955.
7. *Ibid.,* December 11, 1956.
8. *Ibid.,* August 19, 1956.
9. *Ibid.*
10. *Tarybinis Mokytojas,* December 21, 1958.
11. *Mokslas ir Gyvenimas,* No. 6 (1956).
12. Radio Monitoring Service (in Europe).
13. *Tiesa,* January 8, 1961.
14. Cf. *Švyturys,* No. 2 (1961).
15. *Ogioniok,* No. 39 (1960).
16. *Tiesa,* December 22, 1960.

11. SOVIET SOCIAL ENGINEERING IN LITHUANIA: AN APPRAISAL
(pp. 237–59)

1. See, for example, the reminiscences of fellow-traveling writer Augustinas Gricius, in *Tiesa*, August 3, 1963, pp. 2 ff.

2. *Komjaunimo Tiesa*, July 16, 1963, p. 2.

3. See *Komunistas*, No. 11 (November, 1963), pp. 30–33.

4. For a more detailed examination of this "new man," see V. Stanley Vardys, "Recent Soviet Policy Toward Lithuanian Nationalism," *Journal of Central European Affairs*, No. 3 (October, 1963), esp. pp. 323–31.

5. *Tiesa*, December 4, 1960, p. 2.

6. *Komunistas*, No. 8 (August, 1962), p. 26.

7. See Lothar Schultz, "Die Verfassungsentwicklung der baltischen Staaten seit 1940," *Commentationes Balticae*, No. 6–7 (1958–59), esp. pp. 309 ff.

8. Cf. Albert N. Tarulis, "A Heavy Population Loss in Lithuania," *Journal of Central European Affairs*, No. 4 (January, 1962), pp. 452–64; Andrivs Namsons, "Die nationale Zusammensetzung der Einwohnerschaft der baltischen Staaten," *Acta Baltica* (1962), esp. pp. 70–73; Hellmuth Weiss, "Die baltischen Staaten," in Ernst Birke and Rudolf Neumann (eds.), *Die Sowjetisierung Ost-Mitteleuropas* (Frankfurt, 1959), esp. p. 30; K. Pelėkis, *Genocide* (Germany, 1949), pp. 231–42; A. W. DePorte, "The Population of Lithuania," in B. Mačiuika (ed.), *Lithuania in the Last Thirty Years* (New York, 1955). These authors give somewhat different estimates. The lowest are by Hellmuth Weiss, who gives the total loss of about 400,000 for 1940–41 and 1944–51 and the total of 820,000 for both the German and Soviet occupations, including transfers of population. The highest are those of Tarulis and of DePorte with Mačiuika, running to 1,160,000.

DePorte's and Mačiuika's figures have probably the highest degree of accuracy because their total population estimates, made separately from the Soviet census of 1959, are the most correct. The Soviets do not give total population losses. They acknowledge, however, that in 1959 Lithuania's population was still 5.8 per cent smaller than in 1939 and blame the losses on the war, that is, the German occupation. See I. Iu. Pisarev, *Narodonaselenie SSSR* (Moscow, 1962), pp. 112–14.

9. Pisarev, *op. cit.*

10. These and other population figures for present-day Lithuania, unless otherwise indicated, are taken from *Narodnoe Khozyaistvo Litovskoi SSR v 1961 godu* (Vilnius, 1963). Prewar figures are from A. Simutis, *The Economic Reconstruction of Lithuania After 1918*.

11. Pisarev, *op. cit.*, p. 89.

12. *Tiesa*, January 11, 1964, p. 1.

13. *Kommunist* (Moscow), No. 4 (April, 1962), pp. 46–57.

14. J. Radzevičius, *šluota*, January 1, 1963, p. 4.

15. *Literatūra ir Menas*, February 13, 1963, p. 2.

16. See, for example, *Komjaunimo Tiesa*, October 22, 1963, p. 2; *Tiesa*, July 18, 1963, p. 3.

17. *Tiesa*, July 11, 1963, p. 2.

18. *Ibid.*, January 29, 1963, p. 3; January 30, 1963, p. 3; February 10, 1963, p. 3.

19. *Ibid.*, March 11, 1961, p. 3.

20. *Ibid.*, May 9, 1963, p. 4.

21. Kostas Korsakas, in *Pergalė*, No. 10 (October, 1961), pp. 11 ff.

22. Jonas Macevičius' report on the conference in Frunze, *Komunistas*, No. 11 (November, 1963), p. 31.

23. *Ibid.*

24. *Tiesa*, October 9, 1960, p. 3.

25. K. Navickas, *Lenininės Nacionalinės Politikos Istorinė Reikšmė Lietuvių Tautai* (Vilnius, 1960), p. 87.

26. Genrikas Zimanas, in *Pergalė*, No. 9 (September, 1960), pp. 14 ff.

27. *Tiesa*, March 4, 1964, p. 4.

28. See Navickas, *op. cit.*, pp. 87 ff; *Sovetskaia Litva*, July 29, 1959, pp. 1–4; *Izvestiia*, April 5, 1961, p. 3.

29. *Tarybinis Mokytojas*, May 14, 1961, pp. 2 ff.

30. *Tiesa*, February 13, 1963, p. 3.

31. *Ibid.*, October 2, 1963, p. 4.

32. *Literatūra ir Menas*, December 28, 1963, p. 7.

33. *Ibid.*, October 12, 1963, p. 2.

34. *Komunistas*, No. 1 (January, 1964), p. 16.

35. *Komjaunimo Tiesa*, March 19, 1961, p. 1.

36. *Tiesa*, March 23, 1963, p. 1.

37. For example, *Tiesa*, February 10, 1963, p. 3, reported that parents threw a teenager out of their house for joining the Komsomol. This is a more drastic example of parents' resistance.

38. *Ibid.*, August 31, 1963, p. 4.

39. *Valstiečių Laikraštis*, September 22, 1963, p. 3; September 27, 1963, p. 3; September 29, 1963, p. 3.

40. *Tiesa*, February 25, 1961, p. 2.

41. *Komjaunimo Tiesa*, December 30, 1963, p. 3.

42. *Ibid.*, August 17, 1963, p. 3.

43. *Sovetskaia Litva*, September 20, p. 2.

44. For a detailed examination of this new campaign, see Vardys, *op. cit.*

45. *Komjaunimo Tiesa*, November 29, 1963, p. 3.

46. See, for example, the articles by G. Zimanas, in *Tiesa*, December 30, 1962, p. 2, and J. Vicas, in *Literatūra ir Menas*, March 30, 1963, p. 4. Vicas especially calls for the falsification of history of independent Lithuania to show that there was a real class struggle in Lithuania and that "victory of socialism" was achieved primarily by the Communist-led working class (cliché without foundation in fact).

47. *Komjaunimo Tiesa*, September 27, 1963, p. 3.

48. *Ibid.*, July 16, 1963, p. 2.

49. Romualdas Lankauskas, in a novel "Tiltas į Jūrą" ("Bridge to the Sea"), *Pergalė*, No. 3 (March, 1963), p. 35.

50. *Sovetskaia Litva*, September 20, 1963, p. 2.

51. *Komjaunimo Tiesa*, August 5, 1963, p. 2. Recent expatriates have also reported of a secret trial of some Komsomols, sons of high regime functionaries, who wanted Communism without Moscow. *Draugas*, June 21, 1962, p. 3.

52. Cf. *Tiesa*, May 30, 1963, p. 2.

53. See "Verpetas" ("The Vortex"), in *Pergalė*, No. 6 (June, 1963), pp. 117–28.

54. *Literatūra ir Menas*, August 24, 1963, p. 2.

55. *Ibid.*, August 3, 1963, p. 2.

56. Editorial, "Love and Hatred," in *Tarybinis Mokytojas*, March 26, 1964,

which proposes that teachers conduct hate campaigns against "bourgeois nationalists" abroad, foreign imperialists, and those in Lithuania who "still oppose the Soviet rule and Communism."

57. *Literatūra ir Menas,* August 17, 1963, p. 5.

58. See, for example, a statement by graduate geologist Juozas Miklovas, who escaped to the West in the early 1960s, in *Draugas,* November 20, 1962, p. 7.

59. Lankauskas, *op. cit.,* p. 67.

The Contributors

JONAS GRINIUS holds a Ph.D. from the State University in Kaunas, Lithuania, where he taught literature until 1944. A free-lance literary critic and dramatist, he is the author of numerous books and articles in Lithuanian. His German and French publications include contributions to the *Lexikon der Weltliteratur* and the *Histoire générale des littératures.*

ZENONAS IVINSKIS studied at the universities of Kaunas and Vilnius. He received his doctorate at Berlin, and now teaches Baltic and Lithuanian history at the University of Bonn, where he also directs the Baltic Research Institute. He is the author of many Lithuanian articles and books as well as of the *Geschichte des Bauernstandes in Litauen.* Dr. Ivinskis is a frequent contributor to the *Zeitschrift für Ostforschung, Commentationes Balticae,* and other journals.

THOMAS REMEIKIS, a Ph.D. from the University of Illinois, teaches political science at St. Joseph's College, East Chicago, Illinois. He has contributed articles to *Lituanus,* a journal he now edits.

SIMAS SUŽIEDĖLIS taught Lithuanian history at the State University in Kaunas, Lithuania. He is the author and editor of several books and numerous articles on Lithuanian history.

VYTAUTAS VAITIEKŪNAS, a lawyer and journalist, has written for the *Baltic Review* and other journals. His publications include the annual "Survey of Developments in Occupied Lithuania," published by the Committee for a Free Lithuania.

V. STANLEY VARDYS, the editor of this volume, a Ph.D. of the University of Wisconsin, is Associate Professor of Political Science at the University of Wisconsin-Milwaukee. He has contributed articles to *Slavic Review, Journal of Central European Affairs, Midwest Journal of Political Science,* and other journals.

VITTORIO VIGNIERI received his Ph.D. at Rome, his place of residence. For the past twenty years he has made a study of Soviet religious policy in Lithuania.

PRANAS ZUNDĖ, a civil engineer and journalist, has written for *Osteuropa* and other journals. He is the author of a major work on the sovietization of Lithuanian agriculture entitled *Die Landwirtschaft Sowjetlitauens.*

Selected Bibliography

The purpose of the following bibliography is to suggest to the general reader additional sources of information that are available in English. The listing makes no claim to completeness. A good guide to materials on Lithuania is found in a bibliographical work compiled by Jonas Balys, *Lithuania and Lithuanians* (New York: Frederick A. Praeger, 1961). This bibliography lists both books and articles published in Western as well as East European languages and provides a bibliographical primer for the researcher as well as the general reader.

Since monographs on Lithuanian affairs are rather scarce, it seemed desirable to include in the following listing books that offer substantial chapters on Lithuania in a larger, primarily Baltic, context. For the same reason, some studies in German and French have been entered. Finally, since most of the recent research on Lithuania appears in periodicals, a note was added on journals that specialize in publishing such studies.

LITHUANIA'S GENERAL HISTORY AND PERIOD OF INDEPENDENCE, 1918–40

The Baltic States: Estonia, Latvia, and Lithuania. Prepared by the Information Department of the Royal Institute of International Affairs. London: Oxford University Press, 1938.

BILMANIS, ALFREDS. *Baltic Essays.* Washington, D.C.: The Latvian Legation, 1945.

CHAMBON, HENRI DE. *La Lithuanie moderne.* Paris: Editions de la Revue Parlamentaire, 1933.

CHASE, THOMAS G. *The Story of Lithuania.* New York: Stratford House, 1946.

GIMBUTAS, MARIJA. *The Balts.* New York: Frederick A. Praeger, 1963.

GRAHAM, MALBONE W. *New Governments of Eastern Europe.* New York: Henry Holt, 1927.

HARRISON, ERNEST J. *Lithuania 1928.* London: Hazell, Watson and Viney, 1928.

JUNGFER, VICTOR. *Litauen, Antlitz eines Volkes.* Leipzig: Breitkopf & Härtel, 1938. 2d ed. published in Tübingen by Patria, 1948.

JURGĖLA, CONSTANTINE R. *History of the Lithuanian Nation.* New York: Lithuanian Cultural Institute, 1948.

————. *Tannenberg, 15 July 1410.* New York: Lithuanian Veterans Association, 1961.

KALIJARVI, THORSTEN. *The Memel Statute: Its origin, legal nature, and observation to the present day.* London: R. Hale, 1937.

KELLOR, F., and HATVANY, A. *Security Against War.* Vol. I. New York: The Macmillan Company, 1924. An early American view of the Vilnius and Klaipėda problems.

KRIKŠČIŪNAS, JURGIS. *Agriculture in Lithuania.* Kaunas: The Lithuanian Chamber of Agriculture, 1938.

MACARTNEY, C. A., PALMER, A. W. *Independent Eastern Europe.* London: Macmillan & Co., 1962.

NEWMAN, BERNARD. *Baltic Background.* London: R. Hale, 1948.

NOREM, OWEN J. D. *Timeless Lithuania.* Chicago: Amerlith Press, 1943. An account by the last American minister accredited to Lithuania.

PAGE, STANLEY W. *The Formation of the Baltic States.* Cambridge, Mass.: Harvard University Press, 1959.

PICK, FREDERICK W. *The Baltic Nations: Estonia, Latvia, and Lithuania.* London: Boreas, 1945.

REDDAWAY, W. F. *Problems of the Baltic.* London: Cambridge University Press, 1940.

SENN, ALFRED E. *The Emergence of Modern Lithuania.* New York: Columbia University Press, 1959.

ŠAPOKA, ADOLFAS. *Vilnius in the Life of Lithuania.* Toronto: The Lithuanian Association of Vilnius Region, 1962.

SIMUTIS, ANICETAS. *The Economic Reconstruction of Lithuania After 1918.* New York: Columbia University Press, 1942.

TARULIS, ALBERT N. *Soviet Policy Toward the Baltic States, 1918–1940.* Notre Dame, Ind.: University of Notre Dame Press, 1959.

U.S. HOUSE OF REPRESENTATIVES, SELECT COMMITTEE ON COMMUNIST AGGRESSION. *Third Interim Report,* 82nd Cong., 2nd sess., under authority of H. Res. 346 and H. Res. 438. This is a competently prepared study of Lithuania, Latvia, and Estonia until their forced incorporation into the Soviet Union in 1940. Written and edited by specialists of the Library of Congress.

LITHUANIA UNDER FOREIGN DOMINATION, 1940–

ARMONAS, BARBARA, as told to A. L. NASVYTIS. *Leave Your Tears in Moscow.* Philadelphia and New York: J. B. Lippincott Company, 1961.

BILMANIS, ALFREDS. *The Baltic States in Post-War Europe.* Washington, D.C.: The Latvian Legation, 1944.

CHAMBON, HENRI DE. *La tragedie des nations baltiques.* Paris: Editions des la Revue Parlamentaire, 1946.

BIRKE, ERNST, NEUMANN, RUDOLF, and LEMBERG, EUGEN (eds.). *Die Sowjetisierung Ost-Mitteleuropas.* Vol. I. Frankfurt/Main and Berlin: Alfred Metzner, 1959.

HARRISON, ERNEST J. *Lithuania's Fight for Freedom*. New York: The Lithuanian American Information Center, 1945. The author is the former British Vice-Consul in Lithuania.

KALME, ALBERT. *Total Terror: An Exposé of Genocide in the Baltics*. New York: Appleton-Century-Crofts, 1948.

KERTESZ, STEPHEN D. (ed.). *The Fate of East Central Europe: Hopes and Failures of American Foreign Policy*. Notre Dame, Ind.: University of Notre Dame Press, 1956.

——. *East Central Europe and the World: Developments in the Post-Stalin Era*. Notre Dame, Ind.: University of Notre Dame Press, 1962.

MAČIUIKA, BENEDICT V. (ed.). *Lithuania in the last 30 years*. New Haven, Conn.: Human Relations Area Files, 1955.

MANNING, CLARENCE A. *The Forgotten Republics*. New York: Philosophical Library, 1952.

MEISSNER, BORIS. *Die Sowjetunion, die baltischen Staaten und das Völkerrecht*. Cologne: Verlag für Politik und Wirtschaft, 1956.

ORAS, ANTS. *Baltic Eclipse*. London: Victor Gollancz, 1948.

PAKŠTAS, KAZYS. *Lithuania and World War II*. Chicago: Lithuanian Cultural Institute, 1947.

PELĖKIS, K. *Genocide: Lithuania's Threefold Tragedy*. Germany: Venta, 1949.

SUDUVIS, N. E. *Allein ganz allein: Widerstand am Baltischen Meer*. Germany, 1964.

SWETTENHAM, JOHN ALEXANDER. *The Tragedy of the Baltic States*. London: Hollis and Carter, 1952.

TAURAS, K. V. *Guerilla Warfare on the Amber Coast*. New York: Voyages Press, 1962.

VAITIEKŪNAS, VYTAUTAS. *A Survey of Developments in Captive Lithuania in 1962*. New York: Committee for a Free Lithuania, 1963.

ZUNDĖ, PRANAS. *Die Landwirtschaft Sowjetlitauens: Wissenschaftliche Beiträge zur Geschichte und Landeskunde Ost-Mitteleuropas, No. 58*. Marburg/Lahn: J. G. Herder Institut, 1962.

LITHUANIA: LANGUAGE, LITERATURE, AND THE ARTS

BALTRUŠAITIS, JURGIS. *Lithuanian Folk Art*. Munich: T. J. Vizgirda, 1948.

GIMBUTAS, MARIJA. *Ancient Symbolism in Lithuanian Folk Art*. Philadelphia: American Folklore Society, 1958.

LANDSBERGIS, ALGIRDAS and MILLS, CLARK (eds.). *The Green Oak: Selected Lithuanian Poetry*. New York: Voyages Press, 1962.

KUDIRKA, VINCAS. *Memoirs of a Lithuanian Bridge*. New York: Manyland Books, 1961.

RAMONAS, VINCAS. *Crosses*. Los Angeles: Lithuanian Days, 1954. A novel depicting the 1940–41 Soviet occupation in Lithuania.

SENN, ALFRED. *The Lithuanian Language*. Chicago: Lithuanian Cultural Institute, 1942.

VAIČIULAITIS, ANTANAS. *Outline History of Lithuanian Literature.* Chicago, Lithuanian Cultural Institute, 1942.

ZOBARSKAS, STEPAS (ed.). *Lithuanian Folk Tales.* 2d ed. New York: Voyages Press, 1958.

————. *Selected Lithuanian Short Stories.* 3d ed. New York: Manyland Books, 1963.

————. *Lithuanian Quartet.* New York: Manyland Books, 1962. Short stories by four Lithuanian writers.

A Note on Periodicals

Of the current periodicals that specialize in Lithuanian studies, the broadest in scope is *Lituanus,* published since 1954 by the Lituanus Foundation (now Chicago, Illinois). Its coverage ranges from history to modern art. Another quarterly, *The Baltic Review,* publishes materials on all three Baltic States (since 1953 in the United States) under the direction of the Lithuanian, Latvian, and Estonian panels of the Free Europe Committee. The Assembly of Captive European Nations in New York semiannually publishes a very useful *Survey of Recent Developments in Nine Captive Countries,* based exclusively on Communist sources, and dealing also with Lithuanian developments.

In Germany, two journals of an academic nature currently specialize in Lithuanian, Latvian, and Estonian studies. The *Commentationes Balticae,* published since 1953 under the sponsorship of the Baltic Research Institute (Baltisches Forschungsinstitut), Bonn, has published contributions in English as well as in German. The other, *Acta Baltica,* appears annually in German under the direction of the Baltic Institute (Institutum Balticum) of Königstein im Taunus.

The following select glossary of Lithuanian periodicals should prove of help to the reader:

Ateitis (Future)	German-licensed daily, published in 1942–44 in Kaunas
Draugas (Friend)	Daily newspaper, published by the Lithuanian Marian Fathers in Chicago, Illinois
Į Laisvę (Toward Freedom)	1. 1941–42: Daily newspaper, published in Kaunas by the Lithuanian insurrectionists against the Soviet Union; put under German control and closed down in December, 1942
	2. 1942–44: Underground anti-Nazi periodical, published in Lithuania by the Lithuanian Front
	3. 1953–present: Quarterly of history and politics, published in the United States by the Friends of the Lithuanian Front
Komjaunimo Tiesa (Truth of Communist Youth)	Newspaper published in Vilnius by the Central Committee of the Lithuanian Communist Youth

Komunistas (Communist)	Monthly theoretical journal of the Central Committee of the Lithuanian Communist Party
Laisvės Kovotojas (Freedom Fighter)	Underground anti-Nazi periodical, published in Lithuania in 1941–44 by the Alliance of Lithuanian Freedom Fighters
Liaudies Ūkis (People's Economy)	Monthly journal dealing with problems of the Lithuanian economy, published in Vilnius by the Gosplan of the Lithuanian S.S.R., the Lithuanian sovnarkhoz, and the Economics Institute of the Republic's Academy of Sciences
Lietuvos Pionierius (Pioneer of Lithuania)	Children's newspaper, published in Vilnius by the Central Committee of Lithuania's Communist Youth and the Republic's Council of Pioneers
Literatūra ir Menas (Literature and Art)	Weekly newspaper, published in Vilnius by the Association of Soviet Writers of Lithuania
Mokslas ir Gyvenimas (Science and Life)	Monthly journal of scientific popularization, published in Vilnius by the Soviet Society for the Propagation of Scientific and Political Information
Nepriklausoma Lietuva (Independent Lithuania)	Underground anti-Nazi periodical, published in Lithuania in 1941–44 by the illegally functioning Populist Party
Pergalė (Victory)	Monthly journal of the Association of Soviet Writers of Lithuania, published in Vilnius
Santarvė (Alliance)	Journal, published in London, 1953–58, by the Alliance of Lithuanian Resistance
Sėja (Sowing Time)	Journal of politics, since 1953 published in the United States by the Lithuanian Populist Party in exile
Šluota (Broom)	Monthly humor magazine, published in Vilnius by the Publishing House for Newspapers and Journals of the Central Committee of the Communist Party of Lithuania
Sovetskaia Litva (Soviet Lithuania)	Daily newspaper of the Council of Ministers of the Lithuanian S.S.R., published in Vilnius
Švyturys (Lighthouse)	Illustrated biweekly magazine, a Lithuanian version of *Ogoniok,* published in Vilnius by the Publishing House for Newspapers and Journals of the Central

	Committee of the Communist Party of Lithuania
Tarybinis Mokytojas *(Soviet Teacher)*	Semiweekly journal of the Association of Soviet Lithuanian Teachers, published in Vilnius
Tiesa (Truth)	Daily newspaper of the Central Committee of the Communist Party of Lithuania, published in Vilnius

Index